GUNDOGS: TRAINING AND FIELD TRIALS

By the same author

TRAINING THE ROUGHSHOOTER'S DOG

GUNDOGS
TRAINING AND FIELD TRIALS

P. R. A. MOXON

POPULAR DOGS
London

POPULAR DOGS PUBLISHING CO LTD
3 Fitzroy Square, London W1P 6JD

An imprint of the Hutchinson Publishing Group

London Melbourne Sydney Auckland
Wellington Johannesburg and agencies
throughout the world

First published 1952
Second edition revised 1958
Third edition revised 1960
Fourth edition revised 1962
Fifth edition revised 1965
Sixth edition revised 1967
Seventh edition revised 1970
Eighth edition revised 1971
Ninth edition revised 1973
Tenth edition revised 1974
Eleventh edition revised 1976
Twelfth edition revised 1978

Printed in Great Britain by litho by The Anchor Press Ltd
and bound by Wm Brendon & Son Ltd
both of Tiptree, Essex

ISBN 0 09 134470 0

To my friends and professional colleagues ANDREW WYLIE and JACK CURTIS, in gratitude for their generous encouragement and advice on all training matters. Also to CAPT. A. B. J. GANNON in appreciation of his interest and help in keeping my dogs well during the past ten years; and DONALD THOMPSON, Head Keeper, for opportunities to train my dogs under ideal conditions.

CONTENTS

ILLUSTRATIONS

AUTHOR'S INTRODUCTION TO THE FIRST EDITION

JUST over one hundred years ago, in 1849, a wise and humane gentleman wrote a book which created a mild sensation in sporting circles. General W. N. Hutchinson, a keen shot and a lover of horses, dogs and all animals, had been appalled by the ignorant and usually cruel methods adopted by keepers, trainers (or "breakers" as they were then) and shooting men for the purpose of "breaking" a gundog. Being, as I have said, both wise and humane, General Hutchinson had discovered that not only *could* dogs be trained by kind methods but that by so doing the trainer found the task infinitely easier and the resulting mature worker far more efficient. Thus convinced that he could better the lot of many sadly misused dogs and at the same time improve the sport of his fellow shooters, the General produced his large, informative book and so became the pioneer of dog *training*, as opposed to *breaking*.

It naturally took some years for what I term "psychological" training to become general. The diehards stuck to their ignorant methods and many men then (as today, unfortunately) were temperamentally unsuited for training a dog by anything except force methods. However, as the older generation of keepers, trainers and sportsmen died out, the "new" ideas were tried by those who succeeded them, were found excellent, and were gradually adopted generally by all who had cause to train dogs. Other writers, both in books and in the sporting Press, took up the idea of kindly training, and now—Heaven be praised—it is an exception to hear of anyone using methods other than kindness towards the dogs they train. Indeed, General Hutchinson's ideas have been carried even farther and the "spike collar" and other training impedimenta mentioned by him have fallen into disuse, simply because they are not necessary for anyone who understands the canine mind and what can be accomplished by the process of bribery, example and the interpretation of canine psychology.

In this book I make no claim to be the originator of any particular methods or ideas. Neither do I pretend to understand *fully* the workings of the canine brain. I do not believe any man would be bold enough to make such a claim. Those of us whose lives are closely tied up with dogs find we learn something new about them almost daily; indeed, I realize now, after many years with gundogs, how little I knew at the beginning of my training career! My object, as far as this book is concerned, is to help other sportsmen to enjoy training dogs, by showing them what I have found by practical experience to be the easiest and best methods. I wish, also, to encourage more people, not necessarily shooting men, to take up the training of their own dogs as a pastime. Above all, I seek to improve still further our breeds of gundogs and prevent the appalling waste of good "canine raw material" which every year adds to the scrap-heap of "ruined" dogs. Most of these dogs could, given proper treatment and understanding handling methods, have been turned into useful workers with owners proud to have them out. It is because so few men realize how easy it is to train a gundog, and because many of them go about it in the wrong way, that the average shooting dog is a wild, undisciplined creature, frequently more bother than it is worth. Go to any ordinary shoot and see how many dogs remain steady to falling birds or running "fur". Note just what proportion of dogs present are tethered firmly either to their master's waist or to any handy object! Listen, also, to the yapping and whining that takes place every time birds come over the guns; note, too, when shooting ceases and the dogs are released, how few retrieve cleanly, quickly and to hand. Few, very few, dogs will be observed to behave properly. Such a state of affairs need not exist if dog-owning shooting men knew how easy it is to train a dog properly, and how pleasurable it is to shoot over one so trained.

There are, I realize, many dog trainers far more competent than I am to write a textbook on the subject, but who prefer to devote their time to the practical aspect of their work and leave "pen-pushing" to others. I gladly pay tribute to these men, many of whom have helped me generously, both at Field Trials and in private, and from whom I have learnt more than would be possible from all the books ever written. They will understand that I am not "trying to teach my grandmother . . ." by writing this book, for my words are for the novice and the amateur. They will, I am sure, welcome any work which endeavours to improve gundog handling; every trainer knows, to his sorrow, that a big percentage of the dogs he trains becomes ruined by mishandling on the part of owners.

To turn for a moment to Field Trials, it is noteworthy that these events are becoming increasingly popular with shooting men and all those who like to see dogs at work. But there are many misconceptions in the mind of the general public about Field Trials and not nearly enough private individuals enter for them as would do if only they knew the enjoyment and interest that can be derived from this sport. It is for these reasons that I have devoted several chapters to Field Trials and because, as I said above, I wish still further to improve the working breeds and believe Field Trials to be one of the best means of doing so. I can safely say that I have made more good, true friends through attending Trials than one might reasonably expect to make in a lifetime, and it has been my experience that gundog men, from professional to rawest novice, are about the kindest, most generous and genuine sportsmen that one could wish to meet. In short, gundog training and Field Trials can interest and benefit the mind and the body of anyone who indulges in them, as well as provide an opportunity for social intercourse of the most enjoyable kind, and under healthful conditions. It is high time that the fallacies of Field Trials being only for the very rich, always "wangled", and success attainable only by the professional with a specially trained dog, were done away with and the fact brought home to the ordinary gundog lover that "it is far easier than it seems". Luck plays a large part in Trials, though of course you must have a good dog as well, but a Trial dog is only a shooting dog more highly "polished" and carefully trained and not some phenomenal animal produced, like the conjurer's rabbit, out of a hat. In my opinion any dog considered fit to shoot over should be capable of running in Trials.

As one who has charge of a kennel of between twenty and thirty dogs all the year round I have had some opportunity of acquiring experience about the best methods of feeding, housing and exercising dogs. In some things—diet, for example—I do not hesitate to admit that I am a fanatic. The reader will find in the Chapter dealing with feeding that I consider there is nothing to compare with raw meat for feeding dogs, and that when I can no longer get raw meat I will give up keeping dogs. During these last few years, since I became a devotee of the "Natural Rearing and Feeding" methods of Miss Juliette de Bairacli-Levy, I have definitely proved that dogs reared and fed on a raw foods diet have a higher resistance to disease, are capable of working longer (and better) and cost less to keep in the long run than dogs fed on more orthodox lines. The dog is a carnivorous animal and has a digestion suitable for the assimilation of raw meat and bones. To feed cooked foods is unnatural and therefore wrong, as I hope to prove.

Throughout this book I have tried, as far as possible, to avoid being too technical and to explain my methods in everyday language. That on many subjects I have had, perforce, to leave much unsaid, and that many experts will disagree with me on some details, I am well aware. If I appear long-winded at times, dwelling on some seemingly unimportant item to the irritation of the reader, I apologize, but explain that by experience I know how important some of the little points really are in dog training. I offer this book with the hope and wish that readers may, with its aid, obtain as much enjoyment from their dogs as I have from mine, and that their dogs may, in turn, benefit by being better understood and more thoroughly trained.

P. R. A. M.

1952

AUTHOR'S INTRODUCTION TO THE THIRD EDITION

THE fact that only two years have elapsed since the second edition of this book and already a third edition is necessary is, naturally, very flattering and a source of great pride to me. However, the really important conclusion that can be drawn is that gundog training, and Field Trials, are continuing to increase in popularity, especially with the 'average' shooting man. Also, many people are being introduced to the sport of shooting *because* of their interest in dog training—people who otherwise might never lift a gun. This cannot be otherwise than a good thing for field sports and country life generally.

In this edition the appendices have been brought up to date and, by kind permission of the Kennel Club, I have been allowed to incorporate the recently issued and most valuable *Guide to Field Trial Judges*, which I commend to readers irrespective of their interest in Field Trials as such. The Guide is, in short, a summary of the desirable attributes of a well-trained gundog, be it intended for competition or simply for work in the field. It should also make understandable to Field Trial spectators (and competitors!) some of the more obscure decisions of judges.

In the light of experience since this book was written, my views upon inoculation against distemper and other diseases have undergone a drastic change and these are outlined in Chapters X and XI. Veterinary science has been making rapid strides and while I still maintain that true health in dogs can be achieved only by natural rearing and diet, the new "egg-adapted" inoculations have done, and are doing, much to stamp out the dread diseases of "hard pad" and distemper.

The present-day shortage of rabbits, due to myxomatosis, has created difficulties for the gundog trainer, amateur and professional, especially where spaniels are concerned. However, ingenuity and hard work can overcome these difficulties to a large extent, and a gundog trainer must be possessed of both these qualities.

1960 P. R. A. M.

AUTHOR'S INTRODUCTION TO THE SEVENTH EDITION

THAT a seventh edition of this book has become necessary is, naturally, a source of great gratification to me. Quite obviously my faith in the future of gundog training, and prediction that the pastime would become more and more popular, was well founded, but the success and reception of my work has astounded even me! I am particularly grateful to those satisfied readers who have written to tell me that I have been instrumental in helping them to achieve success with their dogs, both as shooting companions and/or as field trial contestants. "The proof of the pudding is in the eating", so it would appear that the methods of training I advocate have proved successful and withstood the test of time.

Although I have not found it necessary, in this edition, to make many radical alterations I have brought it up-to-date by the inclusion of a completely new final chapter, which deals with modern training aids and discusses the gundog world as it is today. We live in times of rapid change, with which it is sometimes difficult to keep abreast, and whilst techniques and methods remain basically the same, the equipment available to us has been considerably widened in scope and enormously improved over the last few years. In this respect, at least, gundog trainers have "never had it so good"!

I have also replaced some of the more "dated" photographs, and, where they are quoted, given prices and costs at more realistic figures. These days, dog owners have to keep a wary eye upon economics, the same as everyone else! Nothing else remains but to wish you good luck with the young dog that you are training or about to train. May it give you as much pleasure and happiness as have the countless animals which have passed through my hands during the last thirty years.

P. R. A. M.

1970

AUTHOR'S INTRODUCTION TO THE NINTH EDITION

Little did I think, when I sat down to write this book in 1952, that, twenty years later it would still be in print, let alone selling like the proverbial hot cakes! But such has been the escalation of interest in training in general, and field trials in particular, among "ordinary" gundog owners (especially the younger generation, and the fair sex) that a ninth edition has quickly been called for. Something of which I feel proud, because it has proved my points and justified my confidence in the future of field sports—not only in this country but throughout the world. More and more gundog folk have discovered that they *can* "do it themselves" and train their pupils to an acceptable standard by the means that I advocate.

In this edition, the appendices have been revised,* quoted prices brought up to date (and decimalised!) and some additional remarks made upon the subject of feeding, but otherwise the text remains unaltered. There are no short cuts in gundog training—at least I have been unable to discover any—and I feel that the progression of exercises which I suggest have proved themselves adequate to put average owner-trainers on the right lines. So it only remains for me to wish them many happy hours of training, and to remind them at all times to try to see things from the dog's point of view. The ability to "think like a dog" is probably the greatest asset that the trainer can possess!

P. R. A. M.

Beoley Kennels, Redditch, Worcestershire.

1973

* The appendices have been further revised where necessary for the tenth edition, 1974, for the eleventh edition, 1976, and again for the twelfth edition, 1978.

CHAPTER I

CHOICE AND SELECTION OF A GUNDOG PUPPY

Choose from Working Stock. Choice of a Breed. Cross-Breds and Inter-Breds. Pedigrees. Picking a Puppy. Early Days. Canine Psychology and "Dog Sense".

Choose from Working Stock.

THERE is one cardinal rule to remember when choosing a puppy, of any breed, for work with the gun. This is that no matter how well-bred or how good-looking the puppy may be, *unless it is bred from working stock* the chances are that it will be difficult to train and an indifferent worker when training is finished. It is an unfortunate fact that today many people are interested in the gundog breeds purely as show animals, and pay no attention to working qualities, breeding as a rule for looks, type and other show points. The true working dogs, on the other hand, are bred from parents with working histories, and generally with several generations of Field Trial Champions and winners in their pedigrees, often regardless of looks. There are strains in some breeds, fortunately, which combine qualities of good looks and working ability and more breeders are aiming to produce a genuine "dual-purpose" dog. In some breeds, notably Spaniels, Pointers and Setters, two different types of dog have sprung up, which I classify as "working" and "Show" types—self-explanatory terms. Why it is that show people who cannot or will not train and work their dogs do not leave the working breeds alone I cannot tell, but in my opinion such people are doing nothing but disservice to the breeds by concentrating solely on the show side. It is a fact that a puppy, with three generations or so of non-trained forebears, will often display a shameful lack of natural working instinct, making its training exceedingly difficult and tiresome, and usually resulting in a very indifferent worker when mature, displaying all sorts of irritating faults. On the other hand, the true working-bred puppy almost trains itself. Such desirable attributes as gamefinding ability (nose), pace, style, love of cover and water, and natural retrieving will be evident in these puppies from an early age and thus make training very much easier and more enjoyable. Natural ability can be bred out of a dog much more easily than it can be bred in, as so many people have found to their disappointment when trying to produce a dual-purpose type by crossing a working dog with a show bitch and *vice versa*.

No, there is nothing else for it, if you want a really good working gundog, than to choose one of definite working and Field Trial parentage. Some breeds have been all but ruined as workers by show breeders who have not only failed to train and work their dogs but have bred for such exaggerations that physically the dog is incapable of doing the work for which it was originally intended. Take the Show-type Cocker Spaniel as an outstanding example. Long ears which impede it in cover and upon which it almost treads if it puts its head down on a scent, high narrow head, deep-hawed eyelids which collect dust, dirt and seeds, heavy feathering which gets full of burrs and brambles and other rubbish when working cover. Much the same has been attempted with English Springers, though fortunately not to the same degree, whose exaggerated size has helped to make them unpopular with shooting men. In both these Spaniel breeds the shooting man needs to be very careful when buying a puppy for training, and to make sure that it has a history of working forebears. Cockers in particular should be chosen from pure working strains, of which there are a few left in the right hands and which figure prominently in Spaniel Field Trials each year. The Show Cocker seldom makes an appearance at Trials; few owners ever train them and if they did they would stand little chance of winning against the working type. Springers at Trials are also of working type in ninety-nine cases out of a hundred, for much the same reasons, but I am pleased to note that an increasing number of Show kennels are having their dogs trained and running them at Trials, which can do nothing but good for the breed as a whole. Similar conditions exist among Pointers and Setters, and anyone interested cannot help but be struck by the difference in appearance between the two types—Show and working. The working dogs of all the breeds are nearly always smaller and more compact, and without useless exaggerations of long ears, deep haws, heavy "feather" and tremendous bone. Some are almost ugly, but what does that matter so long as they can efficiently perform the work expected of them?

Labradors stand out as a breed which has achieved "dual-purpose" status. Because so many breeders have been able (and willing) to train their dogs, and have maintained a breed standard which takes into account working requirements, it is quite possible to obtain a Labrador capable of winning both on the bench and at Field Trials; there exist at the moment several Dual Champions—that is, dogs that have attained Championship status both at Trials and on the bench. There are no Dual Champions at the present time among Cockers, Springers, Pointers or Setters, or any of the other retriever breeds except Golden Retrievers, to which breed all I say about Labradors applies. As far as Cockers and Springers are concerned it seems unlikely that there will be any Dual Champions for some considerable time at any rate—until more Show breeders train and work their dogs and more Trials men take an interest in the appearance of their animals.

I make no apology for taking up so much space on this one topic. Ever since I became interested in gundogs I have been fighting for recognition of one fact—that breeders should put first things first and concentrate upon natural working ability in their dogs. One has only to look round the kennels of any keen shooting man or trainer to see which type of dog he prefers, or to visit Field Trials and note the proportion of show dogs and workers competing. The shooting man *must buy from working stock*. If he does not he will live to rue the day he ignored this advice, and I should be guilty of neglecting my duty to the shooting fraternity were I to advise him to do anything but buy from the right stock.

Choice of a Breed.

The next consideration is the breed of gundog which will be most suitable for the work you have in mind. The rough shooter, who walks up all his game and shoots mostly alone or with one companion, will probably choose a Spaniel as being the most likely dog to help him work out the thick cover of his shoot. The member of a syndicate, however, whose shooting is mainly of the "driven" variety and who shoots a great deal in company, will probably plump for a Retriever which can be trained to sit quietly at a partridge drive or pheasant stand, or in a grouse butt, and which can be relied upon to retrieve only upon command with the minimum of time and trouble. Pointers and Setters will cater admirably for the man who likes to shoot over dogs and has suitable ground upon which to work them and who will probably also have a Retriever to find dead and wounded birds as well. The type of gundog must be chosen with due regard for the work it will have to do, and it is no good expecting a Retriever to do the work normally performed by a Pointer, or *vice versa*, no matter what your preference for one particular breed may be. Of course a Retriever will find birds and some could be trained even to point after a fashion, in the same way that Pointers are capable of retrieving, but the results of such training would not be worth while. It would certainly not justify the time and temper expended.

Having decided upon the type of gundog you wish to have, you are now faced with a choice of breeds. If you have a particular preference for one or the other, then the choice is obvious, for a man will always make a greater success of a car, horse, gun or dog of the "breed" he likes best. The list of breeds is quite formidable and each has its advantages and disadvantages in various respects. In order to assist the inexperienced reader as far as possible, I name them hereunder and add some notes that are the result of experience with the breeds concerned. Remember, I write only of those *of working strain.*

Among the Spaniels we have first of all the *English Springer*, which to my mind is the ideal rough shooter's dog and for anyone who requires an all-rounder the breed will appeal as being most versatile. English Springers, if of working stock, are natural hunters and retrievers, love working in cover and water, and are easy to train, besides being very hardy and with a high resistance to distemper and other ills.

The *Cocker Spaniel* is my second choice as a working dog. They have a lovely, fast, happy action, a grand nose and are small enough to penetrate the most dense cover, of which they are very fond. In my experience Cockers are not so easy to train as the Springers, being rather more selfish and inclined to think about themselves instead of about what the trainer requires of them.

The *Welsh Springer* is very similar to the English in size, but here the similarity ends, for whereas English Springers can be of many different colours and colour combinations the Welsh dog is always red and white and varies in many other points which do not concern us here. As a worker the Welsh dog has an excellent nose and is not afraid of cover or water, but some strains have an annoying habit of giving tongue when questing, and many are extremely lacking in natural retrieving instinct, though this is now being improved by selective breeding. "Trainability" varies from splendid to very poor, according to strain, but a good one takes a lot of beating as a gamefinder.

The *Clumber Spaniel*, at one time considered the easiest to train and the best worker of all the Spaniel breeds, is becoming rare these days. It is generally too heavily built for Spaniel work in thick cover. However, when one of working strain can be found it will prove to be easy to train and a useful, if slow, all-round worker and retriever.

The *Field Spaniel* is another breed that has declined in popularity during the last twenty years. Much of what has been said about the Cocker Spaniel applies to this breed, and I sincerely hope that breeders will in future devote attention to the production of workers rather than of show animals, for a *good* Field is as good as any Spaniel can be.

The *Sussex Spaniel* has also dwindled in numbers, though an effort is being made by enthusiastic breeders to popularize it again. Those specimens with which I have come into contact have not shown a very great natural working ability, but those bred from parents which have been trained and worked prove useful in the field, though not on a par with Springers, Cockers or Fields.

The *Irish Water Spaniel* is rather out of place in this list; I always look upon him more as a Retriever than a Spaniel. The reason for this is that the thick, curly coat is unsuitable for work in rough cover; it collects all sorts of debris and makes the dog thoroughly uncomfortable. The Irishman is an ideal water retriever and quite a good all-rounder on open land. This breed is not easy to train, being self-willed and rather *too* clever for most handlers, but a good one, properly trained, is hard to beat for marsh shooting and wildfowling generally.

The Retriever breeds are numerous, and each has its staunch supporters who will advance reasons for the superiority of one breed over the others with a loyalty sometimes amazing (and frequently violently prejudiced).

The *Labrador Retriever* is without question the most popular Retriever breed today, both for work and show. A comparatively "new" breed, Labradors have won the esteem of shooting men by their outstanding ability to be trained, find game and become companions and guards. The Labrador, as a breed, can be said to be both fast and stylish in action, unequalled in water and with "trainability" far above that of other breeds, and a devotion to master or mistress that makes them ideal companions. The smooth, short coat has many advantages readily appreciated by the housewife and car owner. Dogs from working strains almost train themselves to the gun.

The *Golden Retriever* runs the Labrador a very close second and is my next choice as a Retriever for work with the gun. This breed has made astonishing headway in recent years, thanks to the enthusiasm of breeders who have wisely insisted that the dogs be "dual-purpose" in every sense. Goldens of the right strains are easy to train and handle, have exceptionally good noses and work well in water. They have kind, gentle natures which befits them as "indoor" dogs even where there are young children, and in appearance they are most attractive, especially to women. Their coats need rather more attention than do those of Labradors and being generally larger in build they take up more room and require greater amounts of food.

The *Flat-coated Retriever*, so popular in the '90s and at the beginning of this century when big shoots were the order of the day, has lost considerable ground to the more popular Labradors and Goldens, but for all that the breed remains popular with gamekeepers and many shooting men. Generally speaking, the Flat-coat is easy to train and nice to handle but I do not consider that he has the pace or the style of a Labrador or Golden Retriever. As gamefinders Flat-coats leave nothing to be desired, and they make very attractive companions on account of their kindly disposition.

The *Curly-coated Retriever*, beloved by the older generation of gamekeepers and shooting men, is something of a rarity today. They are excellent gamefinders and full of courage, and make particularly good water dogs on account of the curly, water-resisting coat, but they are not easy to train, being rather like the Irish Water Spaniel in that they have very decided wills of their own and are apt to be rather scatterbrained. They gained a reputation at one time for being hard in the mouth but I believe that this was quite unjustified, my own experiences of the breed being that it contains no greater proportion of hard-mouthed specimens than the other Retriever breeds.

The *Chesapeake Bay Retriever* is an American variety, largely used in the U.S.A. as a water Retriever, at which work they excel. There are a few specimens in this country but they have never become popular and show no signs of doing so, largely on account of their size and because the native varieties can conveniently do all the work required of a Retriever over here.

Of the "bird-dog" (pointing) breeds, the Setter family can

be divided into three varieties—English, Irish and Gordon, each being a distinctive type and of different colouring. The English Setters are usually black and white, lemon and white, liver and white or tri-colour—that is, any of the above combinations with tan. The Irish Setter is always of a red colour (hence the frequent use of the term "Red Setter") described in the breed standards as "rich golden chestnut". The Gordon Setter is another handsome dog, the colour always being black and tan—they were at one time known as "Black and Tan Setters".

The *English Setter* is probably today the most popular member of the family for work. The breed is always well represented at bird-dog Trials, and the working strains tend to be smaller than the show ones. The two best-known strains are "Laverack" and "Llewellyn", which were developed as workers by the gentlemen who gave their names to them. English Setters are fast and stylish workers with excellent noses and are, I consider, the easiest of the Setter family to train, besides being smaller than the other members of the family and therefore easier to feed and house.

The *Irish Setter* has, unfortunately, become a very popular show bench animal, especially with ladies, and as always when this happens the working qualities of the dog have tended to become overlooked. By nature the Irishman is fast and inclined to wildness, but strains that have been kept for work always manage to give good accounts of themselves at Field Trials, being wide rangers with good noses. I do not find them as easily trained as the English Setter or as "showy" when working.

The *Gordon Setter* is a grand, large dog which has lost popularity in the last twenty years and today is seldom seen at Trials outside Scotland. This seems a great pity, for the breed is a beautiful one and as workers Gordons can hold their own with the other Setters, being of more biddable disposition and willing to please. Perhaps the dogs I have seen lately have not been as fast as might be desired, but they are very staunch and have more sober temperaments than many Setters, and make excellent companions for that reason.

The *Pointer* is too well known to need description, and is my first choice as a bird-dog. A really well-bred working Pointer is a joy to behold in the field, being fast, stylish and an excellent gamefinder; and (in my view) with a very lovable, rather Spaniel-like disposition. Highly strung, like most of the bird-dog breeds, Pointers are probably the easiest of all to train and handle and, though I have a personal preference for black and white dogs, the liver and white and lemon and white markings are very attractive and show up well in the shooting field. One occasionally sees whole-coloured and tri-coloured dogs, which do not appeal so much. But "a good horse is never a bad colour", and if given an opportunity to be a companion a Pointer will be found to be a most intelligent, affectionate animal, gentle and good with children, and with a short coat which has obvious advantages. There are various foreign breeds of Pointer, the German short-haired variety in particular becoming quite popular in England since the occupation of Germany. These dogs are somewhat smaller than the English Pointer, and are often docked for work in thick cover, which I think spoils their appearance. As workers they are generally sound, but highly strung and slow making up.

CROSS-BREDS AND INTER-BREDS.

Apart from the main breeds mentioned, there are various inter-bred and cross-bred gundogs which will work well with the gun and can usually be quite easily trained. I am not myself a lover of either inter-breds or cross-breds, believing that greater satisfaction and better results are obtained from a pure-bred animal. It is often found that if one mixes breeds the progeny of the union generally inherit the worst features of both sides and appearance is often far from pleasing. Some men mistakenly cross a Pointer with a Retriever, for example, in the hope of getting puppies that will point and retrieve, thus serving a dual purpose. In such cases it is often a fact that the puppies favour one parent or the other both in appearance and working ability, and seldom do we hear of cross-breds that are better (or more versatile) workers than one or other of the parents. Inter-breeding—that is, crossing different varieties of the same breed, such as a Cocker Spaniel with an English Springer—is usually more satisfactory, but, except to obtain fresh blood or increase or reduce size, the practice has little to recommend it. Obtain a puppy of a well-known, reliable working strain and train it thoroughly—that is my advice to the beginner, and if the puppy is a pure-bred animal I feel sure the breeder will find it more satisfactory than an experimental cross- or inter-bred.

PEDIGREES.

Pedigrees are all-important when choosing a gundog. This document should be supplied by the breeder with any dog or puppy sold, and should give the names and Trial awards of parents, grandparents, great-grandparents and sometimes great-great-grandparents and even the previous generation as well. The registration numbers of sire and dam should also be recorded on the pedigree copy—that is, the number allotted to the dogs when registered at the Kennel Club, the controlling body of the dog world. Registered dogs are of greater value than unregistered animals, for all shows and Field Trials are supervised by the Kennel Club and an *un*registered dog cannot be entered for either. Registration provides some protection against fraud and false pedigrees, because ancestry is checked as far as possible by the Kennel Club when a dog is registered. The small fees charged are well worth while. Probably the beginner in gundogs will not be able to make head or tail of a pedigree, other than to grasp that it contains a lot of names which convey nothing to him. If this is so he should consult someone well up in that particular breed, who will probably know the strains by name and often from personal experience, and will be able to offer advice on the choice of a puppy. By dealing only with a reliable breeder, who has a reputation to maintain, one may be sure of getting a square deal. In cases of doubt the Kennel Club can always be consulted as to the authenticity of the pedigree of any particular dog.

Pedigrees will often be found to contain some evidence of in-breeding—that is, close breeding between members of the same family. This need not be a bad thing—indeed, it is often the only way to ensure the perpetuation of some desirable characteristic of a breed. In-breeding *in moderation*, using only *healthy* animals, has a lot in its favour. It is promiscuous, uncontrolled in-breeding with unhealthy specimens that has brought the practice into such disrepute. An experienced breeder of dogs, or of any other animals, will know just how far to go in this matter, which is an additional reason why a reliable man should be consulted. There is a mistaken belief that cross-bred or inter-bred (*not in*-bred) dogs will be hardier and healthier than pure-bred animals. This need not necessarily be so; I know that there are just as many unhealthy, diseased mongrels as pure-bred dogs. But a pure-bred dog is valuable and if it becomes ill it is taken to a veterinary surgeon and a lot of money spent. If it dies, the loss is bewailed by the owner because of the value of the dog. We hear nothing of the sick and diseased mongrels; they are valueless (except sentimentally, very often) and usually little is spent on them for cures. Their decease is no matter for the comments made when valuable dogs die.

PICKING A PUPPY.

Even for someone experienced in gundogs, it is extremely difficult to pick the best puppy from a litter—the best puppy for work, that is. Most puppies are offered for sale at about eight weeks of age, when fully weaned, and though some of the working characteristics will be evident by that time (a retrieving instinct, for example), such important things as nose, pace and love of cover and water will be impossible to discover in all but a few exceptional instances. I have usually been very lucky in my choice by nearly always picking the smallest puppy (if sound and healthy), but this *is* admittedly pure luck! Generally speaking, the best bet is the bold puppy, which comes up to you fearlessly, does not back away when you extend your hand to him, or roll on his back. Try clapping your hands loudly, to watch the reaction, and refuse any puppy which shows signs of fear and retires into the kennel. If you can see the puppies all out together, running about in a field or under cover, you will get a better idea of the bold specimens and those which will face the long grass, and willingly retrieve a small dummy or knotted handkerchief. Other things being equal, I like a puppy with a good broad head, straight legs and a good tail. Tail action in a working dog is most important, I consider, and a puppy which "keeps his flag wagging" is likely to be a stylish one. Spaniels should not have been docked too short for work, otherwise they will be deficient in tail action, and Labradors should have good thick "otter" tails. Inspect the mouths of the puppies you fancy, and make sure they are not undershot, or "pig-jawed" as this is called. This may not affect their work, but is unsightly and will probably become more pronounced as the puppy grows up. I also favour a dog with a short back, well developed chest and muscles. You will naturally make sure there is no obvious defect such as rickets, that the ears are clean, the eyes bright and normal, and that the puppy is free from skin vermin. If *all* the puppies appeal to you, and you have difficulty in making a choice yourself, you can perhaps get an experienced friend to help, or simply rely upon intuition and pick the one that takes your fancy by reason of colour, markings or personality. If the puppies are bred right, from good working stock, you will probably not go far wrong, anyway. Do remember to inspect the pedigree and make sure it contains Field Trial winners or, better still, Field Trial *Champions*. If possible, see the sire and dam working, and pay no attention to Show points or Show names in the pedigree unless you particularly wish to show as well as work your dog. Do not forget that any defects, physical or mental, in the parents are likely to be accentuated in the progeny.

If you breed your own puppies, and can do so conveniently, I strongly advise that you run on as many as possible until they are six or eight months of age. By this time it should be possible to pick the most promising worker, for they will have made up and developed personality and character by this age. You will certainly get a better idea of the fast, stylish puppies, the cover-lovers and the water dogs, and also have a good idea which are going to be easiest to train. Even at six or eight months, however, one cannot be certain. One of the best Labradors I ever had was apparently useless until he was ten or eleven months old, being gun-nervy and refusing to retrieve. Once he started learning he never looked back. Generally speaking, you stand a much better chance of picking the best at eight months than at eight weeks, though to have a puppy at the younger age is cheaper and really preferable as it develops under your eye and gets to know you better. You can guide it along the right paths from the very start. An older puppy may have formed bad habits which take some correcting, but from the facts I have given you will be able to make the decision yourself having regard to your particular circumstances.

In this Chapter I have purposely refrained from giving "breed standards" for the breeds of dog mentioned. These will be found in any good reference book dealing with the particular breeds; to quote them would probably tend to muddle the reader. In most instances there is a great discrepancy between the standards laid down by the breed societies and the actual appearance of the *working strains of gundog*. Indeed, except with Labradors and Golden Retrievers, and possibly Welsh Springer Spaniels, the working and show types might almost be taken for different breeds. Labradors and Goldens are, fortunately, real dual-purpose breeds, and so are many Flat-coated Retrievers, but the Cockers, Springers and many others bred for work often do not conform at all to the standards laid down for the breeds. This is a great pity, but it's no use blinking the fact. It is entirely due to Show enthusiasts breeding exaggerations into their dogs without taking work into consideration, and also, to a lesser degree, I believe, because lovers of working dogs have not tried to retain a standard of appearance as well as of ability. We can but hope that this state of affairs will be remedied in the future and that more co-operation between breeders will lead to the production of real "dual-purpose" dogs in the breeds which do not at present produce any.

EARLY DAYS.

Having decided upon your puppy, and got him home, you will wish to know how to feed and manage him. Assuming the youngster to be about eight or ten weeks old (puppies should not be bought any younger), I recommend four meals a day at first, one milk feed in the morning, meat cut up very finely (*raw* meat) at midday, and a cereal soaked in milk or green water about 4 p.m. The last meal of the day should be of raw meat, very finely cut up, and chopped green vegetables or grated onion. Cod liver oil and yeast powder can be added as supplements. When the puppy reaches about four months of age the daily meals can be reduced to three, and at eight months two meals a day can be given. It is impossible for me to advise as to the amounts to be given; so much depends upon the breed, size and appetite of the puppy. You must be guided by common sense and will quickly discover if you are feeding too much or too little.

Unless a puppy appears to be losing condition, or shows other evidence of worms, I do not believe in worming as a matter of routine. I consider that far more harm is done by the use of violent vermifuges than by the worms themselves. If the puppy is fit and in good coat, leave well alone.

Kennels and runs are dealt with in Chaper X. If you decide to keep the puppy indoors, he should be provided with a good box or basket in which to sleep, and should be house trained as recommended in Chapter X. The first things a puppy must learn are to respond to name and whistle, and to retrieve a small dummy, if a Retriever or Spaniel; these items are dealt with in Chapter II. I usually start my puppies retrieving a very small dummy, or a knotted handkerchief, right from the nest stage, and seldom do they require any actual "teaching", for pups of working strain have the instinct. All that is required is to get them used to the idea of bringing whatever they are carrying to *you*, instead of running off to play with it or taking it into their box or kennel. The best way to do this is to stand by the box or kennel and throw the dummy away from it, intercepting the puppy on his return and gently removing the dummy and making a fuss of him.

The puppy should be taken about to meet people and things—in other words, get him "world wise" and confident so that when training is seriously begun he will not roll on his back or in other ways play the fool. The earlier a puppy is accustomed to riding in cars the better, as in that way car-sickness is often prevented or, if it does occur, is quickly cured. Plenty of exercise should be given, but not to such an extent as to tax his strength. The puppy should be allowed a lot of free galloping exercise, and should be taken into woods and other places where he can become used to cover. If you select suitable spots where the cover is not too punishing, and walk on unconcernedly, the puppy will soon learn to follow and in this way grow up to consider work in cover as an everyday affair.

Until training age is reached the less restraint and the more experience of people and things the puppy has the better. Gunfire can be introduced at quite an early age, as recommended in Chapter III.

Canine Psychology and "Dog Sense".

I once so interested the editor of a well-known sporting journal in the expression "canine psychology" that he accepted a series of articles from me almost out of curiosity—or so he tells me! Be that as it may, to be a successful gundog trainer you must realize from the start that no two dogs are alike and that unless you can see things from the dog's point of view, especially when matters go wrong, your chances of turning out a reliable, well-trained dog are remote. So many men like to consider themselves dog-wise, and are quite offended if you point out to them that they are obviously not, that I feel this subject merits attention in any book dealing with dog training.

The old-fashioned brute-force-and-ignorance methods of dog-breaking (I will not call it "training") failed to take into account the nature of a dog's temperament and paid no attention whatsoever to "psychology". At one time the standard way to teach a Spaniel to work was to take him out with the gun when quite a puppy, allow him to hunt, chase and become thoroughly keen and wild, and then proceed to "break" him—steady him, in other words, by trying to thrash out the ideas which had been deliberately implanted. A more senseless procedure is difficult to imagine. It usually resulted either in the pupil becoming so cowed that it was useless for work or such a hardened, wilful sinner that it just accepted the thrashings and continued as before. Even today many dogs are ruined because owners do not give serious thought to the workings of the canine mind.

Throughout this book my aim will be to teach the reader how to train a dog step by step in a series of graduated lessons which will be easily learnt by a dog of average intelligence. I have deliberately indulged in repetitions which might seem unnecessary, in order to impress upon the reader the importance of certain items. One of the most common errors into which man is prone to fall is that of crediting a dog with more reasoning power than it really possesses. Hence many dogs receive punishments the reasons for which, though perfectly clear to the master, are quite unknown to the dog. I will give an example which will help to illustrate what I mean. A man is out for a walk with a dog which goes off self-hunting in the woods. The master whistles and calls with no result, so he returns home in a towering rage and awaits the reappearance of the erring animal. Immediately the dog presents itself it is seized and receives a severe thrashing, and is promptly chained up or shut up. "That will teach him not to run away again," thinks master, smugly. More likely such a treatment will *encourage* the dog to run away again at the first opportunity and stay away even longer.

If the owner would only stop to think about it, it must become obvious that there is nothing to show a dog that a beating given upon its return home has any connection with its running away. The reasoning power of the dog is so limited that it connects any punishment with its very last action, which in the case quoted was coming back home. So next time the dog will probably be very loath to return at all, remembering that the last time it did so it received a thrashing. It would be far more sensible to greet the prodigal with a good meal and a great deal of fuss; this would at least make homecoming a pleasant event, which might induce a reluctance on the dog's part to go away again. I do not seriously suggest this as the solution, but it is certainly a better one than the thrashing.

A dog in the habit of running away can be cured if caught *in the act of stealing off*, and *punished there and then*. Then the reason for the punishment is perfectly clear to the dog and it will be taken to heart. I do not, however, recommend thrashing as the best form of punishment, though a few cuts with a lead or whip (*not* with a stick) do at times have a salutary effect upon a wilful dog. I much prefer scolding in a very gruff, grumbling voice, holding the dog up by the loose skin of the neck and glaring at him, and a thorough shaking. This seems far more effective—particularly the holding part. It is so greatly disliked by the dog that it is a more subtle punishment, without being painful.

This same method of, whenever possible, catching the dog *in the act of doing wrong*, or in some way showing it where it has erred, can be and should be applied throughout training, though by a series of easy, graduated lessons I think it should be quite possible to dispense with punishment throughout the entire course. Take the dog which runs-in to a falling bird and retrieves it. Punishment given when the dog returns does not indicate to the animal that the crime he committed was running-in—he assumes that he is being punished for retrieving, this being his last action, and in future he will tend to refuse to retrieve, or if he does he will be reluctant to come to hand, thinking that he will again be punished. Many dogs are ruined as retrievers in this way, through the thoughtlessness of the owner. The correct procedure is to take the bird as though nothing has occurred, throw it back to its original spot, leave the dog on the drop and walk out and pick it up yourself. The next time you shoot a bird try to stop the dog from running-in, either by command or by having previously attached a check-cord with which it can be halted and then shown the error of its ways. The system of training suggested teaches the dog to be steady to falling game quite naturally as a result of the lessons, but the above treatment can be used when temptation proves too great for the dog, or when early training has not been thorough. However, the whole object of the course is to teach the dog to do right before it learns to do wrong, whereas the old idea of letting a dog please itself in order to get it keen and working, and then eradicating (or trying to) faults by punishment, was "starting at the wrong end". Any worth-while, well-bred dog of working strain will become keen on its work quickly enough if given the opportunity, but this can and should come *after it has learned self-control*, and not before.

The man who sends a dog away for training (or who buys a trained dog) and takes it out shooting the day after getting it home shows clearly that he is lacking in "dog sense". The wise owner, who gives the dog ample time (perhaps weeks) to settle down, accustom itself to new home and handler, before taking it into the field is dog wise, and will make a success of a gundog. There are many little matters to which psychology can be applied in dog training. Take the case of the puppy which refuses to bring the dummy to hand but which goes off with it, or just stands and looks at you with a defiant expression. The ignorant trainer may run after the puppy, and, if he catches it, administer a hiding. The man with "dog sense" will act quite differently and run *away from the puppy*, calling him up whilst he does so. The pupil, afraid of being left behind and curious to see what is happening, runs after the trainer, who then takes the dummy from it whilst still on the move, making a great fuss of the puppy for coming in. Where this treatment fails, as it occasionally does, the trainer who thinks will make use of a check-cord, by means of which the pupil can slowly be towed in with the dummy, then rewarded, praised and generally given to understand that by coming in he has done well. The trainer who runs after the puppy usually makes it think he is indulging in a pleasant game (until he is caught!), and will make matters considerably worse.

It will be noticed that throughout the training Chapters I constantly advise that a dog which has done wrong *be taken back to the very spot where he did so*, and there made to drop and meditate. This is about the only way you can show a dog that he has sinned, for the association of ideas between an action and the place where that action occurred is very strong in a dog. It is no good, for instance, when a dog leaves his drop and walks after you to make him drop again at the point he has reached. He must be dragged back and made to go down at the original spot, as often as necessary, and without fail. In no other way can you impress upon him the necessity for remaining where told and instil the idea of complete, absolute compliance with your orders.

More often than not when things go wrong in training it is the trainer who is at fault, not the dog. It is well worth while trying to "think like a dog", endeavouring to see his point of view, as in this way it will often become clear to the trainer that the fault is his own. The remedy will very likely quickly become obvious. It is easy to give a dog a completely wrong impression and so create endless work and worry for yourself, all of which might have been prevented by a little thought and care. As an example, consider a puppy which shows reluctance to face cover and will not go into it at any price. I have known men who, losing patience at such apparent timidity and softness,

[*Shooting Times*

The Author with his Field Trial Winner, Bekesbourne Sweep, Bekesbourne Paddle and Bekesbourne Briar

[P. R. A. Moxon

Walking to heel on the left side of the handler

[P. R. A. Moxon

Two pupils sitting steadily while the handler walks away

[P. R. A. Moxon

A selection of home-made retrieving dummies of various sizes, weights and materials

[P. R. A. Moxon

Kneeling to encourage a puppy which is reluctant to deliver the dummy

Horace Hall

Laying a scent trail for the pupil to follow, a dead partridge attached to the centre of a long line

have picked up the pupil and flung him bodily into the brambles with an air of "that will teach him". Teach him it certainly does—to loathe cover ever afterwards and associate it in his mind with violence and bad temper on the part of his master. How much simpler and easier it would have been to induce the puppy to enter the brambles by throwing in pieces of bread or meat, which would almost certainly have had the desired result and, what is more important, would ineradicably have associated the facing of cover with something very pleasant. This is, of course, an extreme case as the number of men who would be so foolish must be very small, but it helps to illustrate my point and to prove that a little thought can make all the difference between ruining a dog and succeeding with it.

One further example of psychology as applied to dog training will serve to give the reader more food for thought. A very common and annoying habit exhibited by some trained dogs is refusal to come in when whistled. This generally occurs after the completion of obedience training, when the dog is starting work on game and becoming interested in scents. You suddenly notice the Retriever you imagined to be at heel some way behind, sniffing at an attractive scent, and he ignores your whistle. Go back to him and drag him by the skin of the throat in the direction he should have taken when you whistled, at the same time repeating your "come-in" whistle over and over again. Drop him and return to the place where you were when he disobeyed you, and give your whistle. The dog will come bounding in with eagerness to please and you should show him that he has done right by immediately patting and praising him. In this way cordial relations will be maintained and, having shown him effectively where he was wrong, the dog will respect you all the more. Exactly the same procedure can be applied to any dog which disobeys the return whistle or call, though in the case of a dog out working at the time of disobedience it is advisable to drop him by whistle or command before returning to him and dragging him along the route he should have taken when you first whistled. Indeed, at all times when a dog disobeys commands you should immediately endeavour to stop all motion on his part by putting him on the drop and giving him time to meditate upon his sins. This is just another example of the necessity for *teaching the drop thoroughly* and illustrates the reason for it being truly "the king-pin of training".

CHAPTER II

PRELIMINARY TRAINING—I

Obedience. Age to Start Training. Tact and Firmness. Rewards. Aim in Training. Equipment. Commands and Signals. First Lessons. Retrieving the Dummy. Sitting to Command. Remaining on the Drop. The Check-Cord. Punishment. Dropping at a Distance. Steadiness to Thrown Dummy.

OBEDIENCE.

THE early training of Spaniel, Retriever and bird-dog puppies is, with certain exceptions, the same. This Chapter and the next will therefore serve to give the reader a general outline of the most important early lessons for all breeds. Advanced training for the different breeds will be under separate headings. The reader will do well to consider carefully one outstanding fact, which I shall emphasize throughout the training Chapters. This is that *OBEDIENCE is the first essential of all training*; a dog which is not obedient, no matter how good a gamefinder he may be, *is not trained.* This is why all our efforts in training should be directed towards obtaining an obedient dog, without in any way curtailing his keenness and enthusiasm, and why particular importance must always be attached to the early obedience lessons, generally called "hand training". It is safe to say that the hand training of a gundog puppy is by far the most important part of his education, because (if he is of working stock) his natural aptitude for hunting and retrieving will assert itself when field work is begun but, if we have not already made the puppy obedient, his tendency will be to work for himself and in his own way, instead of for us and in the way we require. Furthermore, the whole object of training is to obtain a steady dog—that is, one which does not retrieve without orders and does not chase game which may rise—and unless the idea of steadiness and obedience is instilled before shooting work begins it is well-nigh impossible to obtain it afterwards. This is where modern, "psychological" methods of training diverge from the old ways of "breaking". In the past it was quite usual to allow a gundog puppy to go out shooting, hunt, chase and generally run riot as his natural instincts dictated, and then try to obtain steadiness and control by unmerciful thrashings. It will be noted throughout this book that physical punishment of the pupil plays a very small part, the whole object of my training methods being to teach the puppy right from wrong *from the start of training*. It is obvious that a puppy taught by kindly methods, regarding most of the early work as a happy game, is much more likely to end up as a bold, merry worker, with love for his master, than is one allowed to do as he likes at the start and then suddenly, for no apparent reason so far as he can see, receiving tremendous hidings that are attempts to eradicate habits which he had been encouraged to adopt. It is true to say that in the past these bad, ignorant training methods produced two main types of mature dog—those which became so hardened that they did as they liked regardless of punishment, and those so cowed and cringing that few, if any, men today would be seen with one in their company. To train a dog on modern lines is far easier and infinitely more enjoyable to both master and pupil, the time taken much shorter and the result more certain and efficient than "breaking" a dog in the old way.

Age to Start Training.

The age at which to start training a puppy must be carefully considered. This depends upon both the pupil and the trainer. A bold puppy can be started on hand training earlier than a shy one. A patient man or woman can begin the training of a puppy at quite a tender age, but anyone inclined to impatience should defer training until the pupil is less likely to be frightened or cowed. Patience is not only a virtue but a *sine qua non* in anyone attempting dog training. My experience has been that it helps to teach the trainer patience—I am a most impatient man in everything except dog training, but even so there are days when my mood is such that I know that to attempt training would be a mistake. I might lose my temper. On such days I do no training at all, for to lose one's temper with a puppy is the first step on the downward path. In such a mood one is liable to do something which the puppy does not understand, and the bond of confidence between master and pupil is broken. Once broken, it is almost impossible to mend, and without mutual confidence between man and dog successful training is impossible. To those who wish to be given a definite average age at which a puppy can begin hand training I suggest six months for a Spaniel and seven, eight or nine months for a Retriever, Pointer or Setter. But all breeds can be started earlier or later according to the temperament of the individual puppy. The earlier one starts the shorter should be the lessons and the course made less intensive. One of the best Labradors I have ever trained, Bekesbourne Tosh, several times winner at Field Trials, did not start his training until he was about a year old, because he was so shy and nervy. He won his first stake at fifteen months and before he was two he had, by careful, kind handling, outgrown all nerviness and shyness. A less promising puppy than Tosh at six months I cannot recall; he would not retrieve even a dummy, but once a glimmer of understanding dawned in his brain he never looked back and learnt more every day. It does not do lightly to discard an apparently unpromising puppy too early, for often the slow starters end up as the best mature workers. I have invariably found that a sensitive dog has brains and usually finishes up a *brilliant* worker. A stolid puppy, on the other hand, whilst easier to train and far less worry to begin with, often ends up as a mediocre worker or one which will riot at the slightest provocation. Trainers have a saying, "Easy to train, easy to spoil", and this I have found very apt. But once the more difficult, sensitive puppy has learnt a lesson he does not forget it easily, and is more likely to excel in the field than his stolid brother.

TACT AND FIRMNESS.

Throughout training, tact and firmness are necessary. "Firmness", as opposed to physical violence, and "tact" to show the puppy what he must do and to make him understand your requirements. It is no good standing over a puppy, for instance, and shouting "Sit!". The word conveys nothing to him, so he must be *shown* what to do. This may seem elementary, but it is surprising how many people seem to think that a dog should be capable of understanding what is wanted without any guidance from the trainer. Equally absurd is it to shout "Sit!", grab the puppy and start whipping it—the invariable result being that instead of sitting it runs away. Yet I have seen this done! I do not think this is intentional cruelty—merely sheer ignorance and lack of thought. A dog must be trained by *being shown what is required*, and not be credited with more brains than it possesses. We can explain what we want to a child, but a puppy must be *shown*, and so by showing it what we require and, whenever possible, associating obedience to a command with something pleasant, we reach the desired end.

Disobedience must be associated with something unpleasant—our displeasure. This can be demonstrated effectively by means other than whipping. A grumbling, scolding tone of voice can be very effective, and catching the puppy, holding him by the slack skin under the throat and shaking him will do more to punish than a severe whipping. Reward for obedience can take the form of an edible titbit, in the early stages, or just a few pats and vocal praise in pleasant tones. Voice control in dog training can be very useful, and I recommend its employment. "Good dog! Good dog!" in a happy, caressing tone for good work, "Arrr! Bad dog! Bad dog!" in a gruff voice when things go wrong.

EDIBLE REWARDS.

A few words on the subject of edible rewards may not come amiss, for these can become a bad habit in training. I believe in the *moderate use* of rewards, with certain pupils for certain items in the early stages, but overdo the business and there will be regrets. To give an example, one of the first puppies I ever trained, a Springer, was reluctant to bring the dummy to me, though she would find it and return to within a few yards of me very quickly. In my ignorance, I imagined that if I gave her a titbit whilst she was circling round me, just out of reach, with the dummy in her mouth, she would come up and deliver. Come up to me she certainly did, but in her eagerness to get at the food she dropped the dummy out of my reach. Furthermore, from that time on she always expected a reward and would persistently drop the dummy when she got to within a few feet of me! A reward *can* be given for retrieving, if necessary and in exceptional circumstances, but only *after* the dummy has been delivered to hand and the puppy has had a period sitting in front of the handler. Once allow a puppy to believe that the moment he comes up to you he is going to receive an eatable, then good-bye to a good delivery, though this is an excellent method of teaching a puppy to return quickly!

In the early stages edible rewards are useful for getting a puppy used to and interested in you and for accustoming him to watch your hands. They can be useful, too, to encourage puppies to quest in cover, and as a reward for dropping to command and stopping on the drop. But it is my opinion that the practice of giving rewards should be stopped as soon as it has achieved its object and indeed should be dispensed with if possible. It will usually be found that a keen, kindly dispositioned puppy of working strain who knows and loves his handler will quickly come to enjoy doing his work for no reward other than a few pats and some words of praise. The whole idea of this system of training is to arrange matters so that the pupil enjoys his lessons, regards them more as a game than as work, and performs his tasks for no reward other than the pleasure of his master and because he has been taught to associate certain commands with certain actions on his part. In other words, habit, instinct and the association of ideas rather than mental reasoning is what causes the pupil to perform the different items on the training agenda. I fully believe, as do so many handlers, that a dog loses respect for anyone who over-indulges in the handing out of edible rewards. The handler comes to be regarded more in the nature of a portable food bin than a respected, loved human being who must be lord and master and loved for his own sake rather than for the "hand-outs" he issues!

The reader may consider that I am being unnecessarily long-winded, and deviating too far from the practical aspect of training. Let me hasten to assure him, therefore, that these preliminary considerations and discussion of the "psychological" side of gundog tuition are far more important than they might at first sight appear to be. I receive a great many letters from enthusiastic gundog owners asking for advice, so I feel that I know only too well the sort of mistakes that the beginner is likely to make. How much better it is to realize from the start that when training a dog the trainer must try to "think like a dog".

Aim in Training. Equipment.

It might now be as well to detail just what is required of a puppy, of any breed, during his "hand-training" period. These, then, are the essentials in order of importance:

All breeds	Response to name and whistle. Familiarity with lead. Familiarity with gunfire. Obedience to the command to drop and remain on the drop. Development of "nose".
Spaniels and Retrievers	Retrieving the dummy. Entering cover. Ranging out in quest of dummy. Walking to heel.

It is clearly useless to attempt to impart obedience to a puppy which does not answer to his name and come when called or whistled, so to teach this is the first essential. The lead may be necessary for several of the early lessons, and the pupil should be accustomed to wearing this before serious training starts. I use and recommend a "choke lead". This consists of a leather

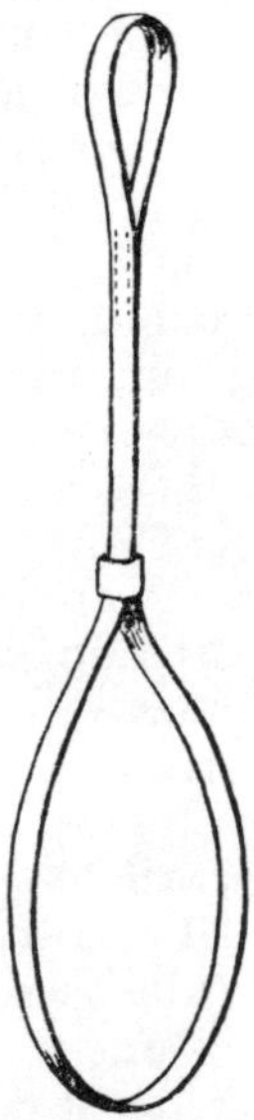

Leather "choke lead" used for training.

strap, one half to three quarters of an inch wide, with a loop for the hand at one end and a metal D at the other. The looped end is slipped through the D to form a noose, which goes round the puppy's neck. This tightens when the puppy pulls, but the moment he ceases to pull the tension relaxes, which is the idea, because he quickly learns not to strain on the lead. This type of lead is much more suitable and easier to remove than the ordinary collar and clip-on lead. It should be between three and four feet long. I treat my leads with a preservative ("Ped-Dri-Tone" is excellent); they last for years and can easily be carried rolled up in the pocket.

The training dummy, used to teach retrieving, can consist of a rabbit skin, old glove, stocking or tobacco pouch, stuffed with rags, wood-wool or *anything soft*. A small puppy requires only a small, light dummy to begin with but as he gets bigger so should the size be increased, as well as the weight, until in the end you are using a dummy about the size and weight of a wild rabbit. I myself generally use a rabbit skin. I find this successful, but some trainers prefer the less tempting stocking or glove, complaining that a puppy often tends to play with and chew a furry skin. If this trouble is encountered, then the dummy should be changed for something less likely to be played with and torn. I do not believe in using any artificial scent on the dummy; I have never found one necessary. The dummy has a slight scent of its own in the first place and after use and being carried in the pocket it probably collects a strong scent of dog and handler, which dogs seem to like. It is amazing how a more-or-less scentless dummy is winded and found by a puppy after very few tries; they can even be used to lay a trail of scent which the puppy will follow for considerable distances, after he has acquired a "nose".

Regarding the whistle, there are many types to choose from, but do not fall into the common error of using the loudest available! Dogs have very sensitive ears. They can hear sounds which are inaudible to us, and a loud whistle is neither necessary nor desirable. I use a very high-pitched "staghorn" whistle, and occasionally the "Acme Silent" whistle, which is capable of being adjusted so that all the human ear can detect is a rushing of air when the whistle is blown, but which is audible to a dog at considerable distances. However, I usually tune this whistle to its loudest pitch, not because it will help the dog but because I like to have the satisfaction of hearing the whistle I am blowing! There are other types, equally suitable, on the market but whichever you use always stick to the same one and, of course, use the same combination of blasts for the same command each time, without exception.

The only other item of training equipment that may be needed is a "check-cord". This consists of a length of cord (a greased clothes-line is very useful, being practically waterproof). This cord should be about ten or twelve yards long, or even longer, and have a metal ring at one end and, as in the case of the choke lead, a noose is made so that it can quickly be slipped over the pupil's head. The use of this cord will become apparent in due course.

Patience is a virtue in dog training—and consistence is of equal importance. Words of command and whistle blasts, as well as hand signals, should always be the same, clearly given and repeated only if necessary. Our aim is to have, at the end of a few weeks' training, a puppy which will: Answer to name and whistle and come dashing in when ordered to do so. Drop quickly to command (or whistle) and remain on the drop until ordered to leave. Drop and remain on the drop at any position in relation to the handler, even when he is out of sight. (All breeds.) Retrieve a thrown or a hidden dummy on command. Enter cover either upon command or in quest of a dummy. Range well out and be guided to any given spot within reason by the handler's commands and signals, the dog using his nose at all times in quest. Walk to heel until bidden to leave. (Retrievers and Spaniels.) Various other minor virtues will be learnt as well—such as jumping gates and fences, and waiting whilst the handler goes through a gate first. Spaniels and bird-dogs will have to learn to drop or stop to shot—this is one of the few differences in early training between Retrievers, Spaniels and bird-dogs; another being that a Retriever should learn more thoroughly to walk to heel, and learn at an earlier age.

COMMANDS AND SIGNALS.

Reverting to commands and signals, use whatever words and combinations of words, whistles and signals you fancy, but let them be short, clear and easily understood. I like to use a whistle as far as possible for certain items instead of the spoken command. A whistle is far less disturbing to game than the human voice, needs less effort by the handler and, above all, dogs seem to respond better than to voice, once taught. For Field Trial purposes the use of a whistle is more spectacular and undoubtedly more efficient than the voice. Whenever possible, when the dog is within sight rely upon signals alone or in conjunction with softly spoken commands. For those who have no idea what words to use, I append those I use myself, together with the whistle combinations and hand signals used for certain actions on the part of the dog. I give this list simply as a guide and leave the reader to use his own ideas, which will more than likely be far better than mine. Remember, however, not to use for any command a word which too closely resembles the dog's name. For instance, if a puppy's name is "Pip", the word "sit" is too confusing, and I suggest the substitution of "hup", "drop" or "down". Another confusing combination is "Rover" and "over", though in this case it is not nearly so important.

Here, then, is the list of commands I use:

Action required of dog	*Command or whistle*	*Signal*
Sit down or stop.	"Hup" or single long blast on whistle.	Raised hand. Stamp of foot if dog is close by.
Come in from a distance (Spaniels and Retrievers).	Dog's name or two quick toots on whistle.	Slap thigh.
Come in (Bird-dogs).	Series of quick blasts.	Slap thigh.
Walk to heel.	"Heel".	Point to left heel.
Retrieve.	"Fetch it".	Swing arm in desired direction.
Turn (Bird-dogs).	Two quick toots on whistle.	Swing arm.
Jump.	"Over".	Point to obstacle.
Enter cover (or water).	"Get in".	Point to cover.
Range out further.	"Get out".	Wave arm forward.
Range to the right.	Stop dog by whistle.	Swing right arm to the right.
Range to the left.	Stop by whistle.	Swing left arm to the left.
Quest ahead (Pointers and Spaniels only).	"Hi-seek" or "Hi-on".	Snap fingers.
Deliver dummy quietly.	"Dead".	—
Prevent wrong action.	"No".	—

From the above it will be seen that I use the whistle, with Retrievers and Spaniels, for only two commands—the most important two—stop or drop, and come in. With bird-dogs *three* commands are given by whistle. To carry the use of the whistle further can be confusing for the dog and complicated for the trainer, but it can be done. Shepherds use whistles for most actions, but generally speaking I think that the average shooting man will find those suggested quite sufficient.

THE FIRST LESSONS.

The first lessons—teaching response to name and whistle and accustoming the puppy to the lead, as well as the drop—are all best taught in a quiet place free from distractions of other dogs, humans or scent of game or animals. A lawn, if secluded, is ideal, or any field or open space will do. Teaching a puppy in a wood, or places where there are obstacles, is trying as the puppy may often run off and hide or investigate the cover, instead of paying attention to the work and to the teacher. Coming to name is easy and simple to teach. Hold the puppy gently and repeat his name and whistle signal over and over again, rewarding him with a pat and a piece of stale brown bread, or crust, if you desire. Let him run about and suddenly call and whistle him, immediately handing out the reward. Cease the reward as soon as a response is obtained, making a fuss of him instead, saying "*Good* dog". If the puppy ignores you, or stands and looks puzzled, turn and walk quickly away in the opposite direction, calling and whistling. Run if needs be and he will soon follow and catch you up, when he can be praised or rewarded. At feeding times always repeat his name a few times just before placing the bowl in front of him, or let someone else hold the puppy whilst you show him the food, walk away, and call him.

The lead should be slipped round the puppy's neck and *allowed to trail* whilst you walk quickly, run and generally play about to distract him and stop him chewing the lead. After a while take hold of the end and encourage him to walk beside you. If he lags behind give a sharp jerk and let the lead relax when he is level with you; if the puppy runs ahead, a sharp jerk back. . . . Never *drag* the puppy. He will quickly find that if he walks without lagging or straining it is quite pleasant. You can help by holding a tempting piece of dry brown bread in your left hand. The puppy should always walk on your *left* side, the lead being held in the left hand. Do not indulge in this practice for too long at a time; give him a few runs and scampers in between. In a short while the pupil will walk quietly on the lead, and you can proceed to the next two items of training, which can be interspersed—the more mixed the better to start with—and can be conducted on the same training ground.

Retrieving the Dummy.

Retrieving is a natural instinct in all worth-while Retrievers and Spaniels, hardly ever absent in those bred from working stock. The tendency is, at first, for the puppy to run off with the dummy for his own amusement, but this soon stops; frequently it never happens at all. It is a good plan always to throw the dummy *away* from home, as the instinct is to return to kennel or home with the retrieve. You must place yourself in a position to intercept the puppy and, after a due interval, relieve him of what he is carrying. Never *snatch* the dummy from him; take it gently whilst you pat him with the free hand, and if he stands holding it in front of you for a few seconds so much the better. Have your puppy running free of the lead and let him see the dummy. Throw it a few yards and when he runs out for it, *the moment his head goes down to pick up give him the whistle to return and call him by name*. If there is any hesitation on his part, turn and walk quickly away, calling and whistling. Nine puppies out of ten will pick up the object and run back but some will either pass you in an endeavour to run off with the prize or will circle round you. If you can conduct this lesson in a position where your back is towards a fence the puppy cannot circle you, and if the trouble persists it is worth while trying him in an alleyway or making a wire *cul-de-sac* where the puppy *must* come to you (without being able to pass out of reach) as he returns. But, generally speaking, if you walk away and call the puppy he will come to you and you can take the dummy whilst on the move. This will almost certainly happen if you taught him his return whistle and name thoroughly, and if he loves and respects you. Never in any circumstances chase the puppy whilst he is carrying the dummy—you have to sow the idea that it is to be brought to you, not that you have to go and get it.

A puppy that refuses to retrieve can be a problem, but usually by trying different objects as dummies you will come across something he likes and will carry; then this can be used to start with and later the dummy proper substituted. A glove, a ball, a rolled handkerchief, even a brush or a raw meat bone can be used—anything so long as you can plant the idea of picking up, carrying and bringing to you. I have found my pocket handkerchief nearly always successfully retrieved when other objects have been disdained. This is first of all knotted into a ball and when the puppy carries it well I tie it round the usual dummy, which he will then almost invariably pick up. After a few more tries the handkerchief can be removed and it will be found that the dummy is retrieved properly. In all these early lessons every effort should be made to avoid boring the puppy; lessons should last only ten or fifteen minutes, though they can be given two or three times a day if desired. When the puppy will retrieve the thrown dummy, increase the distance with each throw, ending up by letting it fall in cover just out of sight. Later on the puppy must wait for orders before retrieving but in these very early stages it is helpful to allow him to run in directly the dummy is thrown—it maintains speed and enthusiasm, which are most desirable. Once the puppy is reliable at picking-up and retrieving the thrown dummy and the lightly hidden dummy, he must be restrained until given the command to "Fetch it", and this can be done only after the lessons in dropping to command have been given. It can be seen, therefore, that obedience to the drop is necessary at an early stage as it is used in conjunction with the retrieving practice. At the end of this Chapter I shall discuss various problems which are liable to arise, explaining how I generally deal with them. It is only by preventing, as far as possible, the development of faults, or arresting them before they have become ingrained, that a dog can be successfully trained to a high standard. I shall return to the subject of retrieving the dummy when the teaching of the drop has been discussed.

Sitting to Command.

Before going on to describe my method of teaching a puppy to drop we must consider what we mean by the word. "Drop", in gundog parlance, may mean the action of sitting down, lying down with head erect, or lying down with head between paws. Different men have different ideas. I like my dogs to sit down so that they are still in a position to watch what is going on round them. Many pupils solve the problem themselves; quite a number will be found to go down flat rather than sit down and if this appears to be a natural inclination I leave well alone. I never insist that head rests on paws, as I fail to see the necessity for that posture. I am content, indeed pleased, if I can teach a dog to sit down on his haunches and remain seated until told to move. The argument that a dog flat down is a step further removed from rioting than one merely sitting is rather splitting hairs, but is nevertheless true. Some people teach both sitting and flat drop to different commands; I know of one man who teaches his dogs *three* drop positions! I shall throughout this book concentrate upon the general terms "sit" and "drop", and not bother whether they mean flat down or merely sitting.

My usual procedure when giving a puppy his first lessons in obedience is to walk him along on the lead at my left side. Suddenly I stop, raise my right hand and say "Hup". This means nothing to the pupil, so I gently but firmly press him down on his haunches and slowly straighten my back. If the puppy remains seated, well and good. Usually he gets up again and I then manipulate the lead to get him back into the sitting position, repeating the command. I retain him thus for a few moments, then pat him and walk him on, repeating the procedure several times. Many puppies get the hang of things very quickly; others seem dense or frightened. With the latter I start giving rewards of pieces of dry brown bread, as well as pats, after holding the puppies on the drop for a while. This usually does the trick; the command becomes associated with something pleasant, the reward eagerly anticipated. *As soon as possible I dispense with the reward*, but I continue to give a pat and say "Good dog! Good dog!" at the conclusion of each successful performance. A stubborn puppy can receive a sharp jerk on the lead if he fails to respond quickly to the command, but be as gentle as possible without giving in to him in any way. The puppy must be put back into position *every* time he gets up and made to see that he must not leave the drop until given permission, in this case a "tchk" made with tongue against teeth (as the waggoner starts his horses). It is one thing to teach a puppy to drop and remain down whilst you are close by; it is quite another to get him to remain down whilst you walk away. For this reason departure should never be attempted until the pupil is perfect on the command and the response is instant, or before he has become proficient at dropping whilst running free from the lead. So what I usually do is this—after three or four lessons the pupil is pretty good at dropping whilst on the lead, so I let it trail, and try him like that. In many cases all goes well and I then try with the lead completely removed. If this, too, is successful I can proceed to the next step. If not, back on the lead again until success is achieved.

The whistle signal to drop (mine is a long single blast) is introduced at the start of this lesson; it can be blown immediately before or immediately after the word of command. In a short while the puppy responds to whistle alone and if I have also made a point of always raising my hand and stamping my foot at the command, it is found that either of these actions will secure a prompt response. When all these items seem to have been mastered by my pupil, and he remains happy, keen and undaunted, I proceed to the next item—remaining on the drop whilst I move away, which part of the curriculum we can discuss next.

REMAINING ON THE DROP.

There are several very good reasons why a gundog puppy should learn to remain on the drop whilst the handler walks away—even letting him get out of sight but still remaining down until called up. For one thing, it is a great help to other items of training, as will become apparent later, and in field work it is often necessary to stop a dog at a distance whilst the handler moves about or changes his position (if pigeon shooting, for instance). Apart from this, if a dog is out questing in the wrong direction he can be stopped, kept stationary for as long as necessary, and then hunted in a different direction. (In point of fact, most dogs, particularly Retrievers, do not *drop* when stopped whilst ranging out questing but instead just *stop* and look towards the handler.) Even so, it is often necessary for them to remain still for some moments before being given the desired hand signal. It is neither necessary nor advisable for a Retriever actually to drop when stopped whilst questing, but this point will be fully considered in the Chapters on advanced training.

Until a puppy has mastered the lessons already given it it is quite pointless to start trying to teach him to remain on the drop whilst the handler walks away. Every item in a particular aspect of training should be learnt before proceeding with the next step; it is a great mistake to hurry through lessons in your eagerness to "get the puppy on". "Make haste slowly" is not a bad maxim as far as training is concerned, and if you remember also that these early lessons are by far the most important part of the curriculum you will avoid the fatal mistakes made by so many amateur and novice trainers.

If you are completely satisfied that your puppy will now drop to whistle and to command whilst beside you, promptly and without any attempt to get up and move about until given permission, you can try moving away whilst he remains sitting. As a beginning, drop the puppy in the normal way and, after giving him a few moments with you standing beside him, unhurriedly back away. Some puppies will immediately either get up to follow or (more annoying still) will crawl forward on their stomachs, as if knowing that they should not follow but cannot resist the temptation! Immediately this happens you must sternly repeat the command to drop and, taking the puppy by the slack skin under the throat, reseat him in exactly the same spot he vacated. Do this gently but firmly, and do it *every time without exception* that the puppy moves. This really becomes a battle of wills—yours versus the puppy's—and it is only by constant repetition, dragging back and reseating, that the puppy will come to realize that he must remain down whilst you leave him. In the early stages always leave the puppy and walk *away from home*. The reason for this is that a puppy is always anxious to run towards his home and if you walk away in that direction the temptation to follow will be greater. For exactly the same reason I suggested previously that the dummy should always at first be thrown away from home, as the pupil would then return more speedily and more readily.

In a very short while, if your tactics have been correct, your pupil will permit you to back away a few paces. When he does so, and remains steady, return to him, give the usual pat and, if desirable, an edible reward. Walk him on a little way, and repeat the procedure, remembering each time to return to the puppy and release him from the drop. It is a mistake to call the puppy in from his drop to start with—though this will have to occur later—because this may unsteady him and make him constantly anticipate the recall. Success in backing away from your pupil having been achieved, now try turning your back upon him and walking away slowly. Quite possibly this will at first cause him to start forward, when you follow exactly the same procedure as outlined above. Rate him sternly and drag him back to the exact spot from which he moved. But by now the idea should be becoming fixed in his mind that he must "stay put", and continual practice (for short spells, but two or three times daily if desired) will quickly have the effect desired. As the puppy gains in steadiness and reliability in this respect you can increase the distance to which you walk, until ultimately you can hide yourself, occasionally glancing at him to make sure he is still steady, and calling on him to drop if necessary. Throughout these lessons you have the opportunity of introducing the useful word "No", using it in a stern tone whenever the puppy attempts to move from the drop. It is always well, when walking away from him, to look back over your shoulder from time to time to see if he is remaining obedient. Take immediate steps to ensure that he is reseated in the correct spot, should he have moved an inch.

Reliability in staying on the drop can usually be accomplished in a few lessons and a week of one lesson daily should see the pupil perfect in this respect. Rewards can be given from time to time, if this seems necessary and desirable, but this must depend upon the disposition of the puppy and the patience of the trainer. As I have continually stressed, the sooner edible rewards are omitted the better. Having achieved reliability on the drop whilst you move away, you can start calling the pupil up without the necessity of returning to him. Throughout these lessons, when I write "command" I mean voice *and* whistle, or whistle only, and use should certainly be made of the whistle for this calling-up practice. I advise alternating calling-up from a distance with returning to the sitting pupil to release him from the drop, otherwise you may find that slight unsteadiness develops. Practice makes perfect and, provided you do not overdo it by continuing for too long at a time, these lessons are quickly mastered and are not irksome to the pupil once the idea has become fixed in his mind.

Now for one or two snags which may occur, though it must be admitted that if the first steps have been taught properly, and the puppy is fond of and respects you, they are unlikely to be encountered. In the case of a sensitive or shy puppy, it may happen that when you first move away and the pupil moves too, he does not take kindly to being taken back and re-seated. In fact, as soon as you move away for the second time the puppy turns tail and makes for home. I always believe that this urge to return home is a sign that you have not obtained the pupil's full confidence and love. A puppy which behaves thus should be very gently treated. If necessary, suspend lessons for a day or two, but concentrate on getting to know the puppy, and letting him know you. Build up confidence, using "cup-board love" in the shape of edible rewards if necessary, at least to begin with. By doing this—even by just taking the puppy for a few long walks each day—I often find that confidence is established sufficiently to eliminate the desire to depart at speed for home when anything not completely understood occurs.

Use of the Check-Cord.

It does sometimes happen, however, that a puppy remains very stubborn in this respect, even though mutual confidence appears to have been established. Then there is nothing else for it but the check-cord, which (as I mentioned earlier) is a cord about twelve or fifteen yards long with a ring at one end, so that a noose can be made and slipped over the puppy's neck. The pupil, having already been accustomed to wearing a lead, should offer no resistance to having the check-cord attached. Before doing so you should have laid the length of cord along the direction in which you intend to walk away from the puppy. By this means, immediately the puppy turns and tries to bolt for home you can quickly tread on the cord, pulling him up with a jerk. This in itself has a very sobering effect on a high-spirited puppy, who should then be gently but firmly taken back to his "seat" and resettled. The check-cord, used thus, is an excellent means of imposing your will upon that of the pupil, and bringing home the fact that you have the upper hand, that you intend to master him at all costs. Never use the cord harshly except to administer a jerk when you stand upon it, and for Heaven's sake dispense with its use as soon as you can. If the check-cord is used too much it loses half its value, for immediately he is free of it the pupil knows that he has "got you where he wants you" and acts accordingly! Usually, however, the tactfully used cord serves its purpose in one or two lessons, and can be kept for later use only after flagrant disobedience. I must admit that at one time I made a great deal of use of the cord, especially in Spaniel training, for all sorts of lessons. But since I moved to a heavily wooded area, where the check-cord is more exasperating to the handler than to the dog (because it gets constantly tangled up in obstructions in the woods), I have been forced to use it less. This has been a blessing in disguise. The cord has its uses, but better never to use it than to make it a be-all and end-all of training. These days I find that only about ten per cent of the dogs I train require it at all, and these only for a few lessons.

PUNISHMENT.

A bold puppy, which constantly irritates by doing wrong whilst lessons are in progress, and which has had sufficient experience to convince you that his behaviour is wilful, can be punished by a shaking and scolding, or a slap. The puppy should be taken by the slack skin under the throat—lifted up bodily and glared at, if this is physically possible—and held thus for some seconds. This treatment has a far more salutary and lasting effect upon most dogs than a whipping; it takes less out of the handler and serves the desired purpose without any loss of respect or temper on the part of either master or dog.

One point I shall stress throughout this book—such an important one that I will put it in capital letters: ANY PUNISHMENT GIVEN MUST BE ADMINISTERED IMMEDIATELY THE OFFENCE IS COMMITTED AND ON THE EXACT SPOT WHERE THE PUPIL DID

WRONG. Never punish a dog when he comes up to you and never, never punish for an offence committed some time previously. I shall have more to say on the subject of punishment in the Chapter dealing with training problems; anyway, in these early lessons punishment is usually unnecessary and is best dispensed with except in extreme cases, when it should be on the mild lines indicated above.

Dropping at a Distance.

Now that our pupil has learnt to drop and stay dropped until called up, and to retrieve a thrown dummy, we can proceed with two more important training items, each of which bears a relation to the other. These are: teaching to drop at a distance in any position in relation to the handler, and waiting for the command before retrieving a dummy. It is advisable to teach the first-mentioned lesson first and it will now become obvious why so much stress has been laid on waiting on the drop. In my experience the best method of teaching a puppy to sit at a distance is to drop him, walk away about twenty yards, whistle him up, and immediately he is almost up to you again drop him by command and/or whistle. Repeat this by walking away again and whistling once more, this time giving the command to drop (in conjunction with whistle, raised hand and stamp of foot, remember) a little sooner, when the puppy is some yards off. By repeating this exercise, and giving the order to drop earlier and earlier, it should soon be possible to stop and drop the puppy at any spot between you and where he was originally seated. From this point it is but a short step to being able to drop the dog wherever he may be. Let him run about without any restraint, then suddenly give your command. I believe you will be agreeably surprised at the ease with which this lesson is mastered, finding that your puppy drops promptly no matter whether he is going away from or coming towards you. Practise this lesson, and all the others so far learnt, in mixed order for a few days, give praise where it is due and rate, scold or mildly punish if necessary, and you have only one more early lesson to teach before you can sit back with a sigh of relief and say, "Well, thank goodness the worst is over!"

Steadiness to Thrown Dummy.

For teaching a puppy to remain steady to the thrown dummy, and not retrieve it until ordered to do so, it may be helpful to have him wearing the short lead, which can be allowed to trail. Take your pupil to his customary training ground and, after a brief walk, drop him beside you. Now place your left foot firmly on the free end of the lead, produce the dummy and throw it in the routine way. Having hitherto known no restraint, the puppy will get up and try to go out for the retrieve, being held back by the lead. Sharply command him to drop, see that he does so, and after half a minute or so slip the lead off and send him out with a command to retrieve, whistling him up in the normal manner. Repeat the performance a few times, and if all goes well remove the lead and let the puppy sit free from all check. When you next throw the dummy he may start up but you can quickly command him to drop again (or use the over-useful "No"), and place yourself in a position to bar his progress towards the dummy. If you are quick the puppy will never elude you, though an occasional failure may occur. If he does break away and your previous training has been thorough, he should stop to command or whistle before he reaches the dummy, in which event go and fetch him, and reseat him whilst you yourself pick up the dummy. In fact, it is a good idea to fetch the dummy yourself every now and again, leaving the puppy on the drop meanwhile. "Temptation is good for the soul" at these times.

This lesson of remaining steady to the thrown dummy and retrieving only upon command is another which is learnt with surprising rapidity by an intelligent puppy to whom previous education has been systematically imparted, and I have found that as a rule the puppy will get the hang of things in one single lesson of fifteen minutes or so, and by the end of the third lesson will be reliable and steady. So much so that many puppies will, if walking free and suddenly aware of a dummy being thrown, drop automatically to it, or at any rate stand and watch.

It will be noticed that the two moments of greatest temptation for the pupil are when the arm is swung to throw a dummy and when the dummy drops to the ground. It is at this second point that most puppies will endeavour to run-in, and the trainer has the unenviable task of trying to keep one eye on the dummy to see where it lands and the other on the puppy to make sure that it does not move. Of the two, it is far more important to watch the pupil; if the trainer himself does not know where the dummy landed the puppy will quickly show him. When the pupil is despatched to retrieve, always give the word of command you use for retrieving and a hand signal, and whistle the puppy up the moment his head goes down to pick-up. Encourage a good delivery to hand and, if you like, try to make him sit to deliver. This looks very pretty, and if the pupil has learnt to drop in front of you when coming in (as described above in the "drop at a distance" lessons) this should be quite easy, though by no means essential. You can, however, encourage your puppy to put his head up to you when delivering the dummy.

The dummy should fall into grass or other light cover, as constantly retrieving an object clearly visible in the open bores a puppy, encourages retrieving by sight rather than by scent, and, worse still, increases the desire to run-in. A puppy which waits for the command to retrieve rather than runs-in as the dummy is falling learns to "mark" the fall each time. This is one of the greatest assets of a shooting dog—the ability to mark accurately the fall of birds whilst master is busy shooting. It can be seen, therefore, that all these artificial training items are intentionally arranged to be of later service, when shooting begins, apart from their being the best method of teaching what is required. It will also have been noted that lessons are given in a certain order, each step being graduated so that the pupil's intelligence is drawn out, each lesson leading on to the next. Thus, if the pupil is hurried through any one item and this is not thoroughly learnt it affects the next lesson, with the result that the puppy is being only half-trained, and will never be reliable. Control, coupled with keenness and natural ability, are the qualifications a shooting man seeks in his dog. Natural ability depends upon breeding but the trainer can certainly impart the control and retain keenness in his pupil by training, little and often, on the lines suggested.

CHAPTER III

PRELIMINARY TRAINING—II

Gunfire. Retrieving Practice. Scent and Scenting. Scent Trail Lesson. Marking. Working in Cover. The Spring Thrower. A Test. Retrieving Birds and Rabbits. Hard Mouth.

TRAINING TO GUNFIRE.

ANY puppy that is ultimately to work as a gundog must very early in his career become accustomed to the sound of gunfire. Provided that the introduction to the gun is tactfully arranged, little trouble should be experienced but there is always a proportion of dogs, even from working strains, that are gun-shy or gun-nervy, though the proportion is undoubtedly higher in the non-working strains. There is a wide difference between a gun-*shy* dog and a gun-*nervy* one. The former is hopeless and is best given away as a pet, or painlessly destroyed, for his life will be a misery to himself and to his master. The latter can, with understanding on the part of the trainer, be completely cured and turned into a useful worker with the gun. Indeed, in my experience some of the best mature workers were often gun-nervy as pups, my Labrador Field Trial winner Bekesbourne Tosh being a case in point, and also my Springer F. T. winner Bekesbourne Rozzi. The first did not get over the trouble until he was about fourteen months, but within a week of cure won an Open Gundog Test against some of the best dogs in the country and has since proved his worth at Field Trials. A dog can easily be made gun-nervy and (though experts have in the past disagreed with me) I am also convinced that they can be made gun-*shy*. However, this does not concern us so much as avoidance of the creation of any nervous reaction whatsoever to the sound of gunfire.

It is worth while to invest in a blank-cartridge pistol or revolver of the race-starter's type. This saves a great deal of expense in cartridges and is a handy weapon to carry about. Failing this, early lessons can be conducted with a .410 shotgun or a larger bore, using blanks with small powder charges or standard cartridges from which some of the shot charge has been removed. The main thing is to work up from a small bang at a distance to a loud one close at hand and for this purpose it is useful to accustom the puppy from an early age to sudden noises. One good idea is to bang a metal tray or a sheet of iron as a signal for feeding time, or to have a pistol or gun fired at a distance (diminishing as the pup becomes accustomed to it) by someone else whilst you stand by and put the bowl of food down directly the shot is fired. In this way the puppy associates the loud noise with something pleasant—his food—and half the battle is won.

When a puppy will tolerate a fairly small charge being fired quite close, the "noises off" can be increased, care being taken to observe the reaction of the pupil. From now on it is a good idea to let him see what is causing the noise, and walks should be taken with a small-bore gun under the arm, which can be fired occasionally, giving the puppy a titbit if there is any nervous reaction. Avoid causing any fear by careless brandishing of the weapon—a good many puppies are more scared of the gun itself than of the noise it makes, having been either foolishly punished with it or because it has been fired too close to them too soon.

I have purposely made rather more of this question of introduction to gunfire than might be thought necessary. In most cases puppies quickly become accustomed both to the weapon and the report it makes, but it is far better to err on the side of safety and make doubly sure. Later on, when more advanced training is undertaken, it will be found that the accepted procedure is to train Retrievers to ignore the sound of gunfire, and for Spaniels, Pointers and Setters to be taught to drop to it. For this reason, with the last breeds, gunfire becomes another "command" to drop, and if you have not already got your pupil quite accustomed to the sound, and suddenly start forcing him to sit to it, the effect on the nerves may be serious. I believe this is why a rather high proportion of Spaniels are found to be gun-shy than is the case in the Retriever breeds. This is usually due to the trainer's mishandling of the situation. Certainly, once the pupil is used to gunfire and has started his sitting lessons, the pistol can be introduced and used in conjunction with the command to drop so that ultimately the puppy will drop to the sound of a shot alone, just as he will to the whistle.

With Pointers and Setters, which are seldom required to retrieve in this country, gunfire must signal a drop. This is fairly easy, for not being retrievers there is little temptation when the gun is fired and something falls. Spaniels and

Retrievers, however, work under much greater temptation, especially Spaniels, which are liable to be nearer the game when it is shot than are Retrievers. Readers will appreciate that the reason Pointers, Setters and Spaniels must drop to shot is to prevent their carrying on with their questing and so flushing other game before that already shot has been picked up and the gun reloaded, and also (as they are questing dogs out in front of the guns) as an additional precaution against running-in and picking-up the bird without command, in the case of Spaniels. Retrievers, walking to heel whilst shooting is in progress, have no obligation to perform any special act when the gun is fired and game drops. They must await a command before going out to retrieve.

Many promising dogs are ruined by the common mistake of allowing the association of ideas between a shot and something to retrieve to be formed too early. This association must come with experience, but under this method of training by that time the pupil should be under such control that he can resist the temptation to run-in to shot. If, however, a puppy is allowed from the start to acquire the knowledge that gunfire probably means something to pick up and retrieve, it is infinitely more difficult to perfect and maintain steadiness to shot, which is essential in a well-trained gundog. If this association of ideas is formed too early a puppy will be found to watch the gun and almost before it reaches the shoulder he will be off looking for something to retrieve, whilst the sound of a shot will cause him to go almost mad with eagerness to get out and search. For these reasons, therefore, we are forced to deceive the pupils for as long as possible. In the case of questing dogs, they must believe that a shot merely signifies that they are to stop all motion and drop. The Retriever must regard the sound of a shot as of no consequence at all; it must never become a signal for a dash out to retrieve.

The case of a puppy which shows serious signs of fright when a gun is fired for the first time (even if at a great distance) must be treated on its merits. If the puppy is really terrified, and bolts for home or into his kennel, you quite likely have a truly gun-shy specimen on your hands. Further tests will prove if this is so. If, however, the fear quickly fades (especially in the presence of a bowl of food!) you may just have to be extra tactful in your future gunfire lessons, but the probability is that all will be well. In these latter cases the practice of firing a gun at a distance at meal times will have to be kept up longer than when there is a more normal reaction, and greater vigilance will have to be observed later if the puppy is of one of the breeds which must drop to shot. All harshness must be avoided and every sudden or loud noise must be associated with something pleasant—an edible reward—until fear of them has abated. It is always as well to get puppies used to strange people, cars, lorries, trains, and all the other noises and sights of everyday life, as early as possible in order to instil confidence about things in general and about gunfire and other loud noises in particular.

In dealing with a gun-nervy puppy a great deal of ingenuity on the part of the trainer may be called for, as with all training incidents where things do not go normally. A very nervy puppy might well have its training deferred for some weeks or months, and an earlier introduction to the connection between retrieving and gunfire be allowed in the special circumstances. This will entail much greater trouble later to steady the puppy, but is well worth while if it cures the gun-nerviness. However, it may be of some consolation to anyone owning a nervy puppy to know that during my training career I have known the above system of training to gunfire to fail only with about five dogs, and three of these were definitely gun-*shy*. The two gun-nervy specimens which did not respond were sold as pets without being given a prolonged course of special treatment which would, I feel, have resulted in success. I am writing now only of the dogs which came to me "untampered with". There have been cases when dogs have been sent in for training that had already been made gun-nervy, or gun-shy, through mishandling on the part of their owners, who have generally been honest enough to admit their mistakes. The great thing is to start off a puppy from an early age to hear gunfire daily and treat it as a matter of course. This is what happens to puppies born in training and working kennels, where they become accustomed to the sound of gunfire right from the time they can hear, especially if training is carried on in close proximity to the kennels, as often happens. Such puppies hardly ever give any trouble with gun-shyness and it is undoubtedly the best of all introductions to gunfire.

I shall deal with the subject of gunfire, as it affects the different breeds, in the Chapters on the advanced training of these breeds. All that is required in the early stages is to accustom your puppy both to the gun and the sound of it being fired and to see that no unpleasant ideas are created.

The connection between a shot and something to retrieve must be concealed until the last possible moment. Puppies which come from working stock and have been well reared on wise and natural diet, especially raw meat, will seldom be found lacking in courage, and such puppies usually have sound nerves as well as sound bodies. In a gundog this is an essential combination.

RETRIEVING PRACTICE.

When your pupil will drop to command, wait for orders before fetching the thrown or hidden dummy, deliver it nicely to hand and can withstand gunfire, you can begin more advanced lessons in retrieving. It is worthy of note that, from the Field Trial angle, a Retriever is expected to be a more "polished" and "finished" retriever of game than a Spaniel. This is as it should be, for a Spaniel's main job is questing for unshot game, whereas the sole job of the Retriever is retrieving, but for all that a good Spaniel should be capable of working to hand signal and ranging well out in quest of shot game to retrieve. The reader who desires to work his Spaniel up to the standard of a Field Trial Retriever should therefore also read the Chapter on Retriever Training as this deals with exceptionally advanced and polished work. But in this section on preliminary training all breeds are catered for, so we can proceed a little further before dividing the breeds.

Now that the puppy remains steady to the thrown dummy whilst the handler walks away, there are three more items of training which should be taught, all very useful practice and tests of steadiness and retrieving ability. The first step is what I call "the going-back lesson", and consists of simply walking the puppy along (at first on the lead) and dropping the dummy. Allow him to watch this, then walk him on another twenty yards or more. Drop the puppy, remove the lead, and after a period of waiting send him back to retrieve with the usual command and signal. Repeat this, extending the distances to which you walk on from the dummy until the puppy will eagerly return for it over a distance of a hundred or a hundred and fifty yards. Finally, practise this without the use of the lead, restraining the puppy from picking up the dummy immediately it is dropped by the command "No". It will be found that after a short while the puppy will hardly notice the dropped dummy and soon you can begin dropping it without letting the pupil see it fall. This practice is extremely useful for several reasons—it encourages the puppy to speed up his departure and return in retrieving, it develops memory and it "trains" the nose, especially if the dummy is dropped into thickish cover from time to time. It will soon be noticed that many pupils become cunning about this, getting into the habit of following the foot scent of the handler back to the spot where the dummy was dropped. This is a good thing and most interesting to the mere human to discover that his puppy can "smell" his trail for long distances and will puzzle out the scent even on bare ground, which does not hold scent so well as grass or other surfaces. It helps to teach a puppy to "take a line", but too much of this kind of thing may make him rely upon finding a trail. As in the shooting field this will not always be possible, practice in this respect should be limited once the puppy starts relying upon a "foot scent" to follow. You can fox him about this by throwing the dummy (unobserved by the puppy, of course) some considerable distance before sending him back, so that when he gets to the end of the trail he must start questing and ranging about to find the dummy. In these cases it is as well at first to throw the dummy up-wind so that a certain amount of help is obtained by the puppy naturally.

Scent and Scenting Conditions.

The whole question of scent and the scenting powers of dogs is a most interesting one, not even now fully understood. You will learn far more (and far better) than I can explain by watching your puppy questing for the dummy and following your scent trail, puzzling out a faint scent by "trial and error" methods and making every possible use of whatever wind is blowing. Whilst on this subject I should mention that on hot, sultry, windless days, when the ground is dry, scenting conditions are liable to be very bad and too much retrieving practice will discourage and weary a puppy. During those days it is better to do the training in the early morning or late in the evening, when it is cooler and there is a dew to dampen the grass and make scenting better. Never go on too long on bad scenting days and avoid discouraging the pupil at all costs. In all early retrieving lessons it is most desirable that the puppy's quest should end in success (especially if the pupil is not an over-keen retriever) and it is as well to make sure that a persevering quest is rewarded with a find, even if it means almost showing the puppy where the dummy lies. This may entail quite a lot of work and walking on your part but it is worth the trouble. Puppies vary a great deal in diligence in quest, some pupils almost refusing to give up the hunt even if called upon to do so, others being easily discouraged if they do not find quickly and therefore needing more assistance and encouragement.

Referring once again to the difference between a Retriever and a Spaniel, I do not consider it advisable (should the pupil be intended for Spaniel work pure and simple) to allow a Spaniel to range out such long distances or go back so far in quest of the dummy—in other words, do not give the puppy the impression that he can continually be working at a great distance from you. If this is done, it will usually be found that a Spaniel needs constant recalling when questing *unshot* game, the idea having been inculcated that he can range as wide as he likes. A Spaniel should therefore be trained to range well out on occasions, but never so far or so frequently as a Retriever. A Retriever, on the other hand, can be allowed to consider that his range is unlimited in quest, and every encouragement should be given to "get him out into the country", to use the expression of a well-known Field Trial handler. Indeed, I consider that a Retriever cannot be given too wide a range in quest, always provided that he can be controlled at any distance within hearing, though this should not be to the exclusion of close-range questing.

The Scent Trail Lesson.

Having already referred to the average puppy's early ability to follow his master's scent trail, his efforts can now be turned into more useful channels by laying definite scent trails for him to follow. In the initial stages the dummy can be used; later on, a dead rabbit or bird, once the pupil has been introduced to the "real thing". As we have seen that puppies will follow their master's scent, it is obviously useless to lay a drag by simply drawing the dummy along behind you and later sending the puppy off—he is just as likely to follow your scent as that of the retrieve. The idea to implant is that (on occasions) the object which he is seeking will lay him a trail, as in the case of a "winged" bird or a crippled rabbit—not that master's scent will always be present. The best method of laying a scent trail is for two people to walk along, each holding the end of a string (as long as is practicable) to the centre of which has been attached the dummy and, later on, a game specimen. The dummy should be allowed to trail along the ground for increasing distances, the puppy being out of sight of this operation. Lay the drag into the wind on the first few occasions, then fetch the pupil and send him from the start of the drag to retrieve the dummy, which has of course been detached from the string and dropped at the end of the trail. Twenty or thirty yards is an ample distance to trail the dummy for a start, increasing to sixty and then to eighty and one hundred yards or more, according to the progress of the pupil. Once he starts taking the line do not distract him with calls and shouts every time he deviates (remember that the scent probably fluctuates here and there for reasons unknown to us) but encourage him to puzzle out the line for himself. Success will inspire the puppy, and later on drags can be laid down-wind and across-wind to give more advanced practice.

Another method of achieving the same object is to use a long pole, or a fishing rod and line—to avoid mixing your own scent with that of the trailed dummy—to lay the trail single-handed. With this method always come back after dropping the dummy by making a wide detour so as not to confuse the scent. If no rod or pole is available an alternative is to lay a long line out, attach the dummy to the far end and then, after an interval to allow your own scent to fade, draw the line in and drop the dummy, again returning by a wide detour, down-wind. To make this practice really valuable the pupil should be put on to the line after intervals of increasing length from the time the drag was laid, and a further diversion can be made by sending the puppy out to the start of the drag from some little distance, as in the shooting field it will not always be practicable to walk the dog right up to the fall—often the exact fall is not known. By using your imagination and common sense this useful lesson can be made most valuable, and steadily more difficult for the puppy, but you must be guided by results and not attempt too much too quickly.

MARKING.

The last item of retrieving practice with which I shall deal here is intended to develop accurate "marking", and to encourage the puppy to range well out in quest of his dummy. The pupil is left sitting on the drop whilst the handler walks away twenty or more yards and throws the dummy as far out as he can. Throw it into light cover for a start, then later into thicker stuff, return to the puppy and send him off to retrieve.

According to the progress made, extend the distance to which you walk before throwing the dummy; with Retrievers the farther you go the better ultimately. It is very handy to have a special command to instruct the pupil to range out, and this can be taught now. Personally, I always use "Get out" for this, and teach it in conjunction with the "going back" lesson and the one under discussion now. The pupil having already learnt to drop on command at a distance, I send him out to retrieve and when he has gone twenty yards or so I stop him by whistle or command. The puppy naturally looks round at me, and then I wave my hand forward and say "Get out", followed by "Fetch it" if the pupil appears puzzled. This is a very good test of obedience to the stop command as well, for the puppy is naturally eager to get to the retrieve, and if you can stop him going out in this manner it is certain evidence that you have correctly taught the drop or stop at a distance. The puppy can soon be stopped two or three times on his way out to retrieve, each time being given a moment or two for consideration, then ordered to "Get out". Most puppies quickly learn to associate the command with going away from the handler, and this will be useful later in the field for getting the dog farther out to a retrieve which he has not marked down. A Spaniel should, I feel, be made to drop as well as stop, whereas with a Retriever all that is necessary is a halt of motion. Most puppies will soon stop only when the command is given (or the whistle blown), so that with Spaniels you can insist that they drop, whereas with Retrievers you can permit them to stand and look at you, without insisting on a complete drop. The reason why a Spaniel should drop is that he is of a more impetuous breed and more liable than a Retriever to proceed without orders, and in Spaniel work the dog will be expected to drop to shot at a distance and may well have live game getting up round him, so that his temptation is greater. This, however, is a matter for the handler to decide on its merits as applied to his particular requirements and is merely a suggestion on my part. If, when you stop him going out to retrieve, the puppy starts to come back to you instead of going forward to your command and signal, take a few steps forward and indicate once again that he is to go away from you. It is inadvisable to overdo this stopping whilst the pupil is on the way out; it may be found to slow down the departure of a dog in quest, which is undesirable. The amount of practice you give will therefore depend, like many other training items, upon the individual temperament of your puppy and the speed with which he realizes what is required of him.

Working in Cover.

In all these more advanced lessons in retrieving every effort should be made to accustom the puppy to work in cover of increasing thickness and toughness, starting with grass or light root crops and finishing after a week or two in thick brambles and undergrowth which will test the drive and courage of any puppy. I should also stress that the sooner you get the puppy used to questing for a dummy he has not seen thrown the better, and in most of these lessons this is easily arranged—after, of course, a good start has been made and progress on the dummy (watched, thrown or dropped) is satisfactory.

The Spring Thrower.

As an additional aid to training, some trainers make use of a contrivance known as a "spring thrower". This is designed on the lines of a simple clay pigeon trap and is intended to fling the dummy some distance. It is fired by pulling a string at any required distance from the trap. This is very useful for teaching marking, and it saves the handler a bit of walking in the matter of distant retrieves, but to be really efficient one needs to have several throwers concealed all over the training ground. Either way, if single-handed the trainer has a good deal of walking to do in order to reload. It is a convenient method of teaching a dog steadiness at a drive; the handler can seat the dog beside him and pull the string, releasing the dummy into the air at any desired distance from him, so more nearly simulating the "real thing". The use of a thrower has several disadvantages, one being that a lot of puppies are scared by the noise made when the spring is released—and I have not come across a silent one yet! Another snag is that if only one thrower is employed, to be effective it has frequently to be moved to different positions, or the pupil becomes used to it and bored by it, and though I do on occasions make use of one I do not consider that it is an essential piece of training equipment. To be a real convenience one needs an assistant to work it, and if you have an assistant he could quite easily do all that is necessary without using the thrower at all! For instance, an assistant hidden behind a hedge, throwing dummies towards you, effectively imitates birds coming over at a drive, without the use of a thrower. What is more, an assistant could be told in which directions and how high to throw the "birds", whereas a thrower unless readjusted can eject them in only one direction, and only one at a time. Possibly with an ingenious arrangement of pulleys, runners and strings several throwers could be arranged to the satisfaction of the most particular trainer, but frankly I think they are, for the average man, quite unnecessary and a waste of time and effort, to say nothing of money.

A Little Test.

As I have already stressed, the preliminary course is all-important and so the wise trainer before proceeding further will set his dog a little test to make quite certain that the instruction so far given has been mastered. If the dog comes through this test with honours, training can proceed to the more advanced work and the retrieving of real fur and feather. If not, the weak items will have to be gone over again and the pupil kept on "hand training" until as perfect as it is possible to make him. I make a point of conducting this test with all my pupils and until I can "pass" them I do not allow training to progress any further. It is simply a waste of effort to do so.

Choose if possible a fine, good scenting day and take your pupil into a field or other quiet place where you are unlikely to be disturbed, either by people or by the presence of birds or rabbits (or the scent of either). There should be some cover available—a few bushes, a thick hedge or some long grass. Walk the puppy along at heel for a hundred yards or so and drop him by command. Continue to walk on for fifty or more yards, then call the puppy up, stopping him by whistle when half-way to you. Walk round him in a wide circle to test for steadiness on the drop. If all goes well, call him up and walk him on at heel, then suddenly produce your dummy, throw it away from you and fire a blank. If steady, allow the puppy to retrieve this. The next test consists of leaving the pupil on the drop and walking away, throwing the dummy into cover. Return to the sitting puppy and, after a suitable interval, send him to retrieve. The next test can be for steadiness on the drop when you are out of sight. Whilst you are hidden from view throw the dummy away. Return to the puppy and after an interval (as usual) send him to retrieve. Try to stop him on the way out to this retrieve, then wave him on with a "Get out".

[*P. R. A. Moxon*

Early hand training can be given under cover in bad weather, a fact which is appreciated by the growing band of lady handlers

[*P. R. A. Moxon*

Group training of Spaniels using the Windrush dummy-launcher

[*Horace Hall*

Retrieving a pigeon across water

[*A. Sparrow*

A stiff climb after retrieving from the far side of the river

[*Horace Hall*

Retrieving a runner over a woodland fence

[*Horace Hall*

A small Spaniel takes a flying leap with her retrieve

[Horace Hall

Working to hand. Stopping at a distance

[Horace Hall

Changing direction by hand signal

If the puppy has a long distance to go back on this retrieve you can stop him two or three times in this manner.

It will be found that most puppies will pass this test quite easily after eight or ten weeks of daily lessons, some even sooner. Backward pupils may take longer to get to this stage, but this is of no great importance as long as the lessons are mastered. All subsequent field training will depend upon how well and how completely these earlier lessons were taught, and, at the risk of being told that I repeat myself too frequently, I will say again that THE PRELIMINARY COURSE IS BY FAR THE MOST IMPORTANT.

Retrieving Birds and Rabbits.

The time has now come for your puppy to have a retrieve of the real thing. I usually start them off on rabbits, because these are easier to obtain at any season of the year and, as the dummy has been a rabbit-skin one, a rabbit is at first more likely to be readily picked up than a bird. Whatever specimen you use for the first retrieve, make sure it is cold (preferably shot the previous day) and is clean and not bloody or dirty in any way. Blood and "innards" spattered all over the fur will only encourage the puppy to stop and lick (possibly even play with and bite) the specimen, whereas we want a speedy pick-up and retrieve. I think that the best method of introducing a puppy to the genuine article is to take him out and, after giving him a "going-back" retrieve or two with the dummy, dropping the rabbit in just the same way. I should point out that the rabbit ought to be concealed from the puppy up to this stage, and for this purpose (and for carrying leads, dummies and for shooting work) I always have a large inside "poacher's pocket" sewn into all my jackets. Send the pupil back in the ordinary way but station yourself so that you can see what happens when he finds the rabbit. Directly you see his head go down to pick-up, give the "come-back" whistle and do all in your power to speed him. Generally the puppy will grab the rabbit and come dashing back, in which event you can feel well pleased and, instead of repeating the test, put the rabbit back in your inside pocket and leave well alone for that day. Avoid whenever possible giving more than one retrieve with the same specimen, otherwise the puppy may start to play with it and bite. If you have other rabbits handy you can use them by all means, but do not overdo it at first; be satisfied that the puppy behaved himself.

It may happen that instead of the puppy retrieving promptly and well he stops and sniffs the rabbit suspiciously, or starts playing. If this happens do all you can to get him back to you, but if he leaves the rabbit do not send him back. Leave the puppy on the drop and fetch it yourself, then show it to him, wave it about in front of his nose to get him interested, then throw it a short distance like a dummy. Get him away to it immediately, if necessary without any waiting on the drop, and start running away quickly, whistling and calling the puppy to follow. In nine cases out of ten this works and thereafter no trouble about retrieving rabbits is experienced. A puppy which refuses to pick up his first rabbit will almost always do his job if he is allowed to see a keen retrieving dog at work. Jealousy comes into play where all else fails. My method is to have both dogs sitting down. I walk out about fifteen or twenty yards and drop the rabbit in full view, then return and despatch the puppy to retrieve. When he is nearly up to the rabbit I send out the experienced dog, and usually I am rewarded by the sight of the puppy grabbing the rabbit the moment he notices the other dog coming, and bringing it back to me at speed. There are other tricks that may induce a shy retriever to lift his first real specimen. You can cover the rabbit with the skin previously used on the dummy, or attach the rabbit to a length of string and, when the pupil gets up to it, jerk and drag it along. However, these stratagems seldom need be employed with puppies of genuine working strain. Their inherent instinct tells them to pick up and retrieve fur and feather in the same way as they have hitherto done with dummies.

Once a puppy will retrieve a cold rabbit he can be tried with other cold specimens—pheasant, partridge, wild duck, etc. Pigeons are not suitable for early lessons as they have loose feathers which irritate dogs by adhering to their mouths, and often cause a puppy to bite and play with the retrieve. Pigeons can come later, and generally no trouble will be met with, though many dogs seem to dislike them, either because of the loose feathers or because of their peculiar scent. The same thing will be found with snipe, woodcock and some vermin birds, such as magpie and jay.

From retrieving cold specimens to carrying warm ones is but a short step. The rabbit or bird used should be clean; particular attention should be paid to this as with freshly shot specimens the scent is stronger, and urine, faeces or blood on the fur or feathers may distract the dog and cause trouble. Usually a puppy which has behaved well on cold game will soon become quite happy about retrieving warm stuff and exactly the same procedure should be followed for the first few occasions.

HARD MOUTH.

A dog is termed "hard-mouthed" when he bites the game sufficiently to break the ribs, not necessarily to break the flesh, as so many people imagine. A hard-mouthed dog will almost invariably pick up the bird or rabbit across the back and crush the ribs—a dog which picks up by a bunch of feathers or a fold of skin, so tearing it, is usually extremely soft-mouthed and will soon learn to pick up properly. Experienced trainers and handlers, and also Field Trial judges, always *feel the ribs* of anything retrieved. To detect breakage is an art and requires practice, unless the carcase is really badly mauled. A young rabbit, partridge or a hen pheasant will crush much more easily than an old buck or cock bird and particular attention should be paid to the examination of anything the dog took a long time to pick up, mouthed or put down on the way back to the handler. Some dogs will always bite their game if they put it down, which is an additional reason for us to like a fast pick-up and return from our dogs.

This subject of hard mouth is an extensive one and a book could be written about it alone. It is one of those things about which you keep on learning, as dogs vary a great deal in this direction. Some are always soft-mouthed and never cause a moment's worry; others will bite certain types of game or only live game—I know of one Spaniel who always bit his game on a short (close at hand) retrieve but never on a distant one. Sometimes injury to the game is accidental; occasionally it is injured in falling (by striking a tree or bush) and the dog is unjustly blamed. Some animals become hard-mouthed with age, a failing which certain strains of Labrador seem to have, and the old fashioned Curly-coated Retriever was always accused of being hard-mouthed as a breed. This was unfair, in my judgment. However, there is no doubt that a dog can easily become hard-mouthed as a consequence of accident or mishandling, and it is my opinion that many do so through fear of their handler. Imagine a dog dashing out to retrieve and knowing full well that upon his return his irate master is going to give him a thrashing—of all the silly things to do. Such a dog may well "clench his teeth" in nervous expectation of the flogging (just as we used to do at school if we knew we were in for a beating), and whatever game is being carried becomes crushed. This illustration is just another good example of the folly and cruelty of punishing a dog for running-in to retrieve *when he returns to you.* He does not know the punishment is for running-in; he thinks it is for his last action (retrieving and returning), so not only is the beating useless as a cure for running-in but it causes confusion and loss of confidence. A dog which is bitten by a rat, or even by a rabbit, may easily become hard-mouthed. I once sent a Spaniel to retrieve a grey squirrel which was not quite dead and this gave the bitch a nasty bite. She dropped it quickly, then bit and killed it, afterwards retrieving it to hand. From that time this bitch has always bitten live fur and feather but has remained as tender as ever with completely dead stuff. A squealing rabbit will often upset a nervy dog to the point of making him bite and anything caught up in wire or brambles may have the same effect. For these reasons the too-early retrieving of wounded birds and rabbits is to be avoided, and in the sections on field work I shall go more fully into the best procedure to follow.

Finally, it should be clearly understood by the novice trainer that many puppies will play with and bite their first few retrieves, sometimes quite badly, but that in most cases time and experience will put everything right. I never worry if any of my pupils are rough with their first few retrieves of real game, but if the habit persists there is little that can be done. Temporary cures for hard mouth may be possible but I do not believe there is any magic remedy for confirmed biting. If a dog brings in a bird you know he has bitten badly he can be scolded and the lips pressed against the teeth; some people even advocate showing the damaged bird to the culprit and giving him a severe whipping. My view is that it is best to deal with each situation on its merits, having regard to the temperament of the individual and to allow time and experience in the case of a puppy with his first few birds or rabbits. Once again, pups from true working strains are seldom found to offend in this respect, but too early introduction to real game can cause trouble with any dog, which is another reason why the wise trainer always starts his puppies off on dummies instead of the real thing. From the very start of training a puppy can be encouraged towards a soft mouth by taking anything he is carrying very gently from him, never snatching or grabbing, or indulging in a tug-of-war. Other dogs should always be out of the way when a puppy is undergoing retrieving lessons, for the same reason, as a dog running up and grabbing the dummy (or game) can cause the other dog to grip his retrieves tightly ever afterwards. I had one or two promising pups ruined in this way years ago, and ever since I have been very, very careful.

A dog which has successfully passed the test of early work, and has done well in his few retrieves of firstly cold and then warm game, may now proceed to much more advanced training. From now on the breeds and their work are separated, except for the extra items of water training and jumping.

CHAPTER IV

RETRIEVING FROM WATER. JUMPING FENCES AND GATES.

Working in Water. First Introduction to Water. Water-shyness. Advanced Water-Work. Working in Reeds. Jumping Fences and Gates.

WORKING IN WATER.

ANY retrieving gundog worthy of the name should be capable of retrieving from water (and from *across* water) in any weather at any time of the year. As far as Field Trials are concerned, a water test is often included in the schedule for Retrievers, and sometimes for Spaniels as well. It is therefore highly desirable that any Retriever or Spaniel should be trained to water, no matter whether it is intended for ordinary shooting or Field Trials. Nothing is more exasperating than to be out shooting and have game fall into water, or on the far bank of a stream or river, with no dog present that will face water to retrieve. Even if you never normally go duck shooting and your own ground contains no water, there may come a time when you are invited out on to ground where much of the stuff may fall into water—and what a fool you will appear if your dog refuses to wet his feet!

It is fairly safe to say that most *working* strains of both Retrievers and Spaniels are water-loving dogs and quickly become adept at retrieving from it if given sufficient early encouragement and experience. There are, of course, exceptions—I have known even an Irish Water Spaniel to be absolutely water-shy—but most dogs will sooner or later come to love working in water. A good many end up by being more difficult to get out of it than into it. The old Springer stud dog "Spitfire Pilot" would always prefer to swim the river for about a mile whilst I walked along the tow-path to get to our duck-shooting hide on the local marshes. If I called him out he would pop in again as soon as he thought my attention had been distracted and in the end I gave up and allowed him to please himself. This love of water he passed on to his offspring and even now I find pups four generations removed from Pilot mad to work in water. One of his grandsons—Sam—will always lie down in any handy puddle given the opportunity, no matter how cold the weather may be! He will even break ice in order to have a bath when nobody is looking!

Perhaps the most popular dog for water-work and the duck-shooting specialist is the Labrador Retriever. This breed is undoubtedly ideal for water, the sleek water-resisting coat and "otter" tail seeming almost designed for the job. After immersion a Labrador dries very quickly—a few shakes and a brisk run and he is ready to go into a car or indoors, whereas most other breeds take longer to dry and, what is more, feel the cold to a greater extent. Anyone who has ever had the job of bathing a Labrador to rid him of skin vermin or to treat him for skin trouble knows only too well how difficult it is to get his actual skin really wet, the dense coat being almost waterproof unless deliberately rubbed the wrong way and massaged. For a man who does little else but duck and marsh shooting I should unhesitatingly recommend a Labrador, especially as the breed is so easy to train and very hardy.

FIRST INTRODUCTION TO WATER.

The first introduction to water should be made when the weather is warm and sunny, as this will encourage the puppy to immerse himself, and a young dog must be guarded against chills, especially if he is still teething. As to the age at which to start a puppy in water, this must also large depend upon the weather, though many keen puppies will solve the problem themselves by entering water unbidden should they come across any. Only a few weeks ago I was in the woods with a Springer bitch who loves water (a daughter of old Pilot, incidentally) and a Labrador puppy aged thirteen weeks. The little bitch as usual made straight for the muddy pond in the middle of the wood, and whilst lighting my pipe I heard a splash and to my amusement saw the Labrador puppy swimming out to her, for all the world as though he had done it many times before. Another puppy last year surprised me—this time a Springer dog about four months old—who stood on the bank of the Kentish Stour and, after a moment's contemplation of the ripples, dived in and swam about with obvious enjoyment, though he was quite alone with me and had never before even *seen* water. Such dogs are "naturals", and apart from practice in retrieving from an opposite bank and marking in water, will require little specialized training. These are the sort of dogs that, with experience, start using the currents to their advantage and will dive after a wounded duck that has disappeared beneath the surface. Apropos of making use of currents, I have many times seen a good water dog wait on the bank until a duck floated down to him, then swim in to intercept it, so saving a tiring battle against the current, but if the bird showed any signs of life when it first hit the water the dog would be after it at once. If this sort of thing is not reasoning, it is very near to it, as also is the art of catching a wounded duck which has dived several times. After two or three unsuccessful dives in pursuit of such a bird, many dogs will swim round watching the surface of the water. Immediately there is a slight ripple and the duck's bill appears they will swim quickly and almost noiselessly to the spot and make a grab, or even dive down and come up below the bird.

There can be no hard and fast rule, then, about the age for first introduction, though few will attempt to get pups into water until they are about six months old or even later. Choose, as I have said, a warm sunny day, and select a pond or stream with a gentle slope into the water, so that the pupil does not have to make a leap or suddenly find himself out of his depth. If you can have with you a keen water dog this will be a great asset and will go a long way towards ensuring success; the puppy will be eager to imitate his companion and jealousy will do much to help. Assuming, however, that you have no other dog, take along some dummies which will float (or rubber balls) and a few pieces of hard-baked brown bread. It is a good plan to wear rubber boots or waders, to keep your legs dry from splashes or to enable you to walk about in the shallows should this be necessary. Stand on the edge of the water and let the puppy play about, and note his reactions. If he starts paddling in the shallow water, throw a dummy or ball a little way ahead of him, and encourage him to bring it to you. If he does, continue the game, each time throwing the dummy a little farther from the puppy so that ultimately he will have to swim a short way for it. If, at this critical juncture, he jibs at going out of depth, try a piece or two of the bread, which will often prove successful. When the puppy has swum a few strokes and found that there is nothing to fear, confidence will be quickly gained and if you achieve that much on your first visit to water you can be well satisfied. When your puppy will swim about to retrieve he should be made to come and wait on the bank while you throw the dummy, and then be despatched for it upon command—that is, if he has already reached the stage of training where he has to wait for orders before retrieving. If he has not, then allow him to retrieve directly you throw. Make him used to retrieving from greater distances until ultimately you can throw the dummy on to the far bank of the stream or pond and get him across.

WATER-SHYNESS.

A really water-shy puppy will require more time and patience, and a youngster that refuses to wet his feet will need special attention. First of all, try using a keen water dog as an example—borrow one if necessary or ask a friend to bring his along. If this does not work then you must try fording a stream yourself, encouraging the puppy to follow, which it will often do if you walk on and disappear over the far bank. Another alternative is to take the puppy out in a boat and gently lower him over the side when, once he has swum a little way, it will often be found that confidence in water has been gained.

At all costs avoid frightening the water-shy puppy in any way and defer the use of force until all else has failed. There are, I know, many advocates of the system of throwing a dog bodily into water time and again, until it will swim, but this is seldom necessary and should be adopted only as a last resort. In all gundog training the object is to get the pupil to work of his own free will and because he likes and enjoys it, and the use of force with any dog which already shows signs of nervousness seems to be more likely to make matters worse instead of better.

ADVANCED WATER-WORK.

The puppy having taken to water, it will willingly swim out a fair distance to retrieve the thrown dummy, and further progress can be made. If you can make use of a wide stream or river, and obtain the assistance of a friend, much useful and interesting work can be done about retrieving from the far side. Progress in this direction will depend on the age of the puppy and the stage to which general retrieving training has advanced. It should not be attempted until the pupil is capable of being sent out, stopped by whistle or command, and directed by hand to any given spot. This stage reached, you can go ahead and practise on the far bank of a river or stream, an assistant being on the opposite bank and concealed from view throwing up dummies which can occasionally be saluted with blank cartridges, whilst you stay with your dog on the near bank. At first the dummy should be thrown so that it falls just on the water's edge, then farther and farther inland, and in cover, to the right and left, the puppy being despatched across the water after the usual proper interval. Success achieved, you can next try getting the dog across to unseen dummies, starting with easy ones close to the water and building up to difficult retrieves well out on the far side, working the dog by command, whistle and signal as in the advanced retriever work on land.

A special command may be introduced and used only for sending the pupil across water. "Over" is probably used for jumping, but "*Get* Over" or "Cross" could be used, or it may be found that "Get out" (as used in land training for sending the dog farther out) is effective. If it is it can be used for both circumstances. It is extremely useful to have a dog that can be sent across water to quest the far bank by command, and many Retriever Field Trials have been won by dogs capable of doing this and working by signal to find birds which they had not been able to mark down, well out on the far side of a river. Being able to get the dog across a river is quite useless unless, when he is there, he can be directed to within reasonable scenting distance of a bird which has not been marked by him. So it will be seen that the advanced Retriever training as intended for land work serves a dual purpose.

It is difficult to direct a dog working actually *on* a large sheet of water such as a lake, but with practice and experience much can be managed. When in the water, a dog is apt to swim round and round searching for a floating object, and is often deaf to all commands and blind to all signals, no matter how good he may be on land. A dog uses his nose on the water as well as his eyes, but not to the same extent as on land, and direction depends upon the experience which can be given, using dummies in the first stages and indicating their position by a wave of the arm and, if not obeyed, by showing the dog their position by throwing in a stone or empty cartridge case. If the dog realizes that you are trying to help him even when in water he will become more co-operative. Many will, with sufficient experience, become almost as "directable" as when on land.

Working in Reeds.

Experience should also be given of working in thick reeds, rushes and oozy swamps, especially if you intend doing a lot of duck or snipe shooting, for it is to these places that many wounded birds make their way. A duck or teal half buried in stinking mud beneath thick reeds or rushes takes a lot of finding, even by a most experienced dog with a good nose. I have spent many hours searching such places on the local marshes after the other shooters have left, and many an otherwise blank morning's flight has been made profitable by the birds, shot by others, found hours later by my dogs in the thick, swampy places. Once they have had some experience dogs get to love working in these stinking, squelchy spots, but to keep going for long stretches under such conditions they need to be very fit and hardy. Work in mud into which they sink at every step necessitates a "leaping" action and great exertion. I well remember the day when my old Susan (a big Springer who was at that time my "duck specialist") spent over half an hour trying to catch a lightly wounded mallard on the bed of a tidal lake which was nothing less than a sea of mud. The duck flapped over the ooze just in front of the bitch and when Susan paused for a rest the duck stopped too. Big though she was, there were times when the bitch was practically out of sight in the mud and the physical exertion called for during this adventure must have been tremendous. My friends and I waited on the bank in fear and trembling that the task would prove too much and that Susan would collapse and perhaps die of heart failure (I knew it was useless to call her off), but the gallant bitch persevered and slowly wore the duck down, until she was able to retrieve it and, quite exhausted and covered in mud and slime, bear it back to me.

One of the most difficult things to get a dog to do is to cross a river, cross the far bank and hunt the reeds of a lake or pond on the far side, or retrieve *from* the far lake. On the local marsh the river at one spot runs between two large lakes, both over fifty acres in area, and some of the best duck flighting is obtained by hiding at a certain spot on the tow path where any birds shot are almost bound to fall into the lake on the far side of the river. My shooting companions and I used to find that whilst most of our dogs would soon learn to cross the river and hunt the far bank few would at first go *over* the bank and down into the rushes at the edge of the lake, or *into* the lake itself, unless they were directed by thrown stones, or unless they could see the bird. It was impossible for any dog with the guns to mark the bird right down (the far bank being high), so that when our dogs were on the opposite bank we had to try to throw stones across to fall somewhere near where we thought the birds might lie, for *we* could not mark the birds right down, either. This was not easy. The river is about twenty yards wide or even more, the bank another ten, and it takes a good man to throw a stone thirty or thirty-five yards. However, we found that when a dog had been thus directed, and had successfully retrieved a bird, it would in future work more assiduously on the far bank and over it, and with experience learned to hunt the reeds on the other side and even swim about in the lake to look for dead and wounded ducks. Old Susan became very adept at this, as did a little bitch belonging to my shooting companion, and we lost few birds when these two dogs were out, many times being called upon by strangers to retrieve ducks for them from this far lake.

Susan was by way of being a "character". She gained a wonderful reputation on the local duck marsh and was almost infallible once she knew a bird was down. She could mark birds in bad light which made me almost blind, and many times started off to birds at which I had fired but thought I had missed. Somehow the bitch knew otherwise, and found many birds of which my friends had said, "We'll *never* get that one!" Susan was taken to the marshes in the first instance because she was far too wild and unsteady for formal land shooting, whereas for the type of marsh shooting I did then I liked a dog which went off as soon as a bird was hit, without waiting for orders. After she had left me Susan could not be recalled until she was ready to return; if she found a likely-looking patch of reeds she hunted it out regardless of shouts and whistles, in this way bringing to bag many ducks for which my own gun was certainly not responsible! There was the famous adventure when I took Susan to an evening flight on a strange marsh, when the widgeon were in. Susan had never before retrieved a widgeon. After it was dark my first (and last!) successful shot of the night brought down a bird across a shallow pool, and off Susan went to retrieve. My companion had just remarked that she was a long time coming back when we heard an ominous crunching sound across the water and as the moon came out of the clouds we could discern Susan lying half in the water, making a meal off my duck! She remained deaf to my blandishments and entreaties, until finally she decided that she was replete and returned, quite unabashed, and gently placed into my hand the two legs and a few feathers of the unfortunate widgeon! I have never lived down that story; friends on the Medway still take pleasure in reminding me on every possible occasion of the "dog trainer's dog which eats ducks". Susan never bit another bird, though she would sometimes cross the river and find a bird, deposit it in full view on the bank and swim back, refusing to go over for it again until we started to pack up to go home. Then, quite unbidden, Susan would swim over and fetch the bird in perfect style, as though realizing that she was playing a joke upon us! She never dropped a runner or wounded bird and despite her faults was the best dog for rough marsh shooting that I have ever known. She was not, perhaps, the sort of dog a dog trainer *should* take about but even dog trainers cannot always have perfect dogs, as the above stories go to prove!

Jumping Fences and Gates.

To be capable of jumping a natural obstacle, such as a fence or gate, is a very necessary accomplishment in a gundog, although of course a Pointer or Setter may never be required to do so. Any Spaniel or Retriever may, in the normal course of its duties, find its way barred by an obstacle which must either be jumped or climbed, or necessitate a long detour. This particularly applies to rough shooting dogs working in enclosed country. It is no joke trying to heave a 60 lb. Retriever over a fence, and having to do so makes the owner look foolish, yet one sees many dogs out shooting which have only a rudimentary idea of jumping. Anything at all difficult, which cannot be penetrated, is sufficient to start such dogs running up and down trying to find an easy way through, and failure to do so starts them whining and even yapping in vexation and excitement.

Most dogs come to love jumping, though sensible ones will usually seek an easy way through a gate or fence when carrying a retrieve and jump only if they cannot quickly find one. I have found that Labradors in particular become very keen on leaping any obstacle which bars their way, and a stylish jumper returning with a bird in its mouth, taking gates and fences in its stride with ease and grace, is always a pleasing sight. Jumping can, of course, be dangerous to the dog, especially if there are barbed-wire fences on the shoot, or wire netting in which a foot may get caught and perhaps a limb broken. For this reason it is essential that any keen jumping dog be under good control, so that if he is seen making for an obviously dangerous fence he may be stopped and diverted. This element of danger is a sound reason why a gundog should be taught and encouraged to jump *properly*, for a keen, clever jumper is less likely to become entangled or to hurt itself than one which scrambles over a fence anyhow and scrapes the top in so doing.

To begin with, a puppy should be practised in jumping easy places, and it should not be started until it is well grown, somewhere around about five or six months at the earliest, otherwise leg bones may become damaged or deformed. Wire-netting fences, unless there is something fairly solid on the top, should at first be avoided as a puppy is liable to get entangled. At all costs it is desirable to avoid giving the pupil any fright or unpleasant shock which may seriously retard progress in jumping, or even put the pupil off altogether. If you can find a suitably low fence or gate, or erect one in a *cul-de-sac* for the purpose, probably the best plan is to get over yourself and walk on, calling the puppy to follow. The pupil will almost always somehow scramble over and, having thus gained confidence, tackle the obstacle with greater enthusiasm on each succeeding attempt, until in the end he will come over in a flying leap. From this stage more difficult fences and gates can be tackled and the practice further diversified by sending the pupil for a dummy thrown or hidden on the far side.

A reluctant jumper can usually be encouraged to the point of success by seeing another dog, or dogs, jumping freely. He will quickly learn to follow their example. Only very occasionally is it necessary to assist a timid pupil and this should be as a last resort and stopped as soon as possible, otherwise the puppy will expect to be helped every time a fence is reached. When using a dummy it will often be found that, at first, though the pupil will jump keenly enough on the outward journey he will attempt to find an easier way when returning with the retrieve. This is natural and, in many ways, shows good sense on his part, but it should be so arranged for a start that there is no way through or round the fence so that the puppy gets the idea of jumping when carrying something. Hence my suggestion—arranging a jump in a passage or *cul-de-sac* where the pupil cannot possibly go round or get through.

A dog fresh and lively will usually jump a reasonable fence without touching the top, but when tiring will tend to leap on to the top of the fence, balance for a second and then jump down, giving a powerful thrust with his hind legs. The same thing applies to a very high fence or gate whether the dog is fresh or tired, and here he will tend to climb rather than jump, though many keen Labradors will, when fresh, quite easily clear five-foot fencing without touching the top. It is essential, therefore, that early practice is carried out with a jump that has a firm top and no crevices in which the feet may get caught. A dog which has learnt to jump a low fence may show hesitation on the first few occasions when asked to tackle a higher one and can be encouraged by the trainer patting the top of the fence and, if necessary, climbing over and walking away himself. It is as well to have a definite command for jumping and I usually say "Over" or "Get over", which, for a start, is used every time. For ordinary shooting work all that may be required is to have a dog that will jump the average fence or gate reasonably well. This should quickly be accomplished. If the pupil is intended for Field Trials a more intensive training should be given, for although a dog may run at Trials year after year and never see a fence there is always the chance that his ability to negotiate a difficult one may make all the difference between "getting into the money" and being an "also ran". I remember seeing a Spaniel Trial some years ago where a rabbit was wounded and made off through a nasty paling fence into some cover on the far side. One of the dogs then being tried, one up to that time well up in the judge's estimation, was put on to the line. This he followed until he came to the fence. He quickly found the place where the rabbit had got through and tried to squeeze through himself, but was unable to manage it and thereupon started running up and down looking for a gap. The handler tried without success to get the dog to jump by command and in the end walked down and lifted it over. It then proceeded to hunt the far cover for the wounded rabbit, which by this time had presumably got to ground—it was never found. In this example the time wasted was considerable and probably made all the difference between failure and success. Had the dog jumped the fence as soon as he found he could not get through he would have stood a good chance of finding the rabbit before it found sanctuary in a burrow. This, plus a stylish jump on the return journey, would have been spectacular enough to "catch the judge's eye". In fairness to the dog it must be stated that the fence was a difficult one, at least three feet six inches high and made of palings spaced in such a way that a Spaniel could not squeeze through. If it had been a netting fence, or boarded without gaps, the dog might have taken it in his stride. On the other hand, if the dog had previously had plenty of jumping experience on all types of fences he should have tackled it at least when the handler gave the command.

I once had a similar experience with a Spaniel, when competing at a Utility Trial. A cock pheasant was wounded and my Springer bitch found it crouching beside a sheep-netting fence. Before she could pick it up the bird got up and made off up the grassy slope on the far side of the fence and my bitch ran up and down along the fence yapping with excitement—excitement so great at seeing the bird departing that she never thought of jumping over! Sheep netting being of such large mesh, the bitch kept trying to get through and several times nearly got her head stuck, but ultimately I was able to stop her and make her jump without assistance. The pheasant was duly gathered, which was fortunate, for the delay was such that the bird might well have got away altogether. In both the incidents I have quoted, the fact that the dogs could see through the fences, and also could nearly *get* through, made them excited to such a degree (especially as they were both on hot scents) that the thought of jumping did not appear to enter their heads. For all that, either of them should, technically, have been capable of being stopped, given a slight wait to "cool off", then made to jump by command. It is easy to be wise after the event, and it is only by getting first-hand experience of these somewhat rare occurrences that one learns how essential apparently trivial items of training can be in certain circumstances.

CHAPTER V

ADVANCED RETRIEVER TRAINING

Handling from a Distance. Direction and Control. Using two Dummies. Work in Cover. The Weighted Dummy. Walking to Heel. Steadiness. The Rabbit Pen. Steadiness to Feather.

Handling from a Distance.

ADVANCED retriever work is one of the most interesting branches of gundog training and though it requires a good deal of time and patience it should not be found too difficult if early tuition has been mastered by the pupil. We have already taught our dog to retrieve both a dummy and the real thing, as well as to be obedient and to answer to hand signals up to a point. The object now is to amplify the education so that the dog can be made to range well out, be directed to right or left, come nearer or get farther away, by command and hand signal as required. The object of this is, of course, to be able to put the dog within reasonable scenting distance of a shot bird it has not been able to mark down, particularly useful training when a dog is required to retrieve from across a river, or over a fence or hedge which would be difficult to negotiate oneself. Distance work and control is most spectacular at Field Trials, the winning dogs frequently being those which can be handled from afar and which gather birds well out from the line, without necessity for the handler to go forward himself. It has another use in that dogs so taught can work well out in thick kale, or other cover, to a bird not marked down, without the handler having himself to enter the cover, more than likely wet and unpleasant on a shooting day.

The dog must also be made steady to both fur and feather, so that it will not chase or run-in to shot, and must be made accustomed to waiting by the guns and to seeing, without moving an inch, game falling temptingly close. A good deal of this steadiness training has already been instilled by means of the earlier dummy work where a retrieve is never allowed without orders; now all that remains to be done is to offer more practical experience, utilizing the rabbit pen or at least a tame rabbit, if this is possible, for the work on "fur". Opportunities will also be given of taking the dog among real game and the scent of game, checking any inclination to give chase.

The distance work and direction by hand signal require that a Retriever should maintain interest in the artificial training dummy, and most dogs will do so at least until they have had a full season's shooting work—a good many will retain their interest in retrieving artificial objects throughout life—and though this should not be overdone it is most helpful to the owner and gives greater opportunities for practising a dog during the close season. It will be obvious that to use real game throughout the training period is quite impracticable, especially with retrieving in which constant and varied practice is likely to be necessary. The trainer cannot always have a dead bird or rabbit in his hare pocket, but a dummy or rubber ball can always be carried—I am never without the latter in my pocket from one year's end to another, thus being able to practise young dogs at odd moments during the day. A rubber ball requires more finding than a dummy when hidden in cover or grass and so calls for greater use of nose on the part of a dog. It is surprising how quickly a good Retriever will find a ball once accustomed to it; no doubt a certain amount of scent lingers from the trainer's hands and pocket. However, for general purposes the dummy is the better object to use; balls can be kept for special work or for use when the carrying of a dummy (or a couple of dummies) would be inconvenient. Certainly a ball can be thrown farther than a dummy and as it bounces and rolls it is possible to get it quite a distance away with comparative ease.

Direction and Control. Using Two Dummies.

Direction and "remote control" can be quite simply taught by the use of two dummies and a good deal of patience. At first this lesson should be conducted in a grass field or on a lawn where there is not too much cover to conceal the dummies, and the pupil should be fresh and keen. My usual method of teaching direction is to seat the dog in front of and facing me a few yards away, and throwing out two dummies, one to the right and one to the left of the pupil, so that they fall well apart but not too far away from him. I then give a clear signal by throwing the right arm out in the direction of the right-hand dummy and give the usual command to retrieve. In most cases the dog starts off for the other dummy, which was thrown last and which he therefore remembers most clearly. I then immediately give my "stop" whistle and, by signal and by moving parallel to and in the direction of the dummy with right arm extended, encourage the dog to quest in the direction of the right-hand dummy. Each time the pupil attempts to go back towards the left-hand dummy I stop him again, until by moving to the right myself and insisting that he leave the other one I get the dog to pick up the correct dummy. If he disobeys the stop whistle and retrieves the wrong dummy, I take it from him, throw it back to its original position and continue to encourage him to go for the right one. It will be seen now why the "stop" command and whistle are so important, and why we taught in the early stages the habit of dropping to whistle on the way out to a dummy. Unless this has already been absorbed it is useless to attempt this exercise, and a puppy which persistently refuses to answer to the "stop" whistle must be put back in training until he will do so.

After the right-hand dummy has been successfully retrieved I give the same signal with my left hand and in just the same way encourage the puppy to quest to my left, until success is achieved. Sometimes after a puppy has retrieved one dummy he thinks there is nothing else to fetch (having forgotten all about the second dummy), and great patience and persistence must be used to get him out for it, even to the extent of walking him almost up to it and pointing it out! This entire practice with two dummies must be kept up until the pupil learns that he must go in the direction indicated by the arm wave and that there are at least two objects to be retrieved one after the other. This usually happens fairly quickly, but the changes must be rung and sometimes the dog sent first for the last-thrown dummy instead of *vice versa*, so that he does not become accustomed to going always for the right-hand dummy first. Every time the dog moves in the wrong direction he is stopped by whistle and redirected by hand signal, which must be clear and definite, and by the appropriate command to retrieve. When successful with two dummies at close range in this manner you can introduce a third, which you can throw straight ahead and make the dog retrieve them all in varying order. My signal for getting a dog straight out in front is to hold my hand up policeman fashion and wave it straight forward two or three times in quick succession, using the command "Go back".

When this lesson has been completed at close range it must be extended by leaving the dog on the drop and walking well out, throwing the dummies out widely apart and returning to your original position by the dog, sending him from there and again directing him by signal and command, using the stop whistle at every attempt to go in the wrong direction. It will now be found rather more difficult to get him on to the right dummy each time. Frequently it will become necessary to stop him and advance to direct him from close range, but with practice the need for this will disappear. Retrievers vary greatly in the ease or otherwise with which they can be taught to work to hand, but dogs from good working strains usually grasp the idea fairly quickly and prove easy to teach. The whole lesson must be conducted only when the dog is fresh and keen, and the weather reasonably cool, for it can become most exhausting and boring for trainer and dog alike, and should never be continued for too long at one time.

The third variation of this lesson is conducted with dummies previously hidden at a distance and about which the dog knows absolutely nothing. Now he must rely entirely upon you for directions, and if the earlier work has been properly learnt it is amazing how quickly a dog will range out, work to right and left or straight ahead according to your commands and signals. When he realizes (by finding the dummies) that you have not sent him on a fool's errand he will evermore believe you when sent to retrieve and, if he has not marked anything down, will learn to turn and watch you for directions. If a dog appears puzzled when you give the hand signals, move in the direction of but parallel to the dummy, so encouraging him to move similarly. If you already possess a trained Retriever working well to hand signals at a distance, a slow or dull-seeming puppy can often be given the right inspiration by working the two together. Get both dogs out in front, give the stop whistle and a signal for right, left or straight ahead, and when the older dog obeys the youngster will follow. In just the same way a puppy which refuses to range far enough out by command alone can be encouraged. Send out the older dog and stop him, then slip the puppy from the lead and he will almost certainly race out to join his companion.

From early puppyhood I try to encourage my Retrievers to get well out and range about. For this purpose nothing is better than to take them for walks over the fields with an older dog or dogs who *will* get out. The puppies soon start following them, and if as they do so you repeat the command "Get out" they will quickly learn to associate the command with the action. At all times in the beginning the commands to retrieve, to get out or to go back are given in conjunction with hand signals, in as loud a voice as necessary, but in time it may be possible to dispense with commands and work the dog by signals alone. The ultimate aim is to be able to direct your Retriever to any given spot within sight and hearing, and by this step-by-step process the object can be achieved.

The type of ground on which this advanced retrieving training is conducted must depend upon circumstances. With me, most of the work is done on arable fields, stubbles and what few pastures are available in this district. It is advisable (certainly for Field Trial work) to give a dog experience of working out on all types of ground. At first one should choose easy places—grass fields if possible, where scent is likely to be good and cover not thick enough to make the finding of the dummy difficult.

Work in Cover.

Retrievers should have particular attention paid to their work in thick cover—brambles, bracken and bushes. Unlike most Spaniels, many Retrievers do not love cover for its own sake and very few youngsters will enter it unless they know there is something to retrieve. Practice with the dummies must therefore be given in woods, and other places where there is thick cover, until such time as the dog will willingly enter formidable places, no matter whether he has seen the dummies thrown or not. I find that though many Retrievers for some time show reluctance to face punishing cover, if they are the right sort they quickly take to it when they have had a few days' shooting work in the woods during the season. By the end of November few Retrievers will refuse to face cover if they have had a day or two at pheasant shoots and plenty of retrieving to do. From the start of training puppies should have experience of cover of different types, as already pointed out, so that no serious difficulty should be experienced in getting them to face it by the time they come to advanced work. Very often when throwing a dummy in cover it will lodge on a bush or brambles and the dog will at first not easily find it. This is good experience for him, for it often happens at a shoot that a bird will lodge in exactly the same manner. It is surprising how quickly a dog will learn to raise his head to find lodged stuff. But make sure your dummies do not become stuck too high up for the dog to be able to find and gather them, for this may well happen and waste a lot of time and patience.

WEIGHTED DUMMY.

In an earlier Chapter I referred to the use of dummies of increasing weight, so that ultimately the pupil would have no difficulty in properly carrying a dummy weighted up to that of a pheasant or rabbit. A dog will in this way get his neck muscles strengthened so that heavy retrieves can be carried correctly, with head well up. I do not wish readers to assume that I intend them to be encumbered by having to carry round two or three dummies weighing about three pounds apiece. For ordinary, everyday work use a largish dummy, twelve inches or more long and about seven or eight in circumference —I usually use the skins of fully grown rabbits, wrapped round rolled-up sacking, the skins held firmly to the sacking by three or four strong rubber bands, made by cutting wide strips from a cycle inner tube. But occasional practice with a weighted dummy is useful and should be carried out until it is obvious that a well-grown pupil will be able to carry with ease a grown rabbit or pheasant. If your dog is likely to be called upon to retrieve hares it is a good idea to practise with even heavier dummies.

In a thick wood a Retriever cannot, of course, be guided for great distances by signal and command, but except for the occasional "towered" pheasant which falls at a distance long retrieves (other than of runners) should not be necessary. You should be able to get your dog well out into a wood by command should there be need. Any good retriever when seeking a lost bird in cover will range farther and farther out and round until he finds it, if he has been properly educated on more open ground. The handler certainly cannot give the dog much assistance in a wood, but usually either the bird has been marked down fairly accurately, when the dog can promptly be put on to it, or nobody has any idea where it lies and the dog will have to search in the general direction of the supposed fall and the rest be left to luck and a good nose. For practice, therefore, dummies should be hidden in cover from time to time, unseen by the pupil and at varying ranges from the casting-off point. I am lucky in that my woods are immediately behind the kennels, so the dogs can receive almost daily exercise in them right from the start of training, which is a great help. I like to take out several young puppies for walks in the woods and go through cover of increasing stiffness, until the puppies will happily plunge through almost anything to follow me. In this way they grow up to consider cover as an everyday medium in which to work and exercise and seldom regard it with fear. Older dogs which come to my kennel for training also receive exercise in the woods, but usually they take longer to become keen on cover than the dogs which have grown up here, unless their owners were wise enough to give them early experience.

One or two "scent trail" lessons in cover on the lines previously suggested are very valuable for teaching the following of a line and using nose. A little later real game specimens can be used instead of dummies; they can also be used for other retrieving practice but should not be overdone as it is such a great help to retain the pupil's interest in the artificial dummy for as long as possible during the training course. Constant use of the real thing will undoubtedly weaken this interest to a certain extent, but a lot must depend upon circumstances and the amount of game or rabbits available and, above all, the reactions of the dog. Some will become sick of dummy work quite suddenly; if this happens you will be forced to use game more frequently. At all costs a pupil must not be allowed to become bored by the dummy. This would slow him up and might even cause him to start refusing to retrieve anything, which would be disastrous. The happy medium must be struck, and the trainer guided by the reactions of his dog.

Walking to Heel.

Up to the present I have not made much mention of walking to heel. This is a necessary and desirable accomplishment in Retrievers. The dog's place, except when retrieving or waiting at a drive, is close to his master, preferably on his left side and with his nose level or just in front of master's knee. At one time I used to teach both Spaniels and Retrievers to walk to heel almost as soon as they had learnt to wear a lead, and with some impetuous puppies I still do so. Generally speaking, however, I find that too early heel-keeping lessons make a puppy "sticky", by which I mean that he will hang round you and be less eager to rush off to hunt or retrieve when ordered. Retrievers are easy to teach to walk to heel; in most it is such a natural trait that strict heeling can be left to this stage of training unless there are exceptional circumstances which demand earlier introduction. Early lessons on the lead have already half-taught the lesson, for by its use the pupil has learnt to walk quietly at the trainer's side. I always use the command 'Heel" and teach the pupil at first on the leather slip lead previously described. The dog is placed on my left side and the lead held in my left hand and as I walk the dog receives a sharp jerk if he strains forward or lags behind, the command "Heel" being uttered sharply at the moment of giving the jerk. It is quite useless to *drag* the lead; a really hard jerk must be given so that the dog receives a kind of electric shock at the critical moment. When the pupil walks sedately without straining or lagging I allow the lead to trail, and watch for any attempt to lag or get ahead. If the dog starts ahead I step on the lead smartly and say "Heel", or if he lags I stop immediately, utter the command, pick up the lead and give him a sharp jerk if he does not at once obey. The next step is to remove the lead altogether—but keep it in hand and administer a sharp cut with it in conjunction with the command at any sign of lagging or running ahead. I find this a most effective means of teaching heel-keeping, far better than the system of walking a dog along in a narrow path or against a fence and smacking him on the nose with rolled-up paper or a switch if he pokes it too far in front. The snag of this system is that it frequently causes the dog to develop the irritating habit of walking first on one side of you and then the other in an attempt to dodge the smack, a habit likely to become permanent. You end up never knowing on which side of you the dog is going to be. As a signal for putting a dog to heel I hiss and point to heel with my left forefinger. The dog generally responds to this sign without any other command, which is most useful in certain circumstances, such as when ferreting, where noise is taboo. As I have already said, heel-keeping is almost instinctive with many Retrievers and very little education need be given, the earlier lead work probably having done all that is necessary apart from the introduction of the specific command, "Heel".

STEADINESS.

A steady dog—that is, one which does not chase game and rabbits or run-in to falling game—is absolutely necessary for Field Trials and highly desirable for ordinary shooting. The standard of steadiness of most dogs seen out shooting is appalling—indeed, few have any conception of it and run about chasing everything and retrieving without orders, unless tethered to their masters' sides. A Retriever should be capable of walking to heel without this attachment—be a "no-slip" Retriever, in gundog parlance—and ignore birds or rabbits which are put up or which fall to shot, streaking off to retrieve only at the given word. All our training so far has concentrated on obedience and discipline under artificial conditions, and the time has now come to put this early work to practical use on real game and rabbits. Due to this schooling the change-over to real game should not prove unduly difficult, especially if obedience has been adequately taught, and completely assimilated by the pupil.

The Rabbit Pen.

Most trainers, myself included, make use of a rabbit pen. This, as the name implies, is a wired-in area containing live rabbits, usually living naturally, where the dog can be walked about among them and restrained from any attempt to chase. Few readers will, I fear, have access to such a pen, or be able to construct a large one, but most people could, with a little trouble, improvise and make use of a tame rabbit or rabbits, either on the lawn or in a little pen somewhere in the garden. Therefore I propose to describe how I introduce my Retriever pupils to rabbits in the pen; later I shall make suggestions for improvisation. When the training already outlined has been successfully completed I take a Retriever pupil, wearing a check-cord, into the pen. This I use like a lead, coiling up the surplus and carrying it in my left hand. I walk round the pen with the dog at heel, and the moment a rabbit is found and bolts away I stop and watch the dog. If he shows signs of unsteadiness I jerk him back sharply and say "No" firmly, and after a pause continue to walk about until another rabbit is found. Then the procedure is repeated. After three or four rabbits have been put up in this way I allow the cord to trail. If the dog starts to chase I let him get some way, then stand on the cord to bring him up with a jerk. The pupil is then rated and dragged back and the walk continued. If there are repeated attempts to chase sterner measures have to be adopted, and the pupil punished by receiving a shaking, holding, or few cuts with the lead after being jerked up by the cord, the word "No" being repeated again and again meanwhile. At the moment when the dog is jerked up by the cord (or, for that matter, the moment he starts to chase) I attempt to stop him by blowing the drop signal on the whistle or by saying "Hup" or "No", and very often a dog properly trained to start with will stop when ordered to do so. In this way after a short while all but the most headstrong animals learn that chase is taboo and, though they may cast envious glances at the retreating rabbit, they refrain from chasing. It is seldom necessary to take a dog into the pen more than a couple of times before reliability is obtained. Some dogs prove so biddable that they never attempt to chase and by the end of the first lesson they can be walked in the pen without having the check-cord on. That lesson should not have been more than ten or fifteen minutes' duration at the most.

It is often a wise precaution to retain the check-cord for the first two or three lessons, just in case of accidents, after which it can be discarded and the dog walked about free. I then throw a dummy out and allow the dog to retrieve it, each time arranging for the dummy tc fall nearer and nearer a rabbit, until ultimately by good luck and good management I have a Retriever which is under such command that it will retrieve from within a few feet of a rabbit without any attempt to chase. This may sound like a fairy story, but it is surprising how many dogs do quickly reach this standard, but only if early education has been scientific and no opportunities have been given previously for chasing or self-hunting. A dog that remains fairly steady to rabbits yet gives the impression that he may riot at any moment had better wear a check-cord for the first few retrieves near rabbits and the trainer must always be on the alert to stop his pupil, as quickly as possible, from doing wrong. Once a dog has proved reliable in the rabbit pen for several days I give a final test by throwing the dummy into a small pen (about eight yards square) where there are two or three rabbits. The dog must jump in and retrieve the dummy from under the very noses of the rabbits (who can, of course escape into a box if the dog does start to chase) and be promptly and effectively checked if he goes wrong.

The great thing in this rabbit-pen work is to avoid physical punishment of the pupil except as a last resort, and to whistle the pupil up quickly immediately he gets the dummy, allowing no time for him to think about chasing. The purpose of this sort of work is for "familiarity to breed contempt", and the dogs become so accustomed to rabbits that they are almost totally ignored after a few lessons. It must not be thought that because a dog becomes reliable with rabbits in a pen he will for evermore be safe from the temptation to chase. This is not so, but early experience in the confines of the pen teaches him right from wrong, and if he later riots in the fields and chases rabbits he will probably be capable of being stopped by command or whistle before he has gone very far. Certainly any correction administered will be understood and heeded. The rabbit pen must always be considered as a means to an end and not an end in itself. Too much pen work is a great mistake. Once a dog has become reliable he should be taken into the pen every few days just as a "refresher", but daily visits are not necessary after the dog has proved thoroughly steady.

Not all dogs turn out as well as the trainer desires. Some dogs, even though they do not chase, are so interested in the rabbits that they refuse to retrieve the dummy in the pen. There is nothing much that can be done, apart from trying them with a real game specimen lying close to a rabbit, and if this does not succeed it must be hoped that later in the field the occasion will never arise when the dog has to retrieve from close by a live rabbit or bird. In actual practice this seldom happens, but if a dog can be trained to this degree of steadiness it is a great asset. The dog proves itself to be well under control and able to deal with any situation. Almost as important—probably more so—is the need for a dog, returning with a retrieve, to be able to resist temptation on seeing a rabbit bolt. These circumstances can be anticipated if you have the use of a rabbit pen, and a good, keen Retriever will seldom drop what he is carrying in order to chase rabbits. If he does so he must be checked and sent for the retrieve again, and the practice repeated as many times as required.

If you wish to go to extreme lengths in training it is possible to lay scent trails in a good-sized rabbit pen for the dog to follow. Here he will encounter near natural conditions, with live scents to foul the drag and so make success more difficult and temptation much greater. It is undoubtedly excellent practice for the dog's nose and by such means he can be taught to discriminate between scents much more quickly than would normally be possible. Professional trainers find the rabbit pen essential if a number of dogs are to be satisfactorily trained in a short time. Any owner who has several dogs to train and the necessary space is strongly advised to construct one. Advice on this will be found in the section dealing with the advanced training of Spaniels.

In my early days of training I had neither the capital nor the ground available for the construction of a good-sized pen, so I used to improvise with a small pen and a tame rabbit. The pen was about ten yards square and contained a certain amount of natural cover, and the dogs were introduced in exactly the same manner as described above. This scheme could be adopted by many people with limited space at their disposal, and is well worth while. Failing this, a tame rabbit which can be let out on the lawn or in the yard should be used to teach a dog that he must not chase. In a very confined space it may not be possible to give retrieving practice under temptation but at least the habit of steadiness to fur can be cultivated and this is the main essential. Some men even go to the lengths of kennelling Retrievers where they can constantly see rabbits, either in hutches or open pens, so that they become used to them and less inclined to chase when opportunity occurs. It is certainly a sound idea, though at first it may be responsible for a good deal of noise from the dogs in their excitement to get at the rabbits. The reader is therefore advised to adopt at least the suggestion of using rabbits for steadiness training, for a dog which is steady to rabbits is well on the way to becoming trained in every sense of the word.

STEADINESS TO FEATHER.

So far we have discussed only steadiness to rabbits, but it is fairly true to say that a dog which does not chase rabbits will be easy to check on game birds, and that half the battle is already won. In my own rabbit pen I keep a few fowls and a duck, so that puppies automatically become reliable with domestic birds concurrently with their rabbit lessons, and are checked from chasing them in just the same way. To obtain steadiness to the rise of birds under natural conditions, and carry still further the practice of steadiness to fur, it is necessary to take a Retriever to the shoot or other ground holding a stock of game and, if possible, rabbits. At this stage of training it should not be necessary for the pupil to wear a check-cord, but if he is headstrong or not too reliable, or if no rabbit-pen lessons have been possible, then a check-cord is a wise precaution.

Walking through likely game-holding cover, the puppy must be checked and prevented from chasing any birds or rabbits that are flushed. If, despite all care on the part of the handler, the dog does go off on a chase he should be met on his return, taken back to the exact spot from which the chase started and be punished there and then. Certainly never punish a dog when he returns to you; *always take him to the spot where he rioted.* I am not a believer in thrashing a dog, though a few cuts with a lead can often be effective. For general punishment take a dog by the slack skin of the neck, hold him up so that he is dangling, shake and scold him in a very cross tone and repeatedly blow your stop whistle or give, over and over again, the command the dog disobeyed. When a dog starts to chase you must try to stop him by command if he is not wearing a check-cord that can be stood upon to bring him up with a jerk. Once he has got up steam and is in full flight it is most unlikely that you will succeed in stopping him by command; in these circumstances it is better patiently to await his return and punish him as suggested. I hope, however, that this will not be necessary, and that at this stage of training you will have obtained such control over your dog that he responds instantly to command and whistle.

Your walks round the shoot will be enjoyable to the dog (and to you, it is hoped) and so can be of much longer duration than ordinary training periods. Try to find as much game as you can to supply temptation and practise him with the dummy now and again, throwing it where he may come upon game or rabbits when retrieving. After a time the gun, too, should be taken out on these exercises and occasionally fired (to miss) when a bird rises or a rabbit bolts. The pupil must, of course, be kept strictly to heel except when retrieving or sent out to practise control from a distance. Very soon now the association between a shot and something to retrieve will dawn upon the dog, but the aim is to keep up the deception until the last possible moment, never allowing the sound of the gun to mean anything to a Retriever at this stage. If it is the shooting season by the time your dog has reached this point in his training, do not hurry to shoot anything for him to retrieve. Devote several days to walking round as I have described, teaching him to withstand temptation and remain steady to fur and feather. Of course you may practise the pupil in water, if any is available, and at jumping fences and gates as described in Chapter IV, including with this all the earlier work, together with distant retrieves and control, hand signals and the rest. Do not send a dog out to seek too often when there is nothing for him to retrieve. By all means do this sometimes for he must get used to the idea of "failures", but more frequently have dummies hidden and thrown well out which he can find and retrieve successfully, so that he may remain persevering and not become dispirited. It is in matters like these that one must assess the individual temperament of the pupil under training and adjust routine so that whilst retaining control and keenness he does not become too "mechanical" or unenthusiastic. To a large extent the training of a gundog *must be* mechanical—that is to say, the dog must come to regard some orders and signals as indications of a need for certain mechanical actions on his part, but at the same time it is desirable to allow him to develop initiative and not become *too* dependent upon his handler. An intelligent retriever, properly handled, will quickly learn to decide for himself when he can rely upon his own judgment and when help from the handler is required in finding a difficult bird. In regard to distant work, you should content yourself with handling the dog to within reasonable scenting range of a lost bird and then leave the rest to the dog. This applies only in the case of a bird or dummy which the dog has not marked down. If the dog has proved himself a good marker and is out to retrieve, it is folly to try to direct him. Leave him alone and you will usually find that his marking was better than yours. After all, a Retriever is wanted to find something which cannot be picked up by hand and if you are constantly handling him by command and signal when out retrieving he will never become self-reliant, as he must be when seeking out of sight in thick cover or on the trail of a "runner" (i.e., a wounded bird or rabbit which can still run).

After a few days spent out on the shoot, practising all his exercises and learning to remain steady to fur and feather, a dog is almost ready to be taken shooting. If possible, take him out picking-up on a big shoot, as described in the next Chapter. This is the finest "finishing school" for a Retriever at which dogs have been trained to win at Trials, the owners themselves having no shooting or even not being shooting men or women. Take the dog out alone, or with one companion to do the shooting whilst you concentrate on the dog, for a few times, certainly many times before taking him to a shoot where you are to participate as a gun in company. This work I will next describe. Pay particular attention to the retrieving of runners and wounded birds and rabbits.

CHAPTER VI

PRACTICAL SHOOTING WORK AND PICKING-UP

First Shooting Expedition. Retrieving Runners and Wounded Birds. Pigeon Shooting. Retrieving Hares, Woodcock and Snipe. Problems. Picking-up at Shoots. Ferreting.

First Shooting Expedition.

THE first shooting expedition is a great event for the Retriever pupil, as well as for the trainer. Now evidence should be received that the earlier, artificial work has been properly absorbed and that discipline has been firmly fixed in the mind of the pupil. Admittedly, for some time there has been introduction of the "real thing" into the training curriculum, but it has been mainly of a temporary, experimental nature. From now on the pupil will be shot over seriously, and all previous instruction can easily be ruined by wrong handling or undue eagerness to get to work.

Pigeon shooting can be an excellent starting point for Retrievers during the close season for game, but it has serious disadvantages. Unless the puppy has previously gently been introduced to these loose-feathered birds (first cold and then freshly shot) they are liable to be played with and even bitten. Dogs at first hate the loose feathers, which stick to their tongues and lips, and I strongly advise against using pigeons as retrieves until the pupil is completely at home carrying other birds less likely to be maltreated. If the time of year prevents anything else being shot, then pigeons (and rabbits) can be shot to the dog during a stroll round the shoot if you are quite certain by previous experience that he will not play with the birds.

During the game season proper it is far better to go out after partridges or pheasants, and rabbits. You can either shoot over the dog yourself or enlist the aid of a friend to do this whilst you do the training. There should not be more than two of you, and the friend should be one who can do as he is told and leave the management of the dog to you. Nothing is more annoying than the man who gives orders to other people's dogs! Your Retriever will walk to heel and likely game-holding cover should be traversed. The first bird or rabbit shot should definitely *not* be a signal to send the dog off straight away. The gun should reload first and if the dog shows any signs of desiring to run-in to the fall of the bird this should be picked up by hand. If, as I sincerely hope, the dog remains dead steady he can be sent out to retrieve after a pause, provided that the bird has not fallen on bare ground in full view. If the bird proves to be a runner the dog should not be sent; I believe in giving a pupil more experience on stone-dead game before allowing him to pick up live stuff. A runner at this juncture should receive another barrel if possible.

I must make it quite clear that no dog should be taken out shooting until it has had several retrieves of real game, first cold and then warm, and rabbits, as described earlier, and then only if these early tests were carried out in a satisfactory manner. I am taking it for granted that the reader realizes the importance of this, for it is desirable to have as many wrinkles as possible smoothed out during the earlier work, so that few faults or problems may arise during actual shooting. Where so many people make a mistake in training is to rush things (instead of making sure of each item step by step) and so complicate matters that the dog is thoroughly bewildered. Every effort should be made to ensure that actual shooting work appears little different to the pupil from the artificial, "mechanical" training which has been given. In this way faults can be avoided and the dog learns each new step in training easily and automatically. The only real difference is that from now on the dummy is to be replaced by real game and rabbits, and any dog with a nose quickly becomes used to this if first introduced to game away from the excitements of the shooting field.

If the first retrieve in the field is successful, and no signs of unsteadiness appear, you can proceed. If the dog chases, or attempts to, steps must immediately be taken to check him on the lines previously suggested, using a check-cord. If the offence is repeated the dog should be put back for further obedience lessons and work without the gun before going on with the training. It is inadvisable to let a dog think that everything shot is a signal for him to retrieve, and for this reason a proportion of the birds should be picked up by hand, sending the dog only for those which fall into cover, or at least out of his sight, so requiring the use of nose. To allow a dog to pick up every head of game shot, especially during the first

[Horace Hall

Pigeon shooting is valuable training for a young dog

[Horace Hall

Correction by holding and shaking is most effective

[Horace Hall

Whipping should be avoided if possible

[*Horace Hall*

Picking up. The dogs should be seated in front of the handler at a drive

[Horace Hall

Picking up. Spaniels prove most useful at covert shoots

few outings, is one of the quickest ways of encouraging him to run-in to shot or falling game, and the association between gunfire and a retrieve will be grasped much earlier than is desirable. Too much should not be attempted on the first occasion, but it is helpful if one or two retrieves are possible of birds which the dog has not been able to mark down. This will give an opportunity for testing him on direction and control at a distance, and also fix in his mind the fact that he does not always see fall what he has to retrieve. On the first shooting outing, therefore, three, four or five retrieves are all that are required, nothing too difficult or too far being attempted, and on the other hand nothing too easy (bird within plain view) being given. Try not to become excited and confuse the dog, and excite him also; be very deliberate in your handling and do not try to give more assistance than is genuinely required. If no game falls in suitable places for retrieving, on the way home you can arrange that the dog can retrieve some birds which have been planted in cover. It is helpful on the first few occasions always to try to work up-wind, so that the dog may receive the advantage of the wind blowing towards him from the bird when he goes out to retrieve, but as most walking-up shooting is carried out up-wind if possible, this is almost a foregone conclusion.

RETRIEVING RUNNERS AND WOUNDED BIRDS.

After a dog has had two or three outings with the gun and has behaved well he can be allowed to pick up wounded birds with a fair degree of confidence. If started on this too early a dog is liable to develop two tendencies—hard mouth and unsteadiness to live game. Most well-bred working Retrievers quickly become adept at finding and retrieving wounded birds and rabbits without spoiling them in any way—certainly not after the first few attempts. The retrieving of wounded birds that would, without a good dog, almost certainly be lost and die without adding to the bag, is one of the strongest arguments in favour of using a Retriever. No matter how good a shot a man may be there is always a percentage of merely wounded birds or rabbits which make off at speed. These are the times when nose is essential, and when the earlier scent trail lessons prove most valuable.

At first it may be better to walk a dog to the fall of a wounded bird and cast him out from there, though later you should be able to stand and send the dog out to the fall on his own, by signal if he has not marked the fall himself. From now on there is little that can be done to help the dog—his nose must do the rest, and if the day is a good scenting one and the ground scent-holding few dogs that have been properly trained will fail to take the line. A wily old cock pheasant, just "wing-tipped" by the shot, may leg it so far and so fast that the dog fails; or on partridge ground the earth may be bare and dry and hold little scent, producing equal failure, but with perseverance and continual practice success should come. If you are lucky the first few times, and the bird does not run very far before squatting, the dog will quickly find it and you should then immediately give the "come in" signal on the whistle if you can see what is going on. In most cases the dog will pick-up the bird and come dashing back, but there are odd occasions where a youngster, finding a live bird instead of a dead one, lets it go immediately it flutters, and refuses to go after it again, having in mind the times you checked him for chasing or attempting to. This is very natural and understandable, and it is easy to see why being suddenly asked to chase and retrieve live birds causes a good deal of confusion in a canine mind. In due course most dogs, I believe, learn to discriminate between the scents of a wounded bird and an unshot one, and realize that in one case he may chase, in the other he may not. Certainly when you start work on runners there is always a tendency for a dog to lose steadiness to a degree, and great care and tact must be used about this.

A dog which refuses to retrieve a live bird will frequently take to the job if given sufficient time and experience. You can help a lot by practising him with a dead bird attached to a long string. Send him out to the bird and as he comes up to it jerk the string to make the bird move. Repeat this several times until the pupil decides to chase, encouraging meanwhile by repeating "Fetch it! Fetch it!" or whatever command you use for retrieving. I have invariably found this idea successful with dogs reluctant to pick up a moving bird or rabbit.

No dog should be put on to a runner whilst the latter is still in view—certainly no dog in its first season—otherwise a desire to chase all live game will be created. Most wounded birds seek the sanctuary of cover as quickly as they can and the dog should not be put out until they have done so. This may appear to be a waste of time to the gun anxious to have his bird gathered but it is the only way to prevent the dog becoming unsteady and to encourage him to use his nose in a persevering manner. Some very tender-mouthed dogs may let a bird escape whilst they are carrying it but usually they speedily catch it again and are more careful in future. Be very definite when taking a live bird from a dog, and kill it immediately, and whilst you do so discourage the dog from jumping up after it. A dog that once drops a live bird seldom makes that mistake a second time; some even become tight-jawed as a result. I do not mean that they bite their game but that they give it a firmer grip and are more reluctant to let go when you stoop to relieve them of the bird. At all times insist on a good delivery, the dog coming right to hand and either standing or sitting immediately in front of you. After two or three retrieves of live birds a dog becomes keen and is before long an expert at following lines, until he will ultimately follow a runner through a thick wood or across fields for great distances.

When your dog is searching for a runner in what is obviously the wrong direction he can be recalled and put on the line afresh, or directed by signal and command from where he is. Before doing this one must be *absolutely certain* that the bird *has* gone in another direction. I interfere with my dogs only if I have seen the bird elsewhere. Remember that a bird often doubles back on its tracks; also that your dog is going by scent and is therefore far more likely to be right than you are. If you find your dog scratching at a rabbit burrow do not be too quick to rate him for rabbiting. A wounded bird will often take cover in any convenient rabbit hole, and usually goes just far enough down to be out of reach of the dog. Investigate the hole with your arm or a stick. At a Field Trial held quite recently my Labrador was put out after a strong running hen pheasant. After a long interval I went to look for him and found him digging furiously at a burrow. I called him off twice, thinking that he was rabbiting, but the third time he disobeyed me, returned to the hole and emerged with the pheasant in his mouth. This performance won him the stake, and also proved to me that the dog could be trusted. Often the dog is right and the handler wrong, and the best plain is to leave the dog alone and trust him on these occasions.

A wounded rabbit, especially one that starts screaming when the dog picks it up, is a nuisance because with an inexperienced dog it often causes it to let go, and a chase ensues before the rabbit is recaptured. This has an unsteadying effect upon any dog, but here again experience, and care on the part of the handler, soon teaches the pupil right from wrong and he becomes able to differentiate between the scent of wounded and unwounded rabbits. A very lightly injured bird or rabbit, especially if traversing scentless ground, may well puzzle a young dog and get away, whereas a bird which is badly hit and has blood on its feet will lay a much stronger trail of scent and will consequently be easier to find. Experience counts in the retrieving of runners more than in any other item of gundog work, so the more shooting work a dog has, and the more runners to find, the quicker will he become reliable with difficult birds. For all that, I do not consider it advisable to give a pupil too much work on such birds too quickly at the beginning of the season, because of the unsteadying effect. The trainer must be guided by the temperament of the dog concerned.

Strange things sometimes happen when a dog is out after a runner. I heard of one Labrador at an important Field Trial which was on the line of a strong cock pheasant and, unfortunately, came across a rabbit squatting in its "form" a few feet from where the pheasant had taken refuge. The dog quite naturally picked up the rabbit and brought it back, and a good deal of argument ensued as to whether this should be penalized or not. In theory, I suppose the dog should have been capable of differentiating between the scent of a unshot rabbit and that of a wounded pheasant, and should have ignored the rabbit after following the line of a wounded bird for so long. This in practice is asking rather a lot of any dog; there are few, if any, which would have acted differently. It was "just one of those things" and illustrates the truth that trials are largely a matter of luck. Had the dog retrieved the runner instead of the rabbit he would possibly have won the stake. As it was, he was awarded second prize.

A dog which picks up an unwounded rabbit should be made to let it go and watch it run off, without chasing. This is usually insisted upon at Trials. It helps to teach a dog that unshot game must not be touched. Also, it is a valuable lesson in steadiness to fur.

When an owner comes to my kennels to collect a pupil at the end of the training course there is one piece of advice I make a point of giving. This is that when first handling a young dog out shooting the best plan is *always to expect the worst* and assume that the dog *intends to run-in or chase.* For this reason, therefore, to begin with always be prepared to say "No" sharply every time a bird rises or a gun is fired, or when a rabbit bolts. In this way the possible desire to give chase can be forestalled and the earlier steadiness, which you have been at such pains to teach, retained at this critical time. There is an unfortunate fallacy among many shooting men, ignorant of gundog handling, that once a dog has been trained it will do no wrong and consequently calls for no continued effort on their part. Nothing could be further from the truth, though this applies to a greater extent to a dog which has been trained by someone else. Any keen gundog is liable to succumb to temptation, especially during the early part of his first shooting season. Great vigilance should be maintained; the handler will do far better to concentrate upon his dog than upon the shooting. Most men are shooters first and gundog trainers second and when a bird rises their thoughts are about killing. A man who wishes to make a complete success of training a dog must also try to train himself to think first, last and always of the dog. This does not have to become a permanent habit, but should certainly be done during the first part of a young dog's shooting season. It is surely worth while to sacrifice a few shots in order to complete the training of a promising gundog—a dog which if properly finished will give many years of useful service in the field, and over which you can then shoot with confidence.

PIGEON SHOOTING.

Pigeon shooting, to which I referred earlier, can be usefully introduced when your dog has proved reliable on other birds and rabbits. Waiting for pigeons to flight in to roost, or shooting over decoys, is quite an effective means of reproducing the conditions which will be met at a pheasant stand or in a grouse butt. The dog must be made to sit quietly beside or just in front of you and patiently await the arrival of birds. He must become accustomed to seeing them fall round and often quite close to him, without moving, and to go out to retrieve only upon command when there is a lull in the shooting. Here again it is essential that only birds which require finding, as opposed to those which lie fully in view, should be retrieved by the dog; birds exposed to view should be picked up by hand before despatching the dog for any wounded, outlying or hidden ones. If your earlier hand training has been thorough, it should be possible to stop by whistle a Retriever from picking up a particular bird and direct him on to another by signal and command. The need for this admittedly is not often present in the shooting field, except when two birds are down, one dead and one a runner. Then the dog may have to be stopped from retrieving the dead bird and handled on to the fall of the runner. But at Field Trials a judge may ask you to get a certain bird when there is another lying near—and the man who can stop his dog picking up the wrong bird, and handle him on to the correct one, will be well up in the judge's estimation. This is probably the acme of perfection in dog handling, because a dog which has once seen (or winded) the bird he thinks he has to retrieve is not easily stopped from completing the task. He probably thinks you a fool for trying to stop him and carries on, which is quite understandable. For this reason, therefore, practice on the lines suggested will be helpful, using either planted birds or ones which have fallen naturally, if the time can be spared. This is but carrying the earlier dummy training and signal work a step onwards, and of course the farther away from you the birds lie the more difficult the dog will prove to control. It is best to practise the work with near birds at first, extending the range as success in control is achieved.

If a dog shows signs of unsteadiness when pigeon shooting he should be attached to a check-cord, the other end being tied to a tree, fence or held under your boot, the slack being coiled up beside the dog. The next time he runs out he will be pulled up sharp and can be scolded and, if necessary, punished by shaking and holding, and reseated in his former position. Few dogs will fail to respond to such treatment; usually the check-cord can be dispensed with after a very short while.

Any dog which shows a serious distaste for pigeons and refuses to retrieve them, or bites and plays with those he does pick-up, should not be forced to carry them. I see no point in running the risk of ruining an otherwise promising puppy for the sake of the odd pigeon or two, and in reality it is very seldom that a dog is necessary to find shot pigeons. The majority fall dead in the open; the few which are lost in thick cover or are only wounded can generally be found easily, the latter being despatched with another shot. However, few well-bred Retrievers will give trouble over pigeons after the first introduction and the reader should not worry unduly on this score.

Retrieving Hares, Woodcock and Snipe.

There are certain animals and birds which create difficulties from time to time with certain dogs, apart from pigeons. Hares are disliked by many, at any rate at first, either becauseof their peculiar scent or the excessive weight as compared with a bird or rabbit. Also, many dogs will chase, or attempt to chase, hares although dead steady to rabbits, so this is another problem that may have to be faced. But for all practical purposes hares may be treated in the same way as rabbits as far as steadiness training goes, and a dog which seems inclined to unsteadiness with them should be practised as much as possible on ground where hares will be encountered in numbers. In many parts of the country hares are a nuisance to trainers in that there are enough of them to interest a dog but not enough thoroughly to accustom him to them. Most dogs, if they do indulge in a chase after a hare, return utterly exhausted and, I suspect, feeling extremely sheepish. Any correction administered immediately, at the spot where the chase began, will be taken all the more to heart. Few dogs will gallop after hares more than five or six times if properly dealt with, and if the earlier training has been sound it is to be hoped they will never chase at all.

A pupil which shows distaste for retrieving hares can be encouraged by seeing another dog pick them up. Also, a hare-skin dummy, weighted with sand, lead or anything convenient up to about 7 lb., may be an inducement if used discreetly a few times. I have found that whilst many Retrievers exhibit a dislike for hares early in the season, this quickly disappears as experience is gained, and in most cases is nothing to worry about at all. Wounded hares will undoubtedly frighten many shy youngsters, which is not to be wondered at. The cry of a wounded hare is a ghastly sound and has an even greater demoralizing effect upon dogs than that of a wounded rabbit. Owing to its weight and size a hare is difficult for a dog to carry properly and until experience is gained most dogs simply drag them along anyhow. The proper grip is naturally at the point of balance, just behind the ribs, and only experience and experiment will teach a dog how to carry hares.

Woodcock and snipe are quite commonly refused by Retrievers, though I must admit that the proportion of dogs I have *known* to do so is remarkably small. The nature of the birds' food is supposed to impart a scent disagreeable to dogs and is often given as the reason for refusals to pick them up. This may be so, but I believe that the size of the woodcock and its loose feathers have much to do with it as well, together with the fact that few dogs get opportunities for experience with these two rather elusive small birds. A dog accustomed to retrieving pheasants, for instance, may well be excused for exhibiting contempt for the sparrow-like snipe. Difficulty in respect of retrieving snipe and woodcock has often been overcome by attaching the wings of such birds to the ordinary training dummy for a while, and even by encasing a bird in the dummy itself, so that the pupil becomes used to the scent of the strange bird in the easiest manner possible. In all cases where a dog refuses early on to retrieve a different type of bird or animal under normal shooting conditions I pick it up myself and throw it as I would a dummy, sending the dog out to retrieve almost immediately. This is often successful and the dog is made a great fuss of on his return, and generally all is well in future. Do not make the mistake of throwing the bird again and again, so sickening the dog. Once is enough, though of course you can try again later with the same bird should this appear desirable. When dealing with these retrieving problems the trainer must at all times try to discover the reason for snags and aim to help the dog by seeing his point of view.

PROBLEMS.

Many dogs are put off retrieving certain types of game, all game, or made "bad deliverers" by the thoughtlessness of owners. Sickening a dog by over-repetition on one bird in the above manner is a common occurrence. Naturally if you keep throwing the bird away every time the dog brings it back he will get the idea that you do not want it, and start refusing to bring it along. Or, worse still, he may begin biting or playing with it in exasperation. Then we have the man who shoots the rabbit his dog is chasing. The dog promptly grabs the rabbit and retrieves it, and receives a tremendous thrashing for his pains. The dog associates the thrashing with his last action, which was retrieving. Nothing tells him that the punishment was for chasing. Thereafter he may refuse to retrieve rabbits, or refuse to come to hand, circling round his master in fear of another beating. This sort of treatment gives a dog an entirely wrong impression, for few people realize that he cannot think out these problems for himself. Any punishment received is always associated with his last action unless steps are taken to impress upon his mind that it was a prior offence that is being dealt with. This is the reason why a dog should be taken before punishment to the exact spot where the crime was committed. In the event of a chase, take the dog to the spot where he started from—never beat him when he joins you on his return.

Shooting a rabbit or bird to a dog which is already giving chase to it has another serious consequence. If the shot is successful and the dog retrieves to hand, you cannot punish him for running-in without risking his retrieving, as explained above, and this may make him unsteady to all rising birds or flushed rabbits. He got away with it once and may imagine that he can do so in future. Never, never shoot when your dog is giving chase. Let the bird go, stop the dog if you can. If you cannot, await his return, take him by the scruff of the neck to the place where the chase started and punish him there and then.

If a dog remains steady until you shoot and the bird falls, then runs-in and retrieves to hand, here again you cannot punish for running-in without creating a wrong impression in the dog's mind. The only thing to do is to take the bird from the dog, throw it away, restrain him for going after it, leave him on the drop and walk out and pick it up yourself. Thereafter keep a watchful eye on the dog when you shoot (a difficult feat, this!) and command "No" as you fire. Try to stop by command the dog running-in, and if he does stop walk out, drag him back and rate him. If he does not stop the only thing for it is the check-cord, which the dog should wear for the next few shots and until he shows that he is profiting by being pulled up short every time he starts to run-in. The check-cord is useful if kept for grave offences and is used as a really degrading punishment in this way. If you make too frequent use of it the dog comes to accept it, and all value is lost.

Whenever a dog begins a bad habit, such as chasing or running-in to shot, *take steps to deal with it immediately*. Let it go on, even for a day, and you will have a job to cure him, no matter how steady he may have been previously. Frequently a brief respite from work for a few days ("hand training" and obedience lessons being substituted) will do a great deal of good. Never let a dog "try it on" and get away with it more than once. If you do, he has "bested" you, and knows it. Thereafter he will ever be ready to riot whenever he feels that your attention is distracted.

Picking-up at Shoots.

Probably the finest "finishing school" for a Retriever is to be taken picking-up at big shoots. The handler does not participate in the actual shooting but works his dog and is thus able to give it full attention. There is no need to hurry; many different types of retrieve are bound to be available and excellent opportunities will occur to check any signs of unsteadiness which the puppy may develop. If you have a promising dog it should be fairly easy to get an invitation to a big shoot, where very often picking-up is left to keepers and others whilst the guns concentrate on the shooting. Keepers usually welcome a man with a good dog, and if you know of a big shoot within easy reach your best plan is to contact the head keeper and ask him to let you attend the next shoot. If you are personally acquainted with the owner of the shoot, or with one of the guns in a syndicate, matters are made very much easier for you.

Assuming you have secured an invitation to pick-up, the appointed day arrives and you are punctual at the meet. Find out from the head keeper where he wishes you to be—put yourself completely under his orders—and make certain that you do not get in the way of the guns or the beaters. I usually station myself beside one of the "dogless" guns, after asking him where he would like me to stand, or in between two guns in the line. Whilst the drive is in progress watch your dog closely for any signs of unsteadiness, or of nervousness at the heavy gunfire. Check the former at once, and endeavour to allay the latter by making a fuss of the dog and, if possible, moving away from the guns out of the actual line *but keeping level with it.* Mark well the falls of any bird shot by "your" gun or guns, paying particular attention to any which seem likely to prove runners. Do not talk to or interfere with the guns in any way; do your own job and nothing else. At a drive, most birds shot will fall *behind* the line, therefore seat your dog *in front* of you.

When the drive is over and all the beaters are out, and the guns unloaded, you can begin picking-up. Ignore for the moment any obviously dead birds lying in the open, or ask the gun if he will pick them up whilst you attend to more difficult birds and runners. If there is a runner, get your dog on to the fall as quickly as possible, but first make certain that you are not likely to disturb the next beat. Here again the head keeper should be consulted and the direction of the next drive ascertained. If the bird has run into the beat which is to be taken next, you can probably stop behind to look for it when the beaters have been through. Make sure that you know where to find the guns again—I have more than once been lost in a wood when picking-up for the first time at a new place!

On many occasions, especially at pheasant shoots, it is possible to station yourself at a point of vantage behind the guns, somewhere near where the birds will fall. This gives better opportunities for marking birds down accurately and getting on to the line of a runner with the least possible delay. But whatever you do, make sure that the guns know where you are and that you are in no danger of being shot.

When picking-up never send your dog for a bird until the drive is over. Having to sit and watch birds being shot and falling all round is first-rate steadiness training for a dog, and if you start letting him go quickly it will soon unsteady him, apart from annoying the guns and keepers. It may be that there are other dogs at the shoot which are not steady; if this is so keep as far away from them as possible, for if your dog sees others running-in and chasing he will quickly try to imitate them, and this must be avoided. Dogs, like children, seem much quicker in acquiring bad habits than good ones. One of the advantages of acting as picker-up is that you can deal promptly with any problems of steadiness; also, you can attach the dog to a check-cord and control him with it, as previously suggested, without having to bother about the shooting. A dog always seems to know when you are watching him and when you are shooting he soon learns that the moment game rises your attention is distracted, and he is liable to act accordingly. Always try to keep one jump ahead of the dog and anticipate his actions. This is a useful knack, acquired by most professional trainers through years of experience. It is one of the reasons why some men seem to have an almost uncanny power over dogs, which can immediately distinguish a man (or woman) with "dog sense" and so do not "try it on" as they would with a less experienced handler.

When your dog is out seeking dead and wounded birds between the drives there will be many excellent opportunities for checking him on rabbits and hares, as well as on unwounded game which may rise. The dog will also learn to become a good marker if taken picking-up a time or two, and this is a great asset when it comes to shooting over him yourself and not always being able to mark the birds accurately. A good marker saves a great deal of time and trouble and is rightly given high credit by judges at Field Trials. Doubtless there will be chances of working your dog at a distance on open ground, especially at partridge shoots, and early in the season much of the game will be walked up, which (especially for a Field Trial Retriever) is most valuable practice, even if you yourself normally do no walking-up. Almost every type of cover will be met with—another advantage, as you can take your time and encourage the dog to enter stuff which is new to him and for which he apparently does not care.

I have known several Retrievers that have been trained up to Field Trial standards in their first season without ever having been shot over by their owners, solely through having been taken picking-up. Last season I was able to train a very unpromising young Labrador by taking him to shoots, and in one day he picked up seventeen running pheasants, eleven at one stand, which cured him completely of his former dislike for live game. When the time came for me to shoot over him myself he proved dead steady and reliable and, what is more, experienced in both marking falls and finding the game. I am quite certain that had I been forced to complete this dog's education by shooting over him myself he would have taken months, instead of weeks, to reach the high standard that he attained.

To accustom a dog to walking in line with other people, and to seeing game and rabbits put up, you can sometimes go through with the beaters when picking-up. This in itself is valuable education, the dog of course being kept strictly to heel and checked if he displays any signs of unsteadiness or starts dwelling on scents. Part of the time the dog can, if desired, be allowed to range out in front of you to quest (if the keeper has no objections). In this way many wounded birds will be picked up which might otherwise not be accounted for.

On many estates it is the custom of the keepers to go out "picking-up cold" on the morning after a big day's shoot. This is also most valuable practice for a dog, the birds naturally being stone cold and having little scent. Most keepers will willingly give you permission to accompany them and you can hunt your dog through the woods without having to worry about anything except finding birds. The approximate whereabouts of many of the birds will be known to the keepers (who should always be told at the end of a shoot about any birds you failed to find), but others will be found quite accidentally and in the most unlikely places. There will probably also be some wounded birds to gather—birds which were either believed to have been missed on the previous day or which could not be found at the time. These jaunts are therefore valuable for teaching a dog to use his nose and distinguish between the scents of wounded and unwounded birds, for of course many unshot birds will be flushed during these operations, which the dog will have to ignore.

There are few shoots at which you will not be welcome with your dog to act as picker-up, both "on the day" and on the day after. If you do your job properly you will receive further invitations at the end of the day, together with a brace of birds and a word of praise for your dog.

FERRETING.

A good gundog is a great asset when shooting rabbits bolted by ferrets, and ferreting offers the trainer excellent opportunities for teaching his dog steadiness to fur and shot, and patience on the drop. A lot of people have the mistaken idea that the only dogs of any use to the ferreter are lurchers or terriers, but when shooting bolted rabbits a dog is useful for retrieving cripples and those which are lost in thick cover.

No dog should be taken out ferreting until it is obedient, a practised retriever of fur (or at least accustomed to carrying it), and patient on the long drop. The trainer may or may not himself be shooting, but on the first outing with the dog he *should* leave the shooting to others. As a precaution against unsteadiness the dog should wear a light lead or check cord, which may be anchored to a convenient fence or bush, or be held by the handler. He may prefer to stand on the loose end of the lead, especially when shooting.

The pupil must be kept on the drop whilst the ferrets are working, and whining must be immediately discouraged. Silence is golden whilst ferreting, so commands should be given in a very low voice, and it is useful to teach the dog to sit to a sharp hiss. At all times the whistle is less disturbing to game than the human voice, and this rule applies even more forcibly when out with the ferrets.

Be watchful when the first few rabbits bolt, and if your dog shows signs of unsteadiness jerk him back sharply with the lead or cord, hiss him to sit or give a low drop whistle. Refrain from stamping your foot—this is a warning signal to rabbits underground, and may cause them to "lie up" and refuse to bolt.

Never send the dog to retrieve until the ferrets have all reappeared and have been picked up. (It is useful, incidentally, to accustom your dog to watching a ferret running about on the ground prior to his first expedition in the field, forcibly restraining any attempt to "have a go" at it.) *Never send your dog to pick up rabbits lying in the open in full view*—pick these up by hand before sending him for the cripples or those which lie in cover.

CHAPTER VII

ADVANCED SPANIEL TRAINING

What is Expected of a Spaniel. Questing. Facing Cover. Dropping to Shot. Steadiness and the Rabbit Pen. Constructing a Rabbit Pen. Introduction to Fur by Other Means. Work in the Field. Retrieving Practice. Shooting over a Spaniel. Retrieving Runners.

What is Expected of a Spaniel.

OF all branches of gundog work I think I like Spaniel training best, though advanced Retriever training runs a very close second. Spaniels are such lively, bustling animals, so bursting with energy and enthusiasm that one cannot remain unaffected by their high spirits. Spaniels—*good* ones—are the rough shooters' "maids-of-all-work" and are expected to do their own job as well as that of a Retriever. It is probably because when working Spaniel one is constantly on the move, and finding game, that they make such an appeal. There is never a dull moment; there is something doing all the time. Quite apart from this, the nature of their work means that Spaniels are the whole time subjected to much greater temptation than are Retrievers or bird-dogs. The art of Spaniel training may be said to be the attainment of complete control without in any way lessening the keenness of the dog, for a Spaniel which lacks drive and style is a poor creature over which to shoot, whilst a wild, uncontrollable dog is a menace and an abomination.

What do we expect of a well-trained Spaniel? We require a dog which will quest ahead of us within gunshot, facing any cover no matter how thick or prickly. When game or rabbits are found the dog must put them up yet remain dead steady, and when something is shot he is expected to retrieve speedily and to hand upon command. Very frequently the dog will have to take to water, even on a bitter winter day. This is asking a lot of any dog, and the relative ease with which the desired results are obtained—from a dog of *good working strain*—often surprises me. Spaniels, more than any other breed, vary tremendously in their working ability, and it is most essential for success to choose a puppy from parents of working and Field Trial stock.

Shooting men often require a dog which, in addition to performing orthodox Spaniel work as above, will also act as a "no-slip" Retriever at formal shoots, where game is driven over the guns, and the fact that so many dogs are trained to perform all these different functions in a satisfactory manner is proof that the Spaniel is a very versatile little dog. It also emphasizes the necessity for efficient early training in obedience and control, and for a trainer who is both patient and active.

No Spaniel should be put on to advanced work until well grounded in preliminary obedience and retrieving work, as described in the Chapter on Preliminary Training, to which readers are referred. Once a puppy has reached the standard suggested, and has successfully "passed the test", retrieved cold and then warm rabbits and game, and will face cover in quest of the dummy, the main work can begin. This will consist of questing for unshot game, and steadiness to fur, feather and shot. I will therefore describe how I set about "finishing" a Spaniel, and also make some suggestions to guide those who have not access to such valuable aids to training as a rabbit pen and an easily reached shoot.

Questing and Facing Cover.

In the natural order of things, if my advice on preliminary training has been carried out a Spaniel puppy has learnt to quest and face cover of methodically increased degrees of density. The questing hitherto has been in search of the dummy and has been conducted as far as possible on ground that does not hold game or rabbits. Questing ("hunting", if you prefer) is an instinct in most well-bred Spaniels, though many fail to become very keen on it until they are eight, nine or ten months old. The puppy has also learnt to watch your hand movements and to work in the direction indicated when seeking the dummy, and should by now be so keen on his work that you can take him into a field, or a wood, and set him out questing with a snap of the fingers and a command. With Spaniels I believe in having separate and distinct commands for retrieving and questing of unshot game. "Fetch it" is used to send the pupil to retrieve, "Hi seek" to get him out questing. I believe that in time an intelligent dog learns that when commanded to "Fetch it" he has unlimited range and is seeking a dead or wounded scent, whilst "Hi seek" indicates to him that he must seek unshot game and keep within range. At first, of course, the introduction of the new words "Hi seek" means nothing, but if the customary signal to get out is given simultaneously the Spaniel soon learns that he is to get away from you and quest. When there is any hesitation on the part of the pupil I introduce an older, fully trained Spaniel into the proceedings, and the puppy quickly starts following and imitating his canine tutor. Sometimes I take out several puppies at the same stage of training, allowing them to quest about at will, though keeping a watchful eye to see that none strays beyond effective range—20 or 25 yards—recalling by whistle or name any that do so.

Assuming that the puppy is keen and intelligent, I take him into a section of the wood where cover is not so dense that I cannot see him, or into a grass meadow or some crop with suitable light cover. I walk straight ahead, up-wind to start with if possible, and give the command "Hi seek" and a wave of the arm, snapping my fingers as I do so. The puppy quests out, nosing through the cover, and by judicious use of the whistle and hand signals I try to keep him questing from side to side within range. If he gets too far to one side I drop him by whistle, and after a pause wave him over to the other side with a "Hi seek". Most puppies quickly come to realize what is wanted and respond to the hand signal, though some seem dense and come back to me instead of continuing the quest in the indicated direction. When this happens the puppy is put out again on the opposite side and the whole process repeated. Love of questing, for its own sake, is so strong in a Spaniel that usually the moment he is released from the drop he "gets on with it" naturally, and by being repeatedly stopped by whistle if questing in the wrong direction he soon learns to respond to your hand signal. If he should remain obtuse in this respect, move over in the direction you wish the puppy to take, at the same time encouraging him to do so by clear signal with your arm. In exactly the same way, if the puppy ranges too far in front I whistle him back to within range and signal him to one side or the other. If necessary I back away at the same time as I give the "come back" whistle to show what I require. When the puppy will quest in front of me, from side to side covering all the required ground, keeping within 20 to 25 yards' range of me whilst I walk straight ahead, I am well on the way to attaining my object. Naturally, the puppy will at first do all sorts of strange things, frequently going in the wrong direction, getting too far out, or not going out far enough. Too much cannot be expected as yet, especially if the ground is comparatively free from game and rabbits, as it should be.

All I wish to do at this stage is to give the pupil some idea of questing and regular quartering before introducing him to rabbits and game, and making him steady. If any game or rabbits are put up, the puppy is stopped immediately by command or whistle, and in most cases will do so. Control over him should be such that he stops at once on command, especially as so far there has been no introduction to the real thing and the temptation to give chase is not so strong as it will be later.

DROPPING TO SHOT.

A questing Spaniel is expected to drop, or at least stop, when the gun is fired. This is useful control and the object is to prevent the dog from running-in to retrieve or from continuing to quest and so risk putting other game up before the gun has a chance to reload. Although an actual drop looks better, and is a stage further removed from running-in than simply standing, I am usually content if my dog just becomes motionless at the sound of the shot. This happens with most dogs when they have been shot over once or twice, but to start with I think that an actual drop should be insisted upon. It is quite easy to teach. The pupil has already been made accustomed to gunfire, and has been taught to drop to command. You merely introduce the gun or the training pistol when the dog is out for his lessons, fire into the air, and give either the whistle or the command to drop. The dog, also having been used to the raised hand signal for sitting, will quickly get the idea, and after that voice or whistle can be dispensed with, the pupil dropping to shot alone, being reminded by voice only when necessary. The time will come when your puppy will associate the sound of a shot with something to retrieve, but for as long as possible try to let the report of the gun constitute yet another order to drop and one which must be obeyed at once. This lesson must be repeated after it has been learnt, and the gun fired during the early quartering lessons at odd moments when the dog is working ahead and least expects a report.

If serious difficulty is found in getting a puppy to quest, I throw out pieces of bread or biscuit on either side of me as I walk, thus encouraging the pupil to work from side to side. This method has the advantage of making the dog watch hand movements, and if necessary can be extended by hiding pieces of bread in such a way that the dog can be brought out later and as you walk in a straight line he will hunt from side to side seeking the rewards. Such treatment is seldom necessary with a working-bred Spaniel puppy; I doubt if I have had to resort to it more than half a dozen times in the last ten years.

Questing on game-free ground should not be continued for more than a few days or it may bore the puppy and cause loss of pace and style. These lessons should be intermingled with practice of all those so far taught, including retrieves of the hidden dummy from cover as previously described. Vary the lessons, not only to revise what has already been taught but also to prevent monotony from creeping in, both for yourself and the pupil. Once the puppy shows that he has the idea of questing, even if it is only rudimentary, I introduce him to the rabbit pen, in which the main training can be said to take place for the next week or two, at any rate.

STEADINESS AND THE RABBIT PEN.

My own rabbit pen is about a quarter of an acre in area, the cover including long grass and weeds and piles of hedge clippings, tree branches and brushwood, to form natural cover for the dozen or so rabbits that inhabit the enclosure. These rabbits are of mixed breeding, one or two usually being pure tames, others true wild-breds and several crosses of tame and wild rabbits. The tame ones naturally sit about more and are fairly easily approached, whilst the wild ones make off at speed when disturbed. The tame-wild cross-bred rabbits have the speed and cunning of the pure wild ones, but do not burrow and are more easily found.

When first introducing a Spaniel puppy to the rabbit pen I use a short check-cord. This I hold as a lead, and walk the puppy around until we find a rabbit. Immediately the rabbit bolts I give the command "Hup" to the puppy and if he does not at once drop I jerk him down with the cord and also blow the drop note on the whistle. Puppies vary greatly in their reaction to rabbits. Some become wild with excitement, tugging on the cord and yapping with eagerness to chase. Others appear almost indifferent, and I have known a puppy to exhibit fear the first time or two a rabbit has been put up! However, most puppies show a keen interest but obey the command to drop, whereupon we continue our walk as before, the puppy being made to drop each time a rabbit bolts.

Five or ten minutes at this sort of thing is sufficient at first. During this time I endeavour to sustain the pupil's interest in rabbits, at the same time indicating that once they have moved no further interest is to be taken in them. To achieve this, when a rabbit is put up I turn and walk the dog in a direction different from that taken by the rabbit. In this way the natural inclination to follow the departing rabbit is lessened.

On the second visit to the pen, the next day, the procedure is repeated until two or three rabbits have been put up. The puppy is then allowed to quest about on his own, with the check-cord trailing. When he finds a rabbit, the drop whistle is immediately blown and if obeyed the pupil is kept sitting for a minute or more, then patted and encouraged to quest in a fresh direction. If the dog starts to chase a rabbit I intercept him and stand on the cord, pulling him up with a jerk. The puppy is rated, taken back to the place where the rabbit was flushed and there made to drop and stay down for some time. If this is repeated, the puppy in due course learns that chasing is forbidden, and sits, or at any rate stands still, when the rabbit bolts. Some puppies show a desire to "stand" or "point" a squatting rabbit, and this I encourage in the belief that it is a desirable attribute in a Spaniel. If, therefore, the puppy under tuition becomes rigid in a pointing attitude when he finds a rabbit I go up as quickly and as quietly as I can and take hold of the check-cord, drawing it taut, keeping the pupil in position for as long as possible. What usually happens is that after about a minute or less the puppy loses patience and makes a dive for the rabbit. Then the command to drop is given at once and the pupil made a great fuss of if he obeys. In order to retain this pointing tendency in Spaniels it is necessary to prevent their flushing the rabbit every time, so I make a point, whenever possible, of putting the rabbit up myself after the dog has pointed for some time, making him drop immediately. Many Spaniels can be taught to point in this way, even if they do not show an inclination for pointing, by using the check-cord as described as soon as a rabbit is scented, the dog being brought up and made to remain standing for some time before putting the rabbit out. A Spaniel that will indicate the presence of squatting game or rabbits by pointing in this manner is most useful to the rough shooter, giving him time to get into a favourable position for a shot, and also making the dog easier to control as far as steadiness is concerned. When I allow the dog to put the rabbit out himself I say "Push it out" and make a slight movement, and this is usually sufficient. As already stated, however, it is better to drop the dog and flush the rabbit yourself on most occasions, in order to foster the pointing instinct.

Once a dog has shown that he can be prevented from chasing when hunting in the pen with check-cord trailing I remove it altogether, allowing him to quest free of all restraint, relying upon the whistle or command to remind him to drop should he attempt to break away after the rabbit. It is surprising how quickly a good Spaniel will grasp what is wanted, and quest round the pen bolting rabbits and remaining steady to them. When this proficiency has been achieved, the gun or training pistol is introduced and a blank fired now and again when a rabbit departs, the pupil dropping to the shot, or to the command, if he has not already gone down of his own accord. In this way natural shooting conditions are simulated as nearly as possible so that when the dog is brought to the field later on the change over from artificial, controlled work to practical shooting will not appear vastly different to him. I always try to make the dog quest in the pen in such a way that all the ground is covered, and quartering becomes instinctive. My pen is about 30 yards wide, and if I walk straight up the middle the dog has to turn well within range when casting from side to side. The whistle and hand signals are used as previously described to encourage regular, systematic quartering of the ground.

Usually, a daily ten-minute spell in the pen for a week or ten days is all that is required, by which time the pupil is quite reliable both at finding rabbits and remaining steady to them, and learns to beat out holding cover and often to "point" a squatting rabbit. At the same time quartering the ground and dropping to shot is thoroughly taught. Once this stage has been reached the pupil need not go into the pen every day but only as often as is necessary to keep him up to scratch. The rabbit pen must not be over-used, for although it is an excellent means of introducing a Spaniel to the scent of rabbits, teaching control and steadiness, quartering and cover work, familiarity is apt to breed contempt and the dog to become uninterested or too accustomed to working in the same area. Some people get the impression that because a dog is steady in the pen it will ever afterwards be so when rabbits are encountered under natural conditions. This is definitely not so, but the pen is a very excellent method of teaching a dog right from wrong, so that any tendency to chase in the field can be more easily checked, and any punishment meted out for unsteadiness is then understood, appreciated and taken to heart. For training any number of Spaniels I consider a rabbit pen essential, but for the man with one or two dogs there are other means by which control can be learnt. These I will outline later.

So far I have dealt only with the cases in which the puppy behaves in the pen as I would wish—cases which are, fortunately, numerous, especially if the initial obedience lessons have been effective. However, we have exceptions to deal with—the over-keen puppies and those whose timidity causes them to be almost scared by rabbits. The excitable, keen pupils, especially those that have been allowed too much freedom and have learnt to chase and self-hunt before coming to my kennels, need a firmer hand and greater patience, and the check-cord remains in use for a longer period than with the more tractable pupils. The puppy which makes a dive after the first rabbit he sees, and nearly jerks the arm out of its socket, must be immediately and firmly dealt with. A sharp, forcible jerk on the cord makes him sit, and he is kept down for some time. A cut or two with the lead may be necessary to dampen the enthusiasm of a headstrong youngster, but I try to avoid punishment in the pen, relying mainly upon the check-cord and my own agility! A puppy of this type will require more visits to the pen than the others, and it will be longer before he can be worked loose, but the principle remains the same. Before releasing a dog from his drop after the rabbit has bolted I make a point of patting him and saying "Good dog", to show that he has done well in my estimation.

Puppies which are frightened by rabbits need taking into the pen once or twice only, and to see another dog hunting rabbits freely, before they begin to take an interest themselves. Such puppies can, of course, be allowed loose straight away in the pen, and must in every way possible be encouraged to hunt. With these pups I often catch up one of the rabbits and allow the puppy to sniff at it and to watch it run off when released. This nearly always makes them interested, and I then take them into the small rabbit pen, an enclosure of about eight yards square containing two tame rabbits. The pupil is now put on a check-cord and introduced to the rabbits by being walked about by my side. Before long he is more than willing to "have a go" at them but is restrained by the check-cord. This, I find, often leads to the pupil starting to point the rabbits, and from this stage everything is as it should be. The small rabbit enclosure is a useful place in which to encourage a Spaniel puppy to point, by using the check-cord (or a lead) to hold him, and insisting that he drops the moment a rabbit moves, as described above.

As a conclusion to rabbit-pen work I try to get my Spaniel pupils, like the Retrievers, to retrieve the dummy in such a way that when going out and coming back they have to pass by rabbits and ignore them, and I stop them immediately if they start to chase, making them pick up the dummy should it be dropped in excitement. Many Spaniels, quite understandably I think, refuse to have anything to do with a dummy in the pen, and that is that. The scents and excitements are too much for them. Others will behave just as well as Retrievers, except that they cannot resist first pushing out any nearby rabbit before retrieving the hidden or thrown dummy! Anyhow, the main object is nearly always achieved in the pen—that of encouraging nose and work in cover, coupled with steadiness to fur and shot.

CONSTRUCTING A RABBIT PEN.

The average shooting man does not have a ready-made rabbit pen available. But if you intend training dogs, especially for Field Trials, and you have the necessary room and wire, I seriously recommend the construction of a pen. The bigger the better up to about half or one acre, but even quite a small affair, ten or twelve yards square, will prove most useful and be suitable for early introduction and steadiness to fur. You can stock these small pens with tame rabbits, which will enjoy living in such freedom, and do very well. A small pen for tame rabbits need consist only of small-mesh wire netting with stakes every six feet, well braced at the corners, the wire to be about three feet high. If you intend keeping rabbits in it permanently the wire should be buried or turned-in at the bottom for about six inches. If you are more ambitious, and erect a larger pen for wild and tame rabbits, a good turn in at the bottom is essential, and the height of the wire should be four or five feet with another turn-in at the top, for wild rabbits if they cannot dig out will try to climb out. A turn-in, attached to angle brackets on the supporting stakes, will effectively prevent this. One-inch-mesh wire is advisable; larger mesh will allow young rabbits to escape. The lower half of the gateway should be wired and turned-in at the bottom, and the top of the gate (which should open outwards) should have a turn-in of wire or a board nailed across it to prevent escape of the inmates. Plenty of cover should be available when first turning-down the rabbits, and care should be taken in winter to see that there is sufficient food for the stock. I use mangolds and hay as supplementary feed for my own rabbits in the winter months, and they seem to do very well. I have found the most useful and hardy rabbits to be those obtained by crossing tame does with wild bucks. So when starting a rabbit pen put in a few wild ones of both sexes, as well as a few tame does. The latter can, if necessary, be caught up after a few weeks and the youngsters reared in a hutch until old enough to be released. A lot of tiny "bolters" sitting about in a rabbit pen are undesirable, so artificial burrows and other forms of shelter should be provided. It is essential to have some cover so that the rabbits can get away from an over-eager dog, and somewhere for them to keep out of the rain and wind in bad weather. Piles of faggots and brushwood are recommended and the more natural the cover in the pen the better, though there should be a somewhat "bare" area where puppies can obtain their first sight of rabbits sitting about. In my own pen I keep a few chickens and ducks to accustom pupils to poultry.

If the trainer cannot arrange for even a small enclosure containing at least one rabbit for early work, then perhaps some tame rabbits can be let out on the lawn, or in the kitchen garden, and used in much the same way, the dog being held on a check-cord until all danger of chase is past. A small, square, sectional pen can be made—say nine feet each way—which can easily be dismantled when not in use.

Introduction to Fur by Other Means.

If you cannot construct a pen of any kind there is nothing else for it but to take the pupil out to woods and fields where plenty of rabbits are likely to be encountered in a wild state. This is naturally going to mean a harder and longer job because under such conditions you will not be able to walk your dog up to rabbits and put them out, making him drop, unless you are lucky enough to find some squatting in their "seats" in long grass and other cover. If you do know where you are certain of finding rabbits thus conveniently seated you can proceed as advised for the rabbit pen. If not, you will have to work your dog on a check-cord in places where he will come across rabbits and when he does so drop him by means of voice, whistle and check-cord. The gun can be taken along, but kill nothing at this stage. Your sole object is to get your dog steady to fur, and to quest for it in a workmanlike manner. Clearly, the use of a check-cord in thick woods is almost impossible—it would get tangled up at every step. Open, rough grass fields and heaths or warrens are therefore the best places for such practice. Although with time and perseverance you will get your dog steady and reliable, it may take several weeks and a great deal of activity on your part. If, in the course of these outings, game or hares are flushed, they must be treated in the same way as rabbits. The moment a bird rises the dog must stop or go down, and thereafter be hunted in a different direction.

During the course of these excursions after rabbits the opportunity can be taken of practising retrieving (and everything else the puppy has so far learnt). A dog which refuses to touch the dummy, having been introduced previously to the real thing, can have occasional retrieves of birds or rabbits, but, if possible, use the dummy instead, for many more varying situations, akin to those likely to be encountered in the shooting field, can be created with one dummy than with one bird or rabbit, and it is unlikely that you will wish to carry a bag full of shot game about with you! The check-cord can be discarded as soon as the dog is reliable with rabbits; it need never be worn at all in natural country if the dog is pretty amenable to start with—it all depends upon how well you taught the early obedience work. But keep up practice until the puppy *is* reliable.

Work in the Field.

Spaniel pupils that have had the advantage of rabbit-pen training must also have some preliminary work on the shoot, without the gun being used to kill, before being shot over in the proper sense of the term. After pen work has been mastered the puppy is naturally much keener to hunt and quest when out on the shoot, and you should now take him to places where game and rabbits will be found. Keep him questing from side to side, within range, beating out the odd spots of thick cover that may be encountered, and keep a watchful eye for the flush of game or rabbits. Immediately something gets up, drop the dog by whistle—do not wait to see whether he remains steady. The best plan is *always to expect the worst with a young dog, and assume that he is going to chase or run-in.* For the first part of his first season *give the vocal or whistled order to drop immediately anything gets up or is shot.* In this way steadiness can be maintained, and later you will have every chance of working your dog without having to remind him to drop. Fire the gun sometimes (not necessarily when something gets up) and see that the pupil drops promptly. Several outings on these lines will prove beneficial to any Spaniel in training, but take care not to work the puppy for too long on ground where there is little game. He will become wearied if you do. On the other hand, too much game on the ground is not desirable; it will tend to excite the puppy and also to give him the impression that he can always find plenty. Consequently he would be inclined to "dry up" on badly stocked land; he must have to *work* for his game, using his nose and not just bumping into it without effort. A good Spaniel will work as keenly on barren ground as on well-stocked land; indeed, a Spaniel is a greater asset on the former type of shoot. On the latter, you can pick the game up for yourself if needs be!

Watch your dog all the time, and deal with any unsteadiness right away, stopping him by whistle or command if you can, or waiting for his return. Whatever happens, do not punish him when he comes back to you. Take him by the scruff of the neck back to the spot where he should have remained steady, shake him, rate him and hold him up, glaring at him and repeating the word "Hup" or blowing your drop whistle if this is what he disobeyed. Do this without fail every time he goes wrong—never lose your temper and punish a dog when he rejoins you after a chase, or next time he will not come back so soon, and thereafter take to circling round you and otherwise showing that he has lost confidence in you. By punishing at the scene of the crime you can show the dog the reason for the punishment, and he will understand. Remember that a dog associates punishment with his last action, or with the particular place where he is punished.

Far better than stopping a dog and having to drag him back is to *catch him in the act*. This can be done in a rabbit pen, as I have shown, and the reprimand then sinks in. Suppose, for instance, your dog is starting to chase a rabbit in thick cover, quite close to you. If you are agile you may be able to intercept him whilst he is still in flight, and there administer punishment which will show him that chasing is not tolerated. There is, however, a knotty point here. A Spaniel's duty is to put game out of cover so that it can be shot, and it is difficult to see how a dog can push a rabbit out *without* chasing it, at any rate from a large patch of bracken or brambles. Technically, the dog is chasing only if he goes after the rabbit or bird *when it breaks cover*, so if you can station yourself in such a position (as can be done in the pen) that the dog can be stopped the moment he emerges from cover behind the rabbit, so much the better. You will, in matters like this, have to decide quickly whether your dog is rioting or simply doing his proper job to the best of his ability.

The above suppositions go to prove the effectiveness of the rabbit pen as a means of training Spaniels. So many situations can be created which might be impossible on the shoot—all situations which sooner or later the dog will have to deal with. The man forced to train his dog entirely on the shoot among natural game has far more work and worry, but if time permits this may be in the end the best way. It is certainly a most enjoyable pastime, roaming the shoot with a Spaniel, and the great pity is that the average man has not easy access to suitable land that he can visit at odd times. However, trainers will have to improvise according to their particular circumstances.

Finally, do not forget to practise the dog from time to time at dropping and remaining down whilst you walk away calling him up. Keep all the earlier work in mind as far as possible and practise it whenever practicable. If the shooting season has started, give your dog retrieves on the different game birds, rabbits and hares—dead specimens shot when the dog is not with you. Try to make the retrieves as realistic as possible.

Retrieving Practice.

Before actually shooting over a Spaniel puppy it is as well to give some lessons in advanced retrieving, on the same lines as I have recommended for Labradors. It must be realized, however, that although a Spaniel is expected to do retrieving work to a very large extent, it is inadvisable to allow him to work at extreme ranges in quest of the dummy or game, at any rate until he has a confirmed range and quests within easy gunshot. The reason for this is that to give a young dog too much freedom of range when retrieving will weaken the idea of a close range when questing for unshot game, and I have found that a Spaniel given too much retrieving work, too early, nearly always becomes a wide ranger when hunting, and needs constant recalling. Except for this, the reader who is training a Spaniel will do well to read also the Chapter on advanced retrieving work and apply to his Spaniel as much of it as he deems fit. The particular type of work the dog is intended for must be taken into consideration, and it must also be borne in mind that whereas a Retriever is trained to ignore unshot game, Spaniel work is aimed at fostering an interest in both *dead and unshot game*, so that whatever one does there is the probability that (*a*) control of a Spaniel at a distance will not be so effective as with a Retriever, and (*b*) that when working out the Spaniel will perhaps hunt unshot game and not concentrate on "dead" or "wounded" scents as would a Retriever. Notwithstanding all this, it will be found that by the very opportunity a Spaniel gets for using his nose, both when questing and retrieving, he will usually become a brilliant retriever, especially "on a line" of a wounded bird.

For Spaniel work pure and simple I aim at reaching the following standard: To retrieve game which has been shot and which has been marked down, from cover or water. To retrieve game which the dog has not seen down, and to be handled to within reasonable scenting distance. This may sound exactly like Retriever work, but remember that when shooting over Spaniels the game is normally being walked up and shot, and falls at closer ranges than when driving and shooting over Retrievers. Furthermore, in rough shooting of this nature most of the game is retrieved *at once*, after the dog has had a wait on the drop; there is no waiting until a drive is over (which may be perhaps half an hour or more) as there is with driven game.

If, as often happens, my Spaniel has retained his interest in seeking and carrying the dummy I give him practice with the hidden dummy, indicating the direction of the search by hand signal, giving the command "Fetch it", and stopping him by whistle if he goes in the wrong direction. I methodically extend the range by hiding the dummy farther and farther out, in suitable cover, and I encourage the dog to work out for it by signal and repeating "Fetch it". I give scent trail lessons, as described earlier, using both the dummy and real game or rabbits, and I try to teach a fair standard of working to hand signal at distances up to about forty or fifty yards—no more. (Later, when the dog has proved himself to be reliable in the field, he can be worked if necessary at greater distances in the open.) Spaniels that have been taught to quest by hand-signal direction quickly respond to this training, which of course has to be given in places where you can see the dog (and he you), and not in a thick wood. Get the dog out, whistle him to drop and wave your arm in the required direction. If the dog does not respond, move in that direction, repeating the hand signal and saying "Get out" as taught in the early lessons, or "Fetch it", to emphasize that he is looking for a retrieve and not for unshot game. Each time the dog goes wrong he must be stopped by whistle and the directions repeated until success is reached. Practice with two or three dummies can be given, too, so that the Spaniel comes to realize that there is often more than one object to be retrieved before he can continue with his questing. Shooting over Spaniels is as a rule done in woods and other places with thick cover, where distance work is neither possible nor necessary, but even so it should be possible to get a Spaniel through a thick hedge to search the field on the far side. This can be done by first throwing dummies over a hedge and, when the idea has been grasped, planting them on the far side, increasingly far from the hedge, unseen by the dog, and later sending him to search for them. Water-work should not be forgotten; this is dealt with in the Chapter on that subject.

Anyone training a Spaniel with the intention of using it solely as a no-slip Retriever should read the section on Retriever training and be guided by that. If a dog is meant for both rough shooting and "formal" events, where he must sit quietly during a drive, it is best if the two types of work are intermingled as much as possible, but the early experience of practical work should be given by taking the dog picking-up at a shoot, as advised for Retrievers. For either purpose a good Spaniel, properly trained in obedience and steady to fur and game, should take to driven-game shooting quite easily, though by nature Spaniels are much more restless creatures than Retrievers and are more prone to move, whine and even yap whilst a drive is in progress, especially if they have done much questing work. Here, again, so much depends upon the temperament of the individual dog.

When training, and later when shooting, a Spaniel which does wrong must immediately be dropped by command or whistle. If the dog is out after a retrieve, and puts up a rabbit, whistle him to sit at once, give him a pause on the drop, then by hand signal and command send him on to continue the search. A Spaniel is likely to be made to drop far more frequently than a Retriever, and for this reason the initial lessons should be as thorough as possible. A very useful maxim for the Spaniel trainer is: "When in doubt, drop your dog." A Spaniel's life sometimes seems one long drop!

SHOOTING OVER A SPANIEL. RETRIEVING RUNNERS.

The handler who shoots over his Spaniel for the first time should, if he wants success, pay less attention to his shooting and more to the dog than would normally be the case. Dogs have the ability to sense in some uncanny manner the instant their handler's attention is distracted from them, even momentarily, and if they are going to riot this is the time they will choose. It is rather difficult, I know, for a keen shooting man to train himself to think first of the dog when game rises and rabbits bolt—the normal reaction is to concentrate on the quarry and try to kill. The wise dog handler will adopt the attitude that the missing of a bird or two is well worth while in order to preserve the steadiness of the dog on which so many hours have been spent. It is well known to those of us who train dogs for a living that a young dog can be spoiled permanently by carelessness in this respect. It is equally certain that it is over this point that the bulk of amateur trainers fail, and many of the wild dogs we see have got into that sorry state only because their owners were careless when first shooting over them.

My procedure when shooting over a Spaniel for the first time differs in no wise from the many gunless outings we have had together, except that now when game is flushed or a rabbit pushed up I shoot to kill. At the same time I keep an eye on the dog, so to speak, by dropping him by command the moment the bird rises, and by repeating the command when I fire. I try to mark down anything I shoot, but immediately after the shot I glance at the dog to make certain that he has remained steady. In most cases he has, fortunately, because as yet he has not learnt the delights of running-in to shot and retrieving at once. My intention is to see that he never does, though as time goes on the temptation is liable to grow stronger, as the pupil comes to enjoy his work more and more and gets interested in carrying the real thing. If the dog has started forward he is made to drop by command; even if he has gone quite a way it is often possible (if you are active) to get to him and drag him back before he reaches the retrieve. If a dog has moved so much as a yard *I do not allow him to retrieve* but walk out and pick up the game by hand, leaving the pupil down. Had I allowed him to retrieve after moving, on the next shot he might move even further, if not run-in all the way, and steadiness would be on the decline. Anyway, I do not allow the dog to retrieve everything shot on any occasion, as this would give him the impression that every time a gun goes off there is something to fetch, and so unsteady him. Neither do I allow a dog to retrieve something lying in the open, but if we are shooting on fairly barren ground, where much stuff has to fall in the open, I leave the pupil down and move the game a yard or two into the nearest cover.

Another point to remember is that *on no account* should the dog be despatched to retrieve *immediately* the game falls. A wait on the drop, to which he has been made accustomed during dummy work, is absolutely essential. The shooter's maxim here is *reload first*, keeping the dog down meanwhile. When the dog goes out to retrieve he should be watched carefully, and the moment his head goes down to pick-up he should be whistled in, giving him no time to stop and mouth the game. A quick pick-up and delivery are most important, and though many youngsters will drop their game when returning, because too light a hold has been taken, others with a tendency towards hard mouth may deliberately put the bird down and bite. If one can keep such dogs on the move the chances are that this tendency will be eradicated, for a dog seldom bites whilst on the move, or whilst swimming.

Until my Spaniel is quite at home retrieving stone-dead stuff I do not let him tackle a runner. If a bird or rabbit is wounded and looks like getting away, I despatch it with another barrel as quickly as possible. Too early retrieving of runners, which necessitates a chase, has a most unsteadying effect upon dogs; it may also start a youngster biting game, if only in excitement. A good many dogs will bite and otherwise treat roughly their first few retrieves of the "real thing" purely from nerves, but this practice soon ceases, especially if they are called in quickly. Make a habit of feeling *the ribs* of all game and rabbits retrieved, for the hard-mouthed dog invariably crushes the ribs and often no outward signs of damage are visible. Torn skin on game is more often a sign of damage through falling on to a bush or tree, or of the dog carrying it by a bunch of feathers instead of getting a good body grip, or it may be caused by the dog pulling the bird from brambles or other thick cover.

If after several excursions to the shoot with dog and gun you feel satisfied that the Spaniel is steady and tender-mouthed with his game, the next runner can be tackled. As I stressed in Chapter VI (dealing with Retrievers), it is a cardinal mistake to put a dog on to a runner which is still in sight. This will create a tendency to chase unwounded game and generally unsteady the pupil. The correct procedure is to give the usual wait on the drop, then get the dog on to the fall as quickly as possible and leave the rest to him. Generally, where there is blood on the feet of the bird or rabbit the scent trail is strong and the puppy will have little difficulty in finding it, having been taught to use his nose by the scent trail lessons previously given. The very slightly wounded birds may cause more trouble, and many youngsters will fail with them, but "nothing succeeds like success" and if the pupil is lucky on the first few runners it will make him keen and persevering, and reliability will develop in no time. Try to avoid hindering the dog with signals and directions; leave him to puzzle out the line for himself, unless he is hunting in what is obviously the wrong direction. All too often the handler interferes when he thinks his dog is going in the wrong direction, only to find later that the dog was right and he himself wrong, the bird having doubled back on its tracks, as they so often do. Whether or not the dog will pick up the bird at once is a matter of chance, but most dogs will. If you are lucky and happy to witness the actual pick-up, give your recall whistle without delay and bring the dog in. I have found that very few Spaniels refuse to tackle a live bird or rabbit, but if they do special training must be given to encourage them. Sending them for a rolling ball whilst it is still in motion makes a good start, followed up by retrieves of dead birds attached to a string, which is twitched to cause movement the moment the dog reaches the bird. This lesson seldom fails to produce the desired results. Once a dog has lifted moving stuff he will never afterwards refuse.

A dog which returns with a wounded bird and lets it go, necessitating a chase to recapture it, does not often do this again. Many dogs will hang on to their game rather tightly instead of delivering up willingly, and this must be dealt with tactfully from the start. I usually manage to insert a couple of fingers into the dog's mouth and with upward pressure cause him to relax his hold on whatever he is carrying, at the same time saying "Dead", a command I keep for use when receiving game from a dog. Never indulge in a tug-of-war with the dog, and try to avoid in any way hurting him; pain might create a bad delivery. A dog which persistently hangs on to his game will have to have the lips firmly but gently pressed against the teeth until his hold relaxes, and this if adroitly carried out will not be found to affect the style of delivery.

A young Spaniel does not want too much work or too many retrieves during his first few outings with the gun. Far more important is the quality of the retrieves given and the attention paid to proper questing and quartering, and steadiness. A dog which starts going downhill in any respect must be immediately and firmly checked and given special lessons on the subject in which he seems weakest. At these times shooting must be dispensed with or at least relegated to second place. Special efforts should be made to see that the dog quests within range of the gun; although many will start off by working within the desired 25 yards' radius mounting excitement and keenness with experience of real game will often tempt the dog to pull away from the handler, which must not be allowed to happen. When working very thick cover a dog must be made to range closer than when on more open ground, and one which will point and hold a point can be allowed greater freedom of range than would otherwise be permissible. The great thing in all training is to bring the dog along sufficiently slowly for all former work to be kept in mind and each step thoroughly marked, learnt and inwardly digested!

[Topical Press

A Spaniel puppy questing for rabbits

[Horace Hal

Spaniels have to face any cover, woodpiles included

[*Horace Hall*

Retriever walking to heel whilst Spaniel quests ahead

[Horace Hall

Spaniels in the rabbit pen watching a wild rabbit away

[Horace Hall

Learning to "point" in the pen

Sport and General

A Pointer rigid on point

[Sport and Genera

An English Setter coming up on point

CHAPTER VIII

POINTER AND SETTER TRAINING

The Use of Pointers and Setters. Early Training. Working to Signals and Whistle. Using a Trained Dog as "Schoolmaster". Steadiness to Fur. Dropping to Shot. Quartering. Introduction to Game. Pointing. Shooting over the Dogs. Brace Work.

THE USE OF POINTERS AND SETTERS.

THE training of Pointers and Setters ("bird-dogs", as they are often called) has one great disadvantage compared with Retriever and Spaniel work. Whilst the other gundog breeds can be trained to a large extent without ever seeing game in a wild state, bird-dogs, after initial obedience training has been completed, must be worked upon game. The reasons for this are obvious—a Pointer or Setter is required to range, to find and "point" game, and there is no artificial object which can be used in place of the real thing. In this country bird-dogs are not often expected to retrieve shot game. Their sole job is to find the game and indicate its whereabouts by coming up on point, or "setting". In these days of driven shooting, high cost of shooting rentals and modern farming methods, few men ever have an opportunity to shoot over pointing dogs, though many more could probably do so if they wished. Certainly conditions do not encourage this form of shooting, and except for a few days at the beginning of the grouse season on the moors of Scotland and Yorkshire, and for a few enthusiastic bird-dog men in partridge districts early in September, Pointers and Setters are but little shot over. It is true that the increasing use of combine-harvesters in areas where there are large fields, and the consequently longer stubble, also the trend towards ley farming, has in some measure improved the possibilities of shooting over dogs in many districts. On the other hand, the modern sportsman is inclined to find it too slow and is often more concerned with the bag than with the pleasure that can be derived from watching dogs at work. Admittedly this form of shooting is not productive of heavy bags of game; the sport of shooting over dogs can be said to exist only among a few ardent enthusiasts. It is a pity, but there it is. In America and on the Continent of Europe bird-dogs are widely used, more particularly where game is scarce and large areas have to be walked up,

E

and generally the dogs are trained to retrieve. Over here it is held that allowing a Pointer or Setter to retrieve not only tends to make it unsteady but also induces it to get nearer in to its game and makes it more likely to flush birds, especially in the scanty cover to be found in most areas in the autumn. Further, it induces an interest in "foot scent", which is undesirable. Few bird-dogs bred in Britain are "natural" retrievers, and I believe that in the U.S.A. it is often necessary to use force methods to teach the art. We shall not concern ourselves with retrieving bird-dogs but discuss the more orthodox work normally expected of a Pointer or Setter in these Isles.

EARLY TRAINING.

As in other branches of gundog work, there are different policies and methods. Many men prefer to let a young bird-dog "run wild" until about nine months or a year old, whereas others believe in teaching discipline at an earlier age, and begin field training in the spring when the dog is about a year or eighteen months old. As a Pointer is expected to range wide and fast, quartering his ground in a methodical manner, he must not be curbed too young or he will lose that pace, style and wide range which is so desirable. On the other hand, it is easier to make a dog obedient and steady if taken in hand whilst still of a tender age, and therefore in the training of bird-dogs, as with that of Spaniels, the art lies in gaining control without in any way sacrificing natural ability, keenness and range. It is my view that a Pointer or Setter should start learning to drop to command, to range and turn to whistle, and to be steady to shot, fur and feather at the age of about eight or nine months, or even earlier if a very bold puppy. Puppies of these breeds should receive plenty of free-galloping exercise from an early age, and be encouraged to get well out. Both Pointers and Setters (of all breeds) can be said to be sensitive and somewhat highly strung animals which need careful understanding and kind handling.

Bird-dogs can be taught to drop to command and whistle in exactly the same way as Retrievers and Spaniels, and also be accustomed to gunfire and dropping to shot like their brethren. For some reason or other bird-dogs seldom seem to be taught to walk to heel, and generally one sees them straining at their leashes. There is no obvious reason why they should not learn to walk quietly to heel like Retrievers, and they can be taught this in just the same way as any other dog. In order to avoid unnecessary repetition of early work details I refer readers to the Chapter on Preliminary Training, which, with certain obvious exceptions, applies to all breeds.

Working to Signals and Whistle.

A dog that has learnt to drop to command and whistle, to shot and signal, to answer to name and whistle and possibly to walk to heel, should receive specialized training to hand signals. A Pointer ranging well out on moor or in stubble should have a ranging limit and turn up-wind when he reaches the extremity of this range to right or left. A special whistle to turn the dog, or at least to make him look to you for directions without ceasing to move, is essential. Many of the present-day bird-dogs seen at Trials fail lamentably in this respect; obviously they have not been correctly taught to respond to whistle or signal when quartering. The judicious use of bribes, as discussed in the Chapter on Preliminary Training, is one of the quickest ways of getting a dog to watch your hand movements. This can be carried a step further in the early stages by hiding pieces of biscuit or bread and indicating their direction with a wave of the arm and by moving to right or left yourself, with arm outstretched to encourage the dog to quest in the direction of the tit-bits. The check-cord can be used to turn a dog which persistently ignores your signals. When he has discovered that your signals indicate the position of eatables, an intelligent puppy will soon become proficient at working to hand, and if this practice is carried out at increasing distances between handler and dog the latter will become reliable even when at extreme range. If you decide to use a special whistle to turn the dog, which I consider desirable, this can now be introduced. Having got your puppy used to quartering to right and left as you walk straight ahead, give the turn whistle when he has found one of the hidden rewards and wave him over for the one on the other side of you. If he does not obey, use the check-cord to show him. In a short while there will be no need to use a signal, the whistle being sufficient to turn the puppy to right or left. With many puppies quartering seems to be an instinct and little specialized training need be given, but the use of a whistle when the puppy turns, even if he is doing so of his own accord, will teach him to respond to it in circumstances when his natural inclination would perhaps be to do otherwise.

Regular quartering can be taught in a smallish field with

good fences or hedges. Always walk up-wind, and in the centre of the field. Upon reaching the fence or hedge the puppy will have to turn; at this moment give your hand and whistle signal, and repeat the process again and again. Quite small fields will do for a start, working up to large areas where the puppy will be encouraged to range wide. The value of having a "turn" whistle is that the range can be altered to suit the size of the fields being worked. Otherwise a dog used to ranging wide would tend to "break fence" when worked in a small field, or one used to confined spaces would not sufficiently cover a wide field, and miss much game. The aim is to allow the dog to have a wide range yet be capable of being turned by whistle when desired. The early training ground should be as "gameless" as possible, until some degree of control and steadiness to fur has been instilled. Because of this, long spells of training should not be given (unless the pupil is an exceptionally keen, natural ranger), or he may become dejected and slow down, which is undesirable. Most puppies, however, will gallop happily for considerable periods, especially if this training is given instead of "formal" exercise. In other words, let the exercise periods be training periods, and *vice versa*. If rabbits are flushed and chased it just cannot be helped, and if game is winded almost any well-bred puppy will acknowledge its presence by some sort of point, even if it is only a rudimentary one. Pointing is a natural quality about which the trainer can do little except encourage and prolong. It certainly cannot be taught to a dog lacking the instinct—that is, not to an extent that would make the trouble worth while.

Using a Trained Dog as "Schoolmaster".

It is advisable when possible to work a Pointer or Setter puppy with a well-trained bird-dog in order to teach him to range, quarter and turn to whistle. If such a dog is available the early lessons will be greatly simplified, but (as I have said before) a puppy, like a child, will learn bad habits far quicker than good ones, and any faults in the older dog will be copied by the youngster. For this reason, a canine schoolmaster should not be utilized unless he is really good and reliable. A well-trained dog, of any breed, which will range well out and turn and work to signal and whistle can be made use of for a time in order to give a puppy the right notions. I have often used a wide-ranging, obedient Labrador as a tutor.

Send the older dog out and encourage the puppy to follow.

Work the dogs from side to side by whistle and hand signal as already described; you will be surprised how quickly most youngsters will cotton-on to the idea and thereafter range out alone and respond to whistle and signal. These lessons should not be prolonged, for the tendency will be for the puppy to rely entirely upon the older dog and not develop any initiative. All that is required of the schoolmaster is to teach the pupil to range well out and to turn when whistled and signalled to do so. To continue working a puppy with an older bird-dog is a mistake, especially in early field work, for the older one will find all the game and the puppy will be content to let him.

STEADINESS TO FUR.

Bird-dog puppies should be made steady to rabbits and hares in early training. This can be done in much the same way as recommended for Retrievers—in a rabbit pen if one is available, by use of tame rabbits or merely by taking them on natural ground where plenty of "fur" exists. All inclinations to point fur should be discouraged; the dog should be taught completely to ignore both hares and rabbits. Harshness, however, must be avoided, especially if there is a predisposition to point fur, or the dog in fear of punishment may become what is known as a "blinker", and ignore scents which he should acknowledge. Great tact and care must be used. At a later stage, if all has gone well, the dog can be allowed to range among fur, wearing a long check-cord which can be used to pull him up should he indulge in a chase, or which can be jerked should he come up on point to rabbits or hares. Many trainers teach their dogs to drop to fur, the pupils having to go down the moment a hare or rabbit is seen, but the better plan is to teach the dog that all fur is to be ignored completely. A dog which does break away should be taken up on his return and brought to the spot from where he started the chase, dropped there, rated and punished if necessary. At first a dog should wear the lead when among rabbits, the handler walking about unconcernedly, the lead being jerked for the dog to follow if he shows any interest. Though there are almost bound to be regrettable lapses from time to time, this early training in steadiness should lay the desired foundation and, as with the other breeds, it has the advantage that correction given later in the field is understood and taken to heart. The useful command "No" should always be used if the dog so much as looks at hares or rabbits, both in early training and in the shooting field. Some dogs *cannot* be prevented from pointing "fur", without spoiling them. There is nothing to be done about this fault.

DROPPING TO SHOT.

Having taught the pupil to drop to command and to a special whistle and signal, dropping to shot, as with a Spaniel, is easily taught. The puppy must of course have been acclimatized to gunfire, as set out in Chapter III, and all that remains to be done is to introduce the training pistol or gun and fire it at the same time as the command is given. Having already learnt to drop to the upraised hand, the puppy will quickly associate the raising of the hand and firing of the shot with this action. This must be painstakingly instilled. A Pointer, not having to retrieve, is not inclined (like a Retriever or Spaniel) to associate gunfire with a good gallop out and is consequently much easier to teach to drop to shot than a Spaniel. This work, besides dropping to whistle and signal, should be practised at all distances so that ultimately the dog will go down wherever he may be.

QUARTERING.

When your dog has learnt to drop to command, whistle, signal and shot, to range freely and turn to by whistle or signal, and is reasonably steady to fur, practical field work can begin. From now on the instincts of the dog play the most important part, and except for maintaining discipline and preventing chasing there is little the handler can do. As with other gundogs, in the excitement of field work, where live game is met with under natural conditions, there is a tendency for the pupil to forget some of the earlier obedience lessons, and the handler must ever be prepared to check attempts to chase or run-in. A dog which flushes larks whilst quartering and chases them should be stopped by whistle, rated and then made to continue ranging. Some puppies will start standing to larks and other small birds, and this must be discreetly discouraged without in any way putting them off pointing. Once game has been experienced, and a few points on it enjoyed, most puppies will soon learn to ignore lesser fry.

So far I have made few allusions to words of command. These can be of your own choice. You will need separate commands for the following actions: drop, quarter, turn, heel, as well as the ever useful "No" to prevent a wrong action. There will be distinct whistles, or combinations of whistles, for the drop, turn and recall, but the fewer the commands the better. "Hi on!" is commonly used when casting off to quarter, though after a while no command is necessary with an eager puppy. With Pointers and Setters the aim should be to work the dogs mainly by signal and whistle, which is much less disturbing to game than a lot of shouting, though the voice may have to be used often in the earlier stages of training. Some men even have a special command which they always use when their dogs come up on point ("To Ho" was a popular expression for this purpose in the old days), and in this way a dog can after a time be brought up on point by command alone. There is really little or no sense in this, except in the case of an unscrupulous handler with a poor dog which has to have its points found. A whispered "Steady" can be useful when a puppy first starts pointing if he attempts to creep forward on his birds. This should be used at the moment of taking hold of the check-cord . . . but I am going ahead too fast.

Introduction to Game.

The spring is undoubtedly the best time to introduce the bird-dog to game. When the birds have paired and will sit tight, and are well distributed over the ground, there will be many opportunities of finding easily and quickly, and scenting conditions are likely to be good. The dog should always be worked up-wind, and for the first few times may wear a light yet strong check-cord. This may perhaps impede him and slow him down at first but he will soon become used to it and with a keen puppy it is soon ignored. Cast the dog off with a definite signal learnt in earlier lessons, and walk straight ahead up the middle of the field yourself. When the pupil reaches the extremity of his range to one side, give your turn whistle and wave him over to the other side. Repeat the procedure. Never take your eyes off the dog, and the moment he comes up on point get over to him as quickly yet as quietly as you can. Take hold of the check-cord gently and restrain him from creeping forward by a steady hold, at the same time whispering "Steady". Keep him on point for as long as possible, then softly walk up to him and encourage him to move slowly forward beside you. Immediately birds flush, drop the dog by command or whistle, and by means of the check-cord prevent any attempts to chase. If the dog gets well under way bring him up smartly with the cord, drag him back, make him drop where he should have done, and keep him down for a couple of minutes. Praise and reward the pupil with a few pats, then cast him out again, repeating the procedure. Fire an occasional blank cartridge as the birds depart, insisting that the dog drops to shot if he is not already down.

POINTING.

It will often be found with a youngster that he is "false pointing"—that is, pointing to scent where birds have been but are no longer present. When no birds rise as you and the dog creep forward, cast him off again as quickly as possible. On the other hand, if the birds are not lying well and flush the moment the dog points and before you get up to him, drop him by whistle or command immediately and try to prevent a chase. If there is a chase, stop the dog as soon as you can, or take him up on his return, and make him drop where he should have done, keeping him down for some minutes before continuing. If the birds are flushed whilst the dog is quartering, without any response by him, stop the dog immediately, take him back to the spot and try to get him interested in the scent of the birds. Accidental flushes are unavoidable and happen with some of the best dogs, especially on bad scenting days when cover is scarce or birds are not lying well. If the dog continually flushes without acknowledging birds by pointing, try to find a squatting brace, or an outlying pheasant, and work the dog up to this whilst you hold the end of the check-cord. Slowly increase your pressure to bring him up and almost certainly he will acknowledge the birds when he winds them —naturally you have approached up-wind. Keep him standing for as long as feasible, then go in and flush as described above, dropping the dog the moment the bird rises. This can be repeated several times, but it will generally be found that two or three times are enough to give the pupil the right idea, and at once start him pointing when he strikes the scent of game.

It is a matter of opinion whether a dog should be introduced in the first place to the scent of a freshly shot dead bird, as a means of encouragement. Some trainers make a habit of this, allowing the novice to bury his nose in the feathers and get a really good whiff of the scent so that he can begin to know what he is supposed to be looking for. With a keen, well-bred youngster this should not be necessary, the acknowledgment of the scent of game being instinctive. Furthermore, as I believe the scents of live and dead birds differ quite considerably, it seems likely that one may be giving the dog a false impression.

If you have any tame or penned pheasants or partridges available it is quite a good idea to give a puppy his first introduction to game with them, using the check-cord as described above. This will ensure that he does know what it is all about and give opportunities for teaching staunchness on point and steadiness to flush before ever going into the field. With a large number of trainers reliance will be placed upon finding the birds in their natural surroundings, and upon the pointing instinct of the pupils.

Bird-dog puppies vary considerably in the age at which they start acknowledging the scent of game. Some very well-bred youngsters may do this at four or five months of age, others will flush and try to chase everything they put up until over a year old. But if the breeding is right, success is sure to be obtained in time. Some of the best mature workers result from puppies that were slow to make up in this respect.

Bird-dogs do not require to be introduced to game on ground which is heavily stocked. To be constantly coming across birds can have a demoralizing effect upon a young dog and may start him flushing and chasing. Also, it gives him a wrong impression; a puppy which starts on ground where he finds birds every few yards is going to become very discouraged when worked on more barren land where whole fields may be beaten out without a single point. The ideal ground for early field training should strike a happy medium—enough birds to give the dog a few points on each outing but not enough to excite him or so few that he becomes discouraged. Long stubbles, clover leys and grass fields with sufficient cover to cause the birds to lie well are the most popular types of ground for bird-dog training on partridges in the southern counties. Completely open and barren ground is hopeless, the birds rising wild almost as soon as the dog is cast off. To work a dog on such ground is worse than useless and may easily lead to his ruination. Conversely, very thick, heavy cover is equally undesirable as the birds will tend to creep forward and puzzle the dog, which in turn will probably start creeping after them instead of holding up, and in such cover it is often well-nigh impossible to see the dog working or pointing.

A bird-dog is expected to acknowledge the body scent of squatting birds and not start running the foot scent of birds which have moved. A Pointer or Setter should quarter with head held high, not get his nose down to the ground in the manner of a Hound or Spaniel. A dog which does so quickly becomes a potterer—a slow, poking animal who will be up to his birds and flush them without giving the gun a chance, or acknowledge them only by a very rudimentary "flush point", if that. Bird-dogs are most useful on large, open tracts of country where game is somewhat scarce and not worth driving, and so are expected to cover a wide area and point staunchly to give time for the accompanying gun or guns to come up to them, flush the birds and obtain a shot. If your dog becomes a potterer you might just as well use a Spaniel for all the use the potterer will be.

As with the other gundog breeds, it is well to give Pointers or Setters several days of work without the gun before starting to shoot birds to them. In this way the handler can devote attention to his dog and so retain steadiness and deal with any lapses that may happen. Blank cartridges can be used to imitate the real thing, and then when serious shooting starts the only difference to the dog will be the fall of birds when they are shot. As a bird-dog is not interested in retrieving this should mean little to him and therefore does not have such an unsteadying effect as results with Spaniels or Retrievers. A shot bird, if hit in the head, will jump and flutter in a most tantalizing manner, and many a young dog, hitherto dead steady, has (by running-in) blotted his copybook the first time he has seen a fluttering bird. Some trainers therefore make a point of working their dogs on ground where there are concealed spring throwers, which eject dummies into the air when a string is pulled from a distance. The "bird" is fired at and the dog made to drop, and in the advanced stages is allowed to see a Retriever or Spaniel go forward and pick it up, being restrained from taking any notice when the other dog returns. This carries training a stage nearer the real thing, and can be most useful.

A dog which carries his head low and appears to be hunting foot scents can sometimes, *I am told*, be cured by use of a device known as the "puzzle peg". This consists of a stick which juts out below the dog's chin and effectively prevents him from putting his nose low, the stick being attached to the dog's muzzle by a special harness. I have never had experience of this, and although the theory seems sound I imagine that wearing the contraption would worry a dog and prevent him from enjoying his work. A dog which does not come to quartering with head high in the proper manner after having been given sufficient time should be discarded, though if the above idea is tried and found successful discarding will not be necessary, for once the pupil has learnt by use of the "puzzle peg" not to put his nose down he may give up the objectionable practice and be capable of being worked without the peg.

SHOOTING OVER THE DOGS.

When first shooting over your bird-dog it is quite a good plan to get someone else to handle the gun, so that you can watch the dog. When he comes up on point both you and the gun move over as quickly and as quietly as possible to where he is standing. If you are still working the dog on a light check-cord (and it may well be advisable) take hold of the end in your customary manner and keep him up on point for as long as convenient. Then move forward with the gun beside you, encourage the dog to walk at your side and go in to "make out" the point (which means flush the birds), drop the dog and shoot. If the dog has not gone down to the rise of the birds he should go down to the shot; alternatively, you have your command, whistle or the check-cord to enforce the action. Do so promptly if necessary, and then both you and the gun must remain dead still for a minute or so before collecting the shot bird or birds. During this early training do not have another dog with you to pick up or there may be an unsteadying effect upon your pupil. Make sure that your companion, the gun, is not the excitable sort of man who wants to rush forward with shouts of joy every time he kills, or who will run like a greyhound after any wounded bird which is getting away. If there is a runner down, the gun should give it another barrel at once, and not move a step. An excitable shooting companion is an abomination at the best of times; when dog training is in progress he is an absolute menace and may easily ruin all your hard work. If no reliable friend is available shoot over the dog yourself, giving the commands immediately and keeping your foot on the check-cord in case there is an attempt to chase.

If for any reason you have decided to dispense with the check-cord you will have to be doubly vigilant and try to control the dog by command and whistle should he go wrong. It is a good thing if you can anticipate the actions of a gundog and so have the appropriate command ready for him if he riots. If a chase does develop, and you can stop the dog, back he must go to the place where he should have dropped, *every time*, and there be rated and punished by "holding", shaking and by giving him a cut or two with the lead if advisable. Then keep him on the drop for several minutes at this spot—for meditation and penitence! If you cannot stop your dog when he starts chasing, await his return and then take him back as directed above. *Never* on any account punish the dog *when he comes up to you*; *always take him to the place where he went wrong*.

As a dog gets older and more experienced he will on favourable scenting days start winding birds and coming up on point at greater and greater distances from them, and will be less likely to flush them accidentally. Some shooting men make a habit of always leaving their dogs and walking forward alone to flush the birds, leaving the dog on the drop. I have seen others leave the dog pointing whilst they walked forward, but usually if this is done the dog creeps or races forward, and it serves no useful purpose. The best plan is to take the dog to "make out" each point, and at first to be in no hurry to do so, or you will find that the dog anticipates you by starting to creep forward before you get up to him. The check-cord can be used to begin with to get him to creep along beside you. With it you can prevent him from dashing in to flush the birds.

Dogs vary greatly in their pointing attitudes. Every reader will have seen the classic pictures of Pointers and Setters standing transfixed in a true "cataleptic point", eyes glazed, tail outstretched and one forefoot raised. Not all dogs point like this. Some never raise a foot, others half drop with neck outstretched forward, others crouch very low, some drop completely, but whatever they do they always indicate unmistakably that they are winding game. The scent strikes them "all of a heap", as it were, and has an immediate and automatic effect upon the brain and muscles which results in the "point" or "set".

Today, great store is set by pace, style and ranging in a Field Trial dog. These characteristics must of course be coupled with steadiness and control if they are to be of any value. Many judges are of the opinion that the dogs of today are not nearly as good as were the dogs of thirty years ago. This is understandable when one considers how few opportunities most men get of training their dogs, compared with conditions prevailing in the years gone by, and must be blamed upon "the times we live in". Those who do embark upon the training of bird-dogs should try to be as scientific as possible in their methods, particularly about obtaining steadiness and controlling the range of their dogs. After a dog has been shooting a few times and seems to be getting the right idea, gaining in confidence as far as gamefinding goes, he will often become more difficult to control. In other words, the dog appears to believe that he knows more than you do (which in the finding of birds is undoubtedly true!) and this must not be allowed to develop to an extent that makes the dog ignore you. Any signs of backsliding in control and steadiness should immediately indicate the reintroduction of the check-cord and an intensive "refresher" course of obedience and hand training. If a dog is allowed to get out of control, and continue thus for a day or two, he is on the road to ruin, and salvation may be impossible. See to it, therefore, that discipline is maintained and that you are acknowledged as master from the word "Go". Stand no nonsense; be kind, be firm, and above all be just, but retain the dog's respect by always being undisputed master.

Brace Work.

Working a brace of bird-dogs is more exacting than working a single dog. Your eyes have to be in two places at once; you have two dogs to control and correct when things go wrong, and there is the probability that if one dog riots the other will follow suit. Why then, you may ask, does anyone bother to work a brace of dogs? The answer is that a brace covers twice as much ground and, for two guns out shooting, gives better sport, especially where birds are scattered on wild moors and other open spaces. On the average shoot in this country it is doubtful if, for two guns only, a brace of dogs *is* necessary. Birds are often so few and far between that one properly trained and experienced dog can find them, and with less likelihood of flushing birds which are wild. Agreed, a good brace is very pretty to watch, and for anyone who has the time, the patience and the necessary ground over which to work them there is a good deal to be said for brace work.

No two dogs should be made up into a brace until they have been trained "solo". To take two completely raw puppies out and try to work them as a brace is most difficult. The main problem with a brace is to prevent the dogs chasing each other about, with the result that one dog is doing all the real work and his companion merely following him. To be useful, each partner must range separately, one to the right and one to the left, crossing over in such a way that the whole of a wide area is thoroughly quartered, without the individual range of each dog being in any way restricted. Successful training of two dogs to work as a brace depends mainly upon the qualities of the individual dogs and the patience and perseverance of the trainer.

Upon casting off the brace, signal one dog to the right, the other to the left, and insist that they go their separate ways. This is not easy, for one is almost bound to follow the other at first, in which event both dogs must be dropped, the wrong-doer dragged back and cast out again in the correct direction. Eventually, by insistence on the trainer's part the dogs should go the ways intended. If each dog is trained to drop to a different whistle matters are simplified to some extent as there may be frequent occasions when one dog will have to drop whilst the other continues working. There is also the question of "backing" to be considered, as this is a very important point when working a brace. For a dog to "back" means that when one of a brace sees his companion on point he must immediately freeze and either point himself (which is a true "back") or drop. On no account must he rush forward and take the point from the other dog, nor get so close to the birds that there is a danger of flushing. Luckily, in many bird-dogs backing is quite a natural instinct; they come up the moment they see another dog pointing. Other dogs, if they see their partner pointing, rush up and back only when they themselves get wind of the birds. This is not true backing; it is attempting to steal the point and should be discouraged. Some men save a good deal of time and trouble by dropping the other dog by whistle the moment one comes up on point. This is quite a serviceable method of working for shooting purposes but it is not true Pointer and Setter work. A dog can be trained to back by taking him out with another to find game. When the schoolmaster is firmly on point bring the pupil to view him and with the aid of the check-cord bring the pupil up to back, in the same manner that you encouraged him to point in the early lessons. A dog which obstinately refuses to back will simply have to be taught to drop every time another dog gets a point, and this can be done only by whistling him down every time a point is secured by his partner. This, again, is not true backing but is better than having a dog spoil every point that his partner secures. It will often be found that such a dog will, when he realizes that his partner is pointing game, start backing properly instead of dropping. This will dawn on him after he has once or twice seen birds rise and heard shots fired, especially after occasions (which are bound to happen) when the dogs are fairly close together and one gets a point.

For a start, both members of the brace should wear a long and light check-cord, no matter how reliable they may be individually. If one starts a chase the other is bound to follow, and the cord may be the means of preventing at least one of the brace from getting too far. Further, it is useful as a means of imposing your will on either dog as necessary, without getting too close to him.

When one of the brace secures a point, and the trainer walks over to "make it out", the backing dog is subjected to a great deal of temptation, especially as the birds rise and a shot is fired. It is necessary, therefore, to dispense with actual shooting for the first few days of brace training in the field and concentrate on the dogs, unless you have someone reliable with the gun who will go over and make out the point for you or, alternatively, go over to take up the check-cord of the backing dog whilst you flush the birds. The latter is preferable if the pointing dog is a youngster and you do not wish anyone else to handle him at this stage. If the backer should run-in, he must be stopped and dragged back to where he should have stopped and there kept down for some time. This must be done every time if the dogs are to be steady and reliable. It is a good illustration of the amount of work (both pedestrian and mental!) which is the lot of trainer of a brace of bird-dogs.

It will by now be obvious why the individual dogs must have been trained solo before forming a brace. Without such training complete and utter chaos will result.

On the inevitable occasions when one dog goes wrong you will have to drop both dogs and, leaving the other one down, attend to the culprit, taking him back to the spot where he went wrong and dealing with him there in a suitable manner. It is best to go back to your original position, call up both dogs and cast them off afresh; if you try to start them again from their present positions, at any rate in the early stages, there is bound to be a muddle and the dogs become thoroughly "mixed up". Great care must be taken when dealing with a miscreant not to let the dog which has done no wrong think that he too is in disgrace. All dogs, particularly the sensitive bird-dogs, are apt to get a wrong impression when you punish one of their companions, so tact must be used. A great deal depends on the temperaments of the dogs concerned, and you must be guided by these.

One of the bugbears of the brace trainer is "fur"—particularly hares. These annoying creatures have a nasty habit of lying low and then springing up in front of a dog just at the wrong moment, and unless both members of the brace have received steadiness training they will course "puss" in great glee, deaf to all your calls and whistles. This will happen from time to time even when the dogs are, individually, as steady as rocks. Jealousy, and possibly rebellion at the restraint under which they have been working, does strange things; I have seen highly trained Pointers and Setters go wrong at Trials after having behaved perfectly earlier in the day. In working a brace, therefore, special attention must be paid to steadiness training and instant response to whistle and command the moment hares or rabbits are sighted.

As I wrote at the beginning of this Chapter, Pointer and Setter training is made more difficult because so little of their work can be copied by artificial means, as with Retrievers and Spaniels. Apart from the early obedience lessons, the main work has to be carried out on ground where temptation in every shape and form may exist and the dog or dogs are probably at great distances from you, which makes control so much less certain. Whereas Spaniels and Retrievers can be three parts trained around the house or on the lawn, bird-dogs have to have the scent of game in their nostrils from an early age. That being so, it must be emphasized that what training can be done away from the excitements of game should be carried out very, very conscientiously, and the dogs made absolutely word-perfect in their obedience drill before being worked on game. The one advantage of a pointing dog over a Spaniel or Retriever is that at some time or other it is going to come up on point and "freeze", which does give the handler a chance to get up to it (or at least to within reach of the end of the ever-useful check-cord). But the damage may by that time have been done, and a dog must not associate pointing with any form of punishment, so no matter how irate you may be you must before administering correction take the dog back to the place where he rioted. My advice is to let the correction be holding, rating and shaking rather than a whipping, with a long rest on the drop afterwards. Dogs can never be trained by the whip, bird-dogs least of all, and though a few cuts with the lead can be very sobering, do without whipping if possible.

CHAPTER IX

FIELD TRIALS

Retriever Trials. Spaniel Trials. Pointer and Setter Trials. Training Classes and Gundog Working Tests. Handling at Field Trials.

Retriever Trials.

RETRIEVER TRIALS are particularly popular with private and novice handlers, probably because a Retriever is a more "personal" dog than a Spaniel, and also because (if we look facts squarely in the face) it is far easier to train a dog to one duty—retrieving—than to two—questing *and* retrieving—which are required of Spaniels. A Retriever walks to heel or waits in the butt or at the stand with his master, and his duties start only when there is a bird down to be sought and retrieved. A Spaniel is expected to quest for the unshot game, put it up and remain steady to it, then retrieve upon command. It does not need much imagination, therefore, to understand why the average shooting man finds a Retriever an easier training proposition than a Spaniel. Of course there are many men who train both breeds for their particular duties, and I believe most of these men enjoy Spaniel training more than Retriever training. The reasons for this will be more apparent in the Chapters on Spaniels.

A Retriever Field Trial is conducted in a similar manner to a day's formal shooting, except that the drives are taken more slowly. At a Trial the important factor is the gathering of shot game and the dog work, and the number of drives and the size of the bag take second place. There are always three judges at a Retriever Trial, and two guns are allotted to each. Until every dog has been under the judges each judge has two dogs down under him at one time, spaced between the guns where he can watch both dog and handler. With each judge is a steward and a man to carry the number holder. The dogs are each allotted a number (by ballot as a rule), the judge on the right taking numbers 1 and 2, the centre judge numbers 3 and 4, and the left-hand judge numbers 5 and 6 and so on down the card. When a dog goes out to retrieve his number is put in the holder and displayed to judges and spectators. As the judges finish with each dog they change over dogs, but no dog is called up for a second time under one judge until it has been seen working by the other two. In this way the judges work down the card and all the dogs are seen working by all the judges, who have been taking notes of the performances, and in due time are able to decide which dogs merit a second "run". What usually happens is that several dogs automatically eliminate themselves during the day, either by displaying some obvious fault, such as running-in to shot or chasing, or others stand out by reason of brilliant performances and so the judges are left with several good dogs to see again, and decide the placings. By this process of elimination, in which it must be admitted luck plays an important part, the number of competitors is thinned down to four or five, and then the judges decide to have the "run off", which is Field Trial parlance for the final tests for placing. The three judges now watch the dogs together, and after consultation are able to announce their findings and place the dogs. Some dogs which were not in the final "run off" may be awarded "Certificates of Merit" or "Awards of Honour", these being awards which, though not carrying any prize money, certify that the dog did nothing wrong, satisfied the judges as a competent worker and a good shooting dog, but failed to make the grade into the placings.

Retriever Field Trials are run by various clubs and societies, and the stakes are classified into categories such as "Open", "Puppy", "Non-winner" and "Novice". Some stakes last two days (the number of dogs competing is then usually 24), others with fewer dogs competing are decided in a day, and some societies hold as many as three stakes in a two-day period but limit the total number of competitors. The Open Stakes are the most important, and as Kennel Club Rules stand at present a Retriever which wins two Open Stakes run under K.C. rules by an approved society, under different judges, qualifies for the title of Field Trial Champion. The International Gundog League Retriever Society organize an annual Retriever Championship Stake.

Retriever Trials are, as far as possible, conducted over ground where dogs can be tested both walking in line and waiting at drives, but this is not always possible to arrange and so some Trials consist exclusively of walking-up and others of drives over waiting guns. The handler works his dog in his own way, but no dog must be sent to retrieve until the judges' permission is given, and the handler has to obey the orders of the judges. Each handler wears an armlet bearing his number, and a judge with two dogs down under him tries the lowest numbered dog first. If this dog fails to find his retrieve, the other dog down is given a chance. If neither dog finds, the judge can either try the first dog again or ask the other judges if they wish to try any of their dogs on the bird. Apart from calling in the lowest numbered dog first, the method of judging is left entirely to the judges' discretion, and it is difficult to see how this system can be bettered. In my opinion, judging on a "points" system, previously decided, is difficult and unfair. It is far easier for a man who knows a good gundog (as a Field Trial judge should) to make notes of each dog's performance, good and bad points, and decide in his own mind the best dogs and the order of their merit. Mistakes there will inevitably be from time to time, and luck, good and bad, will always play its part in Trials, because it is quite impossible to give every dog an exactly equal test in precisely the same circumstances. But this element of uncertainly and luck is all part of the sport of Trials, and is understood and appreciated (or should be!) by those who compete at them. "The luck of the draw"—in other words, the number a particular handler draws—may help or hinder his dog as the following true story will illustrate. Four dogs were down under the judges for the "run off" at a Retriever Trial, numbers 3, 5, 10 and 11. All had done good work and were more or less equal in the judges' estimation. After the last drive a strong runner was down, and so the lowest number, number 3 dog, was called up. This dog saw the bird and followed it into a thick wood, but after being allowed about seven minutes by the judges came back without it. I was handling number 5 which was called up next. The dog hunted for several minutes without result and the judges ordered it to be called up. On looking round for the next dog the judges, seeing that the handler and dog were some way off, told me I could continue to hunt my dog until number 10 arrived on the scene, and at that very moment my dog came out of the wood with the runner in his mouth! Now number 10 was a brilliant dog which had had far more experience than my own, and had it drawn a lower number would have had prior chance, and would almost undoubtedly have found the bird. In this instance my dog was placed first and number 10 second, whereas but for "the luck of the draw" the placings might have been reversed.

Spectators at Field Trials are in the charge of a flag steward carrying a red flag, and they must obey his orders. Whenever possible this steward will stand the spectators where they will obtain a good view of the dog work, but it is an unfortunate fact that where the lie of the ground does not permit this the spectators often see little or nothing of what is going on at certain drives. The chief duty of the flag steward is to keep the spectators in a position where they will be safe from the guns and where they will not get in the way of the handlers, dogs or judges, nor foul the scent of the fallen birds. This means, as a rule, that the spectators are kept some way to one side or behind the line of guns, so how much they will see of the shooting and dog work depends upon the conformation of the ground.

What are the actual qualifications of a Field Trial Retriever? Above all else, a judge seeks gamefinding ability. A Retriever's job is to seek, find and retrieve to hand dead or wounded game whose whereabouts is either completely unknown to the guns or which lies in a place inaccessible to them—such as in thorny cover or across a stream or river. To do this a dog needs to have a good nose, a wide range and be under command of his handler, who must be able to direct him, within limits, to any particular spot within view. If you possess such a dog, which is also tender-mouthed and steady both to falling game and fur, then there is no reason at all why he should not compete at Trials. Far too many people seem to believe that Field Trial dogs must have some supernatural ability and their handlers some mystic, secret form of control over them. Nothing could be farther from the truth. The ideal Field Trial dog is simply a good, reliable shooting dog which, through more careful and intensive training, has been brought to (and kept at!) a higher pitch of perfection than are most shooting dogs. It has long been my view that the man with one or two gundogs, and a love of training, is the man who should "wipe the board" at Trials. Professional trainers have to deal with such a large number of clients' dogs that they can seldom give as much time as they would like to any one single animal. The private owner is not so handicapped, yet it is only in recent years that the owner-handler has started to compete in good numbers at Trials and, what is more, to win a good many of them.

Pace and style are two words which can be heard mentioned frequently in any discussion about Trials. Field Trial judges quite rightly like fast, stylish dogs. So does the keen shooting man, provided this is accompanied by gamefinding ability. Both pace and style will be found in many strains of Retriever

—they are natural features which can be either brought out or eliminated by training. There is little one can do to make a naturally slow dog fast, but by wrong handling it is easy to slow up a naturally fast one. This subject has been discussed in more detail in the Training Chapters; it will suffice to say here that a fast dog generally has a good nose and can rely upon that advantage.

In order to win Trials with a Retriever I consider that the dog should be very "handy". By this I mean that it should be possible to direct him to within scenting distance or reasonable questing distance of a bird which he has not seen fall. In other words, the dog should be capable of being directed by hand signal or voice to any given spot within sight. How this result can be obtained I have endeavoured to show in the Training Chapters. With a good dog it is almost easy and makes very interesting work. Nothing, to my mind, is prettier to watch than a fast, stylish retriever ranging out, stopping, as if equipped with four-wheel brakes, at a whistle from his handler, then turning and questing in the direction indicated by a wave of the hand. Yet many people call this "circus stuff", and decry it on the grounds that "the handler is finding the bird, not the dog". Reliance on the handler's directions can be overdone, of course, and at all times we want a dog with initiative and self-reliance. But a dog which cannot be guided when necessary wastes a lot of time and a good deal of temper, whereas a "handy" dog gathers his game speedily and at the same time "catches the judge's eye" as a dog which can be handled and which has been expertly trained. Such a dog will do well at Field Trials and be a pleasure to shoot over at home. The objects of Trials, as I see them, are to demonstrate the best breeds and strains of gundog for shooting, and, incidentally, the best trainers of such. A fast, stylish, wide-ranging and "handy" gamefinder does all these things.

Spaniel Trials.

Field Trials for Spaniels are held during the shooting season from October to January by the various Spaniel societies and clubs and also by societies which cater for Field Trials generally —some clubs even running different meetings for Retrievers, Spaniels and bird-dogs (Pointers and Setters). In order that the Spaniels shall be seen performing their proper duties as questing dogs as well as retrieving, Spaniel Trials have to be held on ground which can be walked over and the game flushed by the dogs. Whenever possible, ground is selected which favours that work and contains cover of such a nature that the judges can see what the dogs are doing, and also test their courage in thick brambles and thorns. Heaths containing plenty of bracken, gorse and brambles are therefore ideal for Spaniel Trials, and shoots on which there are small woods and belts with good undercover are also useful. Plenty of game, including ground game, is desirable if the Trial is to be a real test as Spaniels are expected to find, remain steady to and retrieve fur as well as feather. An abundance of rabbits at a Spaniel Trial offers stiff tests of steadiness, and this is a great help to the judges. What usually happens is that the organizing society contact owners of ground suitable for trials, and after permission has been given to use it, a date is fixed, guns arranged for (usually members of the syndicate which shoot the ground, or are guests of the owner) and the question of beats is gone into with the head keeper, who makes all arrangements for beaters, game carriers and a meeting place.

Two judges and a referee officiate at a Spaniel Trial, each judge having one dog down under him at one time. The competitors are numbered on the official programme (usually by ballot), the handler wearing an armband with the number his dog has drawn. Some men handle two or more dogs in a stake. One judge takes the even numbers, the other the odd ones, for the first run through the card. When each judge has seen all his dogs they change over, so that both judges sees every dog working at least once. The judges walk in line about 40 yards apart, with a gun on either side of each, and there are usually a number of beaters spaced between judges and guns. A dog is expected to work independently, questing within range of its handler, who is beside, or a little in front of, the judge. The judges note the manner in which the dog beats his ground, his courage in cover, and gamefinding ability. They also take into account pace, style and steadiness. When a bird or a rabbit is flushed the dog must remain steady to it and, if it is shot, retrieve promptly to hand on the command of his handler, who awaits orders from the judge before sending his dog out. The judge then watches how quickly the dog finds the game and the manner in which he retrieves it, and carefully examines the bird or rabbit by touch for any signs of it having been bitten or crushed. As in Retriever Trials, hard mouth is one of the offences for which a dog is heavily penalized and, unless there is some extenuating circumstance, put out of the stake. Before this is done, however, both judges must examine the bird and agree that it has been bitten, consulting the referee if necessary. Chasing, or running-in to shot or the fall of a bird, are other crimes which usually mean that a dog is put out of the stake, but where a handler is able to stop his dog before it has gone more than a few yards most judges keep the dog in but note that it has shown signs of unsteadiness but was stopped by good handling.

It sometimes happens that a dog will catch a rabbit which is squatting in cover or in a "form", and when this occurs the judge tells the handler to make the dog release his capture. If this is done, and the dog will sit (or stand) and watch the rabbit run off, resisting the temptation to chase, no black marks are entered against the dog, but it often happens that the handler cannot make his dog let the rabbit go and has to take it from him. That crime is regarded as serious and the dog is marked down.

A great deal of latitude is allowed by most judges to the handler, who handles the dog in his own way, but undue noise is penalized and the handler must obey any instructions a judge sees fit to give. Each dog is given as fair a run as possible, and the judge likes to see it have a retrieve of *at least* one rabbit and one bird before calling up the next dog. If a dog fails to find a shot bird the judge may ask his colleague if he wishes to try the other dog on it, and on occasions (especially if the bird is a strong runner and offers an exceptional test of ability) several dogs may be tried. However, time is a factor and as little as possible is wasted on birds which are unlikely to be gathered. Usually the head keeper of the shoot arranges for pickers-up to search for any birds left behind.

When a judge has seen all he wishes to of one dog he makes notes of its performance in his judging book, then calls in the next dog, when the line proceeds as before. Each time a bird is shot and a dog goes out to retrieve the whole line is halted until the bird is brought to hand. Spectators are kept either behind or to one side of the line, in the charge of a flag steward, whose duty is to see that the crowd does not get in the way of the dogs, handlers or judges and, above all, is safe from the guns. Nothing is more annoying to handler, judge or gun than to have people getting in the way and putting up game which should have been left for the dogs to find, or fouling the scent, and for this reason an efficient flag steward is a most desirable official at any Field Trial. As at Retriever Trials, it often happens that the spectators at times see little of the dog work—it all depends on the ground. For instance, the judges, dogs and guns may be in a small wood whilst the spectators have to wait outside, but such instances are reduced to a minimum and the organizing society does all it can to arrange that the spectators see most of the dog work.

When each judge has seen all his dogs working once, a change-over is made and the judge who previously saw the even numbers working now sees the odd, and *vice versa*. Probably some dogs have already been eliminated on account of glaring faults. At the end of the second run the judges compare notes, and if necessary consult the referee. They then announce which dogs they wish to see working again, usually some four or five that have proved of outstanding merit. Now the judges watch the dogs together and begin to be able to determine placings. If they are in agreement when these dogs have been seen the awards can be proclaimed; if not in agreement they try the dogs again, until by elimination they are able to come to a fair decision as to the merits of the dogs. At most Trials there are four prizes and a "Reserve" award, and Certificates of Merit are given to dogs which went well but did not justify a "place". The prizes at Trials consist of cash (from the entry fees, and allotted on a sweepstake principle) with additional cups and "specials".

At any Field Trial luck plays a part, and this is possibly more so at Spaniel Trials than at any other. One famous handler once remarked that, "At Trials you want a one hundred per cent dog, plus ninety-nine per cent luck!" It is, of course, quite impossible to give every dog at a Spaniel Trial an exactly equal test; conditions must vary according to the ground being worked, the type of cover, and the direction of the wind. In America, some Trials are much more artificial. Birds are "planted" at certain points on the ground and the dogs worked up to them, a bird being shot by a gun stationed in a predetermined spot. In this way much more equal tests can be given, but in this country it is preferred to run Trials as nearly as possible like an ordinary shooting day and under natural conditions, which in my opinion is far preferable. The element of luck makes a wide appeal to British sporting instincts, and I feel perfectly certain in my own mind that any dog if really good, and run consistently at Trials, is bound to come to the top in the end, though it may be unlucky for a start. Certain it is that to win one must have a good dog, one which is not merely a gamefinder but is under good control and has pace and style. The best Spaniel in the world from the gamefinding angle is an uninteresting animal unless he works with a stylish action at a good pace; a pottering dog is a time-waster and fails to give that extra enjoyment to shooting over Spaniels which few men fail to obtain from lively, bustling dogs. It is often said of Field Trial dogs that they work too fast for their noses, but among Spaniels a fast dog usually has drive, a most essential feature in a dog which has to face punishing cover under difficult conditions. Courage and drive in cover will usually be found also in the fast dog, though there are those which will work with pace and style in fairly open country but display lamentable lack of courage when they come to real "Spaniel cover". Trials find out all these things, but what most judges are looking for are gamefinding ability (both unshot and shot game), style, pace, courage in cover and retrieving skill. Retrieving in a Spaniel is not considered quite so important as with a Retriever, by which I mean that though a Spaniel *must* retrieve his method of doing so is not as important as that of the Retrievers. After all, a Spaniel which has had a long, punishing quest in thick cover, seeking unshot game, cannot be expected to retrieve quite so smartly, when the time comes, as a Retriever whose time has probably been spent sitting beside its handler or slowly walking at heel. For all this, the *working* strains of Spaniel which one sees at Trials today do retrieve remarkably well, many as well as (if not better than) lots of Retrievers. A Spaniel being trained for Trials should have a good deal of attention paid to this aspect. Very little game is lost at Spaniel Trials, most dogs having developed good noses, and, owing to the amount of time they spend using this organ, they can distinguish between scents better than can many Retrievers. Hence a Spaniel will frequently succeed on a difficult runner where a Retriever fails.

A regrettable development in the Spaniel world in recent years is that a wide gap exists between the Show animal and the working dog. How this has come about one can only conjecture. It seems likely that this unfortunate state of affairs exists because breeders interested only in showing have concentrated on breeding for looks, whereas breeders for work and Trials have bred their dogs according to working ability and without regard to appearance. Nowadays, the Show Spaniels, particularly Cockers and Springers, are more heavily built and have much more exaggerated features (such as absurdly long ears) than the workers and Field Trial dogs. These latter tend to be smaller, lighter in bone and snipier in face. Few Show dogs ever make their appearance at Trials, still fewer Trial dogs ever grace the Show bench, and a good deal of rivalry exists between breeders of the two types. I have referred in an earlier Chapter to this divergence of opinion and will leave the reader to judge for himself the rights and wrongs of the situation.

Spaniel Field Trials cater for all breeds of Spaniel, though there are some specialist clubs which run stakes only for particular breeds. At most meetings there are Puppy, Novice (or Non-Winner) and Open Stakes, and a Spaniel which wins the Spaniel Championship or two Open or All-aged Stakes under different judges at meetings organized by bodies recognized by the Kennel Club gains the title of Field Trial Champion. Naturally the standard of work in a Open or All-Age Stake is expected to be higher than that in a Puppy or Novice Stake. Many societies also hold Amateur Handlers' Stakes, which have done a lot to encourage novice and amateur handlers and trainers, but nowadays, as is the case with Retriever Trials, many amateurs and novices compete in the other stakes, and with great success. Spaniel training and Trials have an appeal of their own, for a dog questing for live game as well as retrieving has double the temptation of a Retriever, and a far greater degree of control is required by the handler. The shooter's maid-of-all-work, the lively, bustling Spaniel, is pretty to watch and a joy to shoot over, provided it is under control, and spectators at a Trial see dogs working *all the time*—not just when the shooting has finished, as with Retrievers. Trials have undoubtedly done the Spaniel breeds an immense amount of good and popularized them with the shooting man who has to work hard for every head of game, and who enjoys seeing a dog at work as much as, if not more than, his shooting. A good Spaniel to shoot over should also make a good Field Trial dog; the requirements are exactly the same.

POINTER AND SETTER TRIALS.

Field Trials for bird-dogs are held both in the spring, when birds have paired and lie well, and during the shooting season. Thus Pointer and Setter work is more of an all-the-year-round job than is that with Spaniels and Retrievers. In order to demonstrate ability a bird-dog does not have to touch the game, as is necessary with the other breeds. That is the reason why spring Trials are possible, and this is also a popular time for giving puppies their first run in public.

Spring Trials are conducted in the same manner as autumn Trials except that no birds are shot. The organizing Society arranges a suitable ground and fixes a date for the meeting, and the organization of the beats is left to the head keeper of the estate. Two judges and a referee are appointed, and there are different stakes so that dogs in all stages of training are catered for—Puppy, Novice (or Non-Winner) and Open Stakes being the usual classifications. A puppy is generally defined as a dog under two years of age on the date of the meeting; a Novice (or Non-Winner) can be of any age but must never have won a first prize at a Field Trial, and the "Open" stake caters for any dog of any age, whether a winner or not. There are also stakes for single dogs and braces. With single dogs each under one handler two dogs and two handlers are down under the judges at one time, working independently. A brace is worked under the judges by one handler, no other dogs being down at the same time. The beats are taken up-wind and the dogs are run according to a previous draw, each handler wearing an armlet bearing the number his dog has drawn. There is usually a draw for the second round, so that dogs which have not committed serious offences and been put out of the stake are seen twice by the judges, who are then able to make their awards or call up any dogs they wish to try again. In most cases such serious crimes as chasing, running-in to shot or seriously interfering with another dog are sufficient to put a dog out of the stake, but the judging is entirely at the discretion of the judges who, if in doubt, consult the referee. Gun-shyness is also penalized, as it most certainly should be.

The head keeper having indicated the beat, the judges, referee, and one man with a gun (at spring Trials) proceed up-wind, with a handler and dog on either side spaced out so that as far as possible the dogs will not overlap when working. The dogs are cast off and quarter ahead, and the judges watch for the various points such as pace, style, quartering and, above all, gamefinding coupled with steadiness. When a dog comes up on point the handler goes up to it and walks forward with his dog at his side to "make out"—in other words, to flush the bird or birds—at which moment the gun is fired and the dog is expected to drop. The dog belonging to the other handler may "back" the pointing dog either by coming up on point himself, standing stockstill, or dropping, and very often the handler has to drop the dog by whistle or command. In no circumstances must the dog try to steal the point or in any way interfere, or move when the game is flushed. If all goes well, the successful dog has remained steady to shot and rising birds, and the handlers return to the judges and cast the dogs out afresh.

Judges may make mental notes or write up the performance of each dog in their judging books, giving credit for game-finding, style and staunchness on point, "backing", besides the other qualities of quartering, style and pace. Judges vary a good deal in their convictions of what constitutes a good bird-dog, but few if any like a slow, pottering dog, and with all judges gamefinding ability is of prime importance.

The spectators are kept back from the line of handlers and dogs, or to one side, by a flag steward who does his best to prevent any interference with the dogs or with the judges. Owners of the competing dogs, if they are being handled by others, may be in the line, and there are usually Pressmen and photographers there as well, many of whom win the judges' displeasure by getting in the way of the dogs or blocking the judges' view. The spectators at bird-dog Trials are usually more fortunate than those at Retriever and Spaniel meetings, in that the flat, open country on which Pointers and Setters are worked gives the audience a much better chance of seeing all the dog work, and there is no danger (at a spring Trial) of anyone being shot, the cartridges fired being blanks.

Summer and autumn Trials are conducted with grouse and partridges in the same way, except that conditions more nearly resemble a shooting day, as official guns are appointed to do the shooting. Here, when a dog comes up on point the gun goes forward with the handler to flush the birds and shoots a brace if he is lucky. This gives the dogs a good deal more temptation than when the birds merely fly off to the accompaniment of gunfire, for birds may fall quite close and, if hit in the head, flutter in a most exasperating manner that tempts the most steady dog to move without orders.

Considerable luck is required at any Field Trial, as well as possession of a good dog. In some parts of the shoot cover may be better than in others, with more birds lying, and dogs which are down at this time have an easier task. Again, on some fields hares and rabbits may tempt dogs to chase, whilst other dogs in the same Trial may be down when no fur is seen at all. At other times perhaps a good breeze is blowing, giving the first dogs down every assistance, but later in the day it drops and succeeding dogs have to work much harder and come upon their birds suddenly, flushing them without having a chance to point. The fair judge tries to take all these points into consideration, but the reader will appreciate the immensity of the task when so many different sets of conditions have to be taken into account. It is therefore quite understandable how sometimes a quite mediocre dog will win an award out of all proportion to its ability, purely because of luck, the weather, and the ground traversed at the particular time when it was down. This element of luck cannot be avoided, and it helps to make Field Trials the sport they are. Every sportsman loves a gamble, and in Field Trials there is no such things as a "cert". Admittedly, as with the other gundog breeds, if run often enough at Trials a good dog is almost bound in time to receive the recognition he deserves. But Trials are expensive both in time and money, and men who can run their dogs as often as they wish are few and far between.

Handling at bird-dog Trials is, of course, an important point. A good dog can be ruined by a bad handler, and a good handler can sometimes make a mediocre dog appear to be brilliant. The judges leave the handling to the discretion of the handlers, but they will penalize undue noise, or interference with another man's dog. The astute judge will see through many of the little tricks with which some handlers help their dogs, though a less experienced man may be blind to them. To give an example, there was one well-known handler some years ago who used to fool judges over backing. He taught his dogs always to stand stockstill the moment he himself stopped walking—to freeze in their tracks. When one dog secured a point, if his other dog did not immediately back all he had to do was to stop walking. Then the dog appeared to be backing the pointing dog but in reality it was simply obeying a command it knew by repetition!

Men who have attended Pointer and Setter Trials for many years often tell me that the standard of dog work is far lower today than it was thirty or forty years ago. There is every excuse for this. Nowadays when game is scarce, money even scarcer, and everyone is in such a tremendous hurry, people have not the opportunities or the time for getting dogs to a very high standard. One very well-known judge told me at a recent Kennel Club Trial Spring Meeting that the winning dogs would not have been worth a Certificate of Merit years ago, but that the situation was quite understandable. Pointers and Setters, to reach a high pitch in training, need a good deal of time and money spent on them, to say nothing of well-stocked ground over which to work them. So little shooting is done now over bird-dogs that this fact alone has discouraged many would-be trainers. This seems a pity, for pointing dogs and bird-dog Trials could bring a great deal of pleasure to many more people if conditions were otherwise. There is, however, an indication that at least in some districts bird-dogs are regaining popularity and that more men are shooting over them whenever conditions permit.

Prizes at Field Trials usually consist of money, with additional "specials" in the form of cups and other trophies. There are generally four "places", a Reserve and various Certificates of Merit, the latter going to dogs which failed to make the grade "into the money" but were sound workers for all that. The number of competing dogs is limited by the Societies, and there is an annual Championship Stakes run by the Kennel Club.

Training Classes and Gundog Working Tests.

During the last few years there has been a great revival of interest in gundog training, and because of the need for a Show bench Challenge Certificate winner to gain a "qualifying certificate" at a Field Trial before assuming the title of Champion it is not surprising that several Gundog Clubs have started Training Classes. These Training Classes can do nothing but good for the gundog breeds; already several dogs have made their appearance at Trials as a direct result of the Classes—dogs which had hitherto been regarded solely as Show animals.

The United Retriever Club is one of the pioneers of Training Classes, having branches throughout the country which hold classes at regular intervals under experienced instructors. It has been my privilege to act as instructor to the Southern Area of the U.R.C. for the past two years and during that time I have had ample opportunity of observing the enthusiasm and keenness of members, and the great strides made in handling, to say nothing of the improvement noticeable in the dogs themselves. I have also acted as judge at several Tests, and have competed in others, and it is my experience that the art of gundog training and handling is rapidly being assimilated by competing owner-handlers.

Training Classes are held on suitable ground, and the instructor endeavours to teach the handler and the dog at the same time, starting from the very beginning with simple retrieving and obedience lessons and working up to such advanced lessons as control and direction at a distance and water and cover work. At my own classes I try to cut down lectures to the minimum, and concentrate on practical work, at the same time explaining what we are doing, why, and to what end. As far as possible the lessons are arranged so that everyone can join in with their dogs, and I have been agreeably surprised by the speed with which most dogs become used to working in company, human and canine, and the benefits they derive from tuition. We begin each series of Classes with simple obedience work, the handlers and dogs lining out and walking forward, dogs on lead and at heel, stopping every few yards to teach the drop. From that we progress to walking with dogs free and dropping to command alone, then on to dropping at a distance, remaining down and returning to call. Retrieving practice begins with the simple thrown dummy which the dog is allowed to retrieve at once, followed up by the dog having to wait for orders before retrieving, retrieving from cover, over a fence, hidden dummies, direction and control at increasing distances. We usually wind up the classes by staging "partridge" drives and "walked up" shooting, with concealed throwers putting dummies out in front of or over the dogs, to the accompaniment of gunfire. In other words, the intention is to reproduce as nearly as possible natural shooting conditions, teaching gamefinding, steadiness and direction and control. At the conclusion of each series of Classes, Tests are held, usually consisting of two stakes, Novice and Open, so that the more advanced dogs are catered for. In this way many dogs belonging to town people, who have no shoots and only limited opportunities for training, are brought to a comparatively high standard of training, in some instances almost to Field Trial form.

Classes and Tests held throughout the country by other Societies differ only in slight detail. The Tests are usually so designed that they should be suitable for any retrieving gundog which has been properly grounded in the initial work and has reached the stage where it is ready to take the field. Frequently dogs which *have been* shot over in the proper sense of the term compete, as well as others that have competed (and often won) at Field Trials, but generally speaking the Tests are best left for the younger dogs, as too much attention to artificial work and dummies, after a dog has been shot over, is apt to be detrimental. When a dog has become used to retrieving real game, and seeking genuine scents of game and rabbits, the continued use of the dummy is apt to bore him and result in loss of pace and style.

Typical Tests are as under. It will be seen that any Retriever that has undergone proper early training should be capable of performing.

1. Dog walking to heel 100 yards.
2. Dropping and remaining down whilst handler disappears from sight 100 yards away.
3. Handler reappearing and recalling dog.
4. Retrieving hidden dummy from cover.
5. Retrieving dummy over 3 foot jump.
6. Two dummies thrown up 80 yards out, one to the right and one to the left, each being saluted with gunfire. Dog to retrieve only the dummy indicated by the judge, ignoring the other.
7. Retrieving from water, or from cover on the far side of a stream or river.

Some of the clubs also include temptation for the dogs in the form of a rabbit pen containing live rabbits, a dummy being thrown in and the dog expected to retrieve this whilst ignoring the rabbits. Tests for novice dogs are made somewhat simpler. In addition to the above, the Tests often include dogs and handlers walking in line, dummies being ejected ahead of the line and fired at by "official" guns or by the handlers themselves. Dogs are expected to remain steady to throw and shot, and to retrieve upon command. In this way a thorough test of steadiness is given, the situation as far as the dogs are concerned being almost identical with a real shoot.

The great advantage of Training Classes and Gundog Tests is that, apart from giving opportunities for dog training to people whose circumstances would otherwise prevent them from indulging in the sport, they are mostly held during the spring and summer months when there is little else doing—no Field Trials or game shooting. This helps to keep those interested in touch with each other and to compare dogs. Furthermore, many owners will train for and compete at Tests, whereas they would not feel competent to enter for Trials until this experience had been gained. Competitors at these Tests are mostly amateur handlers who are thus given confidence by not having to compete with professional trainers.

[Sport and General

Typical scene at a Retriever Field Trial

[P. R. A. Moxon

The 'Acvoke' adapter which enables a .25 cartridge to be fired from a shotgun

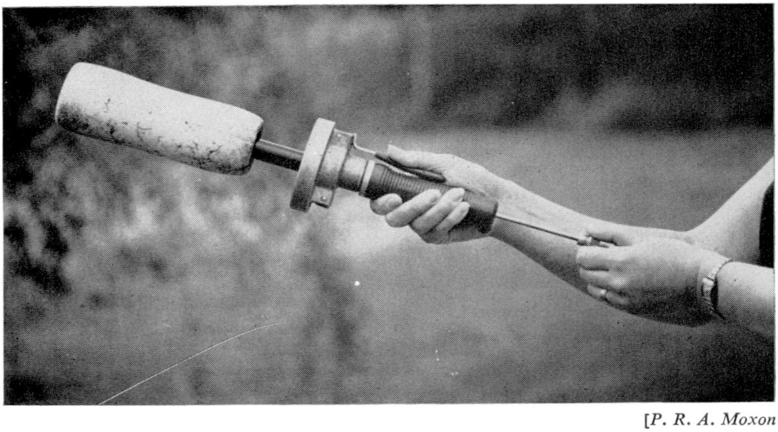

[P. R. A. Moxon

The Windrush dummy-launcher ready for action

[*Sport and General*

Handlers "casting off" at a Pointer and Setter Trial

[*P. R. A. Moxon*

A Spaniel training class in session

As far as the Classes themselves are concerned, we usually find the dogs far easier to teach than the owners! The great stumbling-block seems to be that owners will not be firm enough with their dogs; also, it is very difficult to impress upon them the necessity for taking the course slowly and getting absolute control before attempting advanced work. At my own Classes I have had the greatest difficult in impressing upon owners that they MUST teach their dogs to stop or drop by command or whistle, wherever they may be, so that they can be directed when working at a distance. I find that many handlers can get their dogs out, but once the dog is away from them they have no control. However, great strides have been made in the last year or two. More and more people are coming to appreciate control and direction at a distance, and both handling and dog work have vastly improved.

HANDLING AT FIELD TRIALS.

As one who suffers from "stage fright" as much as the next man when handling at Trials, I am perhaps not as well qualified as I might be to give advice and make suggestions on the subject! I do not think that I am in the minority, for most handlers, if they be honest with themselves, will admit that when "going into the line" the heart has a nasty habit of rising and nearly choking you, and the stomach feels as though it is detached from the body. Once in the line, however, and getting on with the job of handling, most of us forget our nerves by focusing our attention on the dog. I believe that one should, as far as possible, endeavour to handle the dog exactly as one would on a shooting day or when picking-up. A great many, because of nerves, *over-handle* their dogs, and by generally "flapping" and panicking they transmit their nervy state to the dogs, which react by either getting wild or by refusing to "go" as they usually do.

There are one or two professional trainers I know well who are a joy to watch when handling their dogs. One of them, a Scotsman (as are so many trainers), seems oblivious to everything and everybody except his dog. Nothing worries him; he is cool, calm and collected, and though he keeps a wary eye on the judges the dog is his main interest. He will deal with the most delicate situations with such unruffled calm that he might not have a nerve in his body. From him issue no frantic blasts on the whistle whenever the dog appears to be getting too far out, or showing signs of unsteadiness. Not a command, not a whistle or signal is given that is not needed. Consequently, he comes out of the line at the end of his "down" as fresh as when he went in, with a confident, happy dog. No wonder this handler each year figures high in the award lists for many of the major Trials. Above all, he is the most sporting loser I know.

Another "pro", this time an Englishman, wanders into the line hands in pockets, very often hatless, and with a "couldn't care less" attitude about the whole business. When necessary he can move quickly, and blow the "stop" whistle as fast as anyone else, but I honestly believe that he worries not at all, and is so confident in his own ability, and that of his dog, that there is no strain. His record of Field Trial Champions over the last twenty years is very impressive, which shows that his confidence is not misplaced. One thing both these handlers have in common is that they do not "play to the gallery" or try to show off—they simply do the job of work they have to do, remembering all the time that the judges are watching both handler and dog, and that the essential thing is to show the dog to its best advantage.

To take the other extreme, the excitable, nervy handler is all too common at Trials. This type of man almost runs into the line, tugging his dog along on the lead, and arrives before the judges panting and perspiring. When his dog goes out it has only to go a few yards before the whistle is frantically blown, a direction given and almost immediately countermanded! When searching for a bird the handler is constantly shouting "Hi lost, Ben!" or "Get out!" at the wrong times, distracting the dog or, more likely, being ignored by him. Much waving of arms and legs, whistles, "Get outs", "Come backs" and "Hi losts" in rapid succession. When his run is finished, this sort of handler comes out of the line looking "all in", and generally cursing his luck, the dog's behaviour or the ineptitude of the judges. More often than not this man is also a bad loser, and when the results are announced he openly and loudly bemoans his bad luck, the good luck of the winners, and continues to hold an inquest on the Trial in the hotel parlour all the evening, if he can find anyone to listen.

Between these two extremes there lie the representative handlers who run at Trials. The average man does suffer from a certain amount of nerviness, and realizes afterwards that whilst handling his dog he made certain mistakes for that reason. For all that, he handles his dog efficiently and quite frequently gets into the awards, and is quick to go up to winners and shake them by the hand, offering congratulations in true sportsmanlike spirit, vowing to do better himself next time. Such men are the backbone of Field Trials, and the sporting atmosphere, good comradeship and willingness to help others which prevails at most of the meetings is entirely due to the presence of men like these. Indeed, a good loser is probably more popular with the Field Trials fraternity than he realizes. The knowledge that luck, good and bad, must by the very nature of things play a large part in Trials is essential if one is going to get any pleasure out of them. My advice to anyone likely to take the sport too seriously, and be really hurt when defeated, is: "Leave Trials alone, and do not enter for any." After all, Trials *are* a sport, and unless one can accept defeat, as well as success, with good grace it is better to leave participation to those who can display that spirit.

Having cultivated this frame of mind, it will be found that handling at Trials is both interesting and exciting. The essential thing is, of course, to have a really good dog and to be able to trust it and handle it adeptly. Given this, there is no earthly reason why anyone who trains a dog for shooting should not run in Trials and enjoy the experience. There is a widespread impression that the professionals are always going to win, and a good many men get an inferiority complex before they start, all of which is unlikely to lead to success. The professionals do not always win; in recent years more and more amateurs have been successful, even at the major events. The nasty-minded suggestions, frequently heard, that Trials are "fixed" before they begin, and that judges indulge in "back-scratching", can be ignored. Maybe there have been Trials in the past where everything was not quite as it should have been, but at the majority everything is run fairly, the judging all square and above board. So many people criticize from the spectators' line, not realizing that the judges are in a position to see much more detail of the dog work than are the spectators. Furthermore, a judge can be guided only by what he actually sees, and if, as sometimes happens, a dog runs riot in cover unseen by the judges, and subsequently figures in the awards, this is just an outstanding example of good luck for that particular handler and dog, and if we are honest we will admit that there are times when we should like to be equally lucky. It is so futile to turn a blind eye to the other man's point of view.

I have found it a great help, when going into the line with my dog, to say to myself, "I'll do my best, but if things go wrong—so what?" I try, as far as possible, to think about the dog to the exclusion of everything else, except to keep an eye on the judges and make sure that I am not getting too far ahead, or handicapping my dog by over-handling. Whenever in doubt on any point, a good maxim is: "Consult the judge." Then you cannot put yourself in the wrong. Suppose that a bird is down, and you have been asked to get it. The judge may say to you, "Get it from here," which means that you are not to move forward or sideways to help your dog. But if the judge says nothing except "Try to get that bird," and you think you can do better by moving a little to one side or forward, perhaps to give your dog the advantage of the wind, there is nothing to stop you asking the judge if you may do so. If you move *without* asking him, you may be penalized without knowing it, and so ruin your dog's chances of an award. Wherever possible, however, it is much more impressive to judges if a handler can get his dog out and on to a bird without moving about, and with the minimum of noise and directions.

Try not to draw the judges' attention to yourself and the dog by unnecessary whistling and shouting. If your dog is going wrong—getting too far out to one side and working excitedly, for example—you may have a good idea that he will not respond to your stop whistle. The judge does not know this until you blow the whistle and it is ignored, so instead of running the risk of showing up your dog wait and see if he slows up or turns, then whistle him at that moment, when he will probably answer. In this way you have lost nothing but gained everything, whereas had you panicked and whistled before with no result, the judge would have realized that, at that moment, your dog was out of control.

The more quietly a dog can be handled the better. I have seen a Pointer ranging out to one side ignoring frantic blasts of the "turn" whistle, drawing to dog and handler the unfavourable attention of the judges. When the dog neared the hedge, the boundary to that field, he turned automatically and crossed over. Had he been left alone this would have happened anyway, and no marks would have been lost. On the other hand, there are times when a handler lets a dog down by not stopping it. At a recent Setter Trial, an Irish Setter remained steady to a hare that another dog put up, but when cast out immediately took the line of the departed hare. Whether the handler knew what the dog was doing or not, I do not know, but had she whistled the dog to stop immediately he started hunting the line (a crime for a bird-dog) and put him out in another direction all might have been well. Instead, the dog continued on the line unchecked, sighted the hare and a wonderful course ensued—which resulted in the dog being put out of the stake.

I have seen Retrievers at a drive run-in, though this could have been prevented. The line of guns, handler and dogs, and judges, was waiting in a meadow alongside a wood, from which pheasants were being driven. In such circumstances most of the birds will fall *behind* the guns, and a dog should therefore be placed *in front of* the handler. One man in the line had his dog behind and to one side of him, and each time a bird was shot and fell in the meadow this dog became more and more excited, giving clear evidence that he might run-in at any moment. After several birds had been shot another came down and fluttered and jumped as they so often do when shot in the head. This temptation was too strong and off went the dog, deaf to all calls and whistles. Had the dog been properly placed, in front of the handler, so that he would have to pass his master if he started to run-in, the probability is that this would never have occurred, or if it had the handler could doubtless have stopped the dog before it got past him. As it was, he stood no chance once the dog had gone, and I can put this down only to inexperience and thoughtlessness on the part of the handler.

I myself have more than once ruined the chances of my dog through lack of confidence in him or because I was getting panicky. At a Trial near Cambridge a runner was down in a huge sugar-beet field, and after several dogs had been tried mine was called up. I put him out and he worked right across the field and in among the farm buildings on the far side, where I had previously seen some hares squatting. Fearing that the dog might start coursing, and having no idea that the bird might be so far out, I whistled the dog back to me. Later I was told by the secretary, who had happened to be standing in the farmyard at the time, that my dog was on the line of the runner, which he, the secretary, had seen disappear behind a stack a few seconds before. If only I had trusted the dog and not recalled him this might have won me the stake, especially as several dogs had failed on that bird.

Probably an older dog would have ignored my recall whistle, but this young first-season Labrador was fresh from his hand training and responded at once. This is one of the instances where the handler was wrong and the dog was right, and where a disobedient dog might have won the stake despite its handler!

I have also lost a Trial through trusting my dog too much. I remember a Utility Trial in Sussex, where game was very scarce, and it became necessary, in order to make a decision, to "plant" by hand some previously shot birds for the dogs to retrieve. Three handlers and dogs were lined up in front of a hedge, and we were told that under one of the several piles of clippings lay the bird. I sent my bitch out, saw she was working the clumps of hedge trimmings, and thought finding the bird was a foregone conclusion, she being a very experienced, reliable bitch. I turned and started chatting to the judges, and was surprised after a while to hear one of them say: "All right, call your bitch up." I whistled her in, minus the bird, and the next dog found it in a trice. I was told afterwards by one of the judges that Rozzi found the bird, looked back at me, saw I was paying no attention and carried on hunting. As I have said, Rozzi was an experienced bitch. She knew that the bird had been handled, and as she had often been prevented from picking up handled birds left lying about to cool off at lunch time she ignored it. Had I been watching, *as I should have been*, and when she looked round had said "Fetch it" and whistled her in, she would undoubtedly have picked up the bird and brought it along. If the bird had been freshly shot and unhandled she would have retrieved it, but she did not think she was meant to mess about with a handled bird like a raw puppy, so carried on looking for a fresh scent. Since that day I have been careful never to take my eyes from my dog at a Trial, nor to waste time talking when I should be handling!

When judging I have often had experiences of good and bad handling. I remember one stake where a partridge was down in a grass field. It was a bad scenting day, and eight dogs had been tried, all being sent from where the judges were standing against the fence. The next handler down asked if he could move farther along the fence, away from the direction of the bird, in order to cast his dog out into the wind, which was blowing almost parallel with the fence from the bird. I allowed him to do so, and was afterwards taken to task by several unsuccessful handlers for giving this man a better chance than they had. My answer was that the handler was the only one to *ask* to make use of the wind, that anyone else who had made the request would similarly have had it granted, and that in my opinion a man who showed such obvious wisdom was entitled to the advantage. As it happened, his dog did not get the bird, but it might have done—at least the handler had done all he could to help.

There are many ways in which one can help a dog when handling at a Field Trial, if only one will try to think of them. The trouble is that most handlers are too much on edge to be able to work a problem out calmly as they undoubtedly would on a shooting day, when there are no judges or spectators watching, and no hurry. Take the case of two birds being down, one to the right and one to the left, the judge wanting the right-hand bird which was shot first, and about which your dog has forgotten. You send the dog out and it makes straight for the left-hand bird, which it remembered seeing fall. Most handlers will stop their dog all right, then immediately try to handle it by signal on to the other bird. The almost invariable result is that the dog again goes towards the wrong bird, and has to be stopped once more, or it may see the bird and then be incapable of being stopped. The correct and probably successful thing to have done would have been to stop the dog directly it made for the wrong bird, then whistled it back towards you, dropped it again for a second or two to give it time to forget the wrong bird, then directed it out by signal to the one the judge wanted gathered. There is only a very small difference, but it is an important one. It shows what a little thought can do to help a dog towards success at Trials.

When working a Spaniel, a rabbit may get up and run away unshot. It is highly probable that your dog will want to take the line of the vanished rabbit and may, once he has got his nose down, refuse to stop. The sensible thing here is to work your dog in *an entirely new direction* immediately the rabbit has gone, thus causing him to forget all about it, and so avoid any possibility of unsteadiness or disobedience. An experienced judge will give you credit for sensible handling; an inexperienced one may not realize what you are doing but cannot penalize you as he would have to if the dog had got out of hand. A Spaniel may catch a rabbit alive in its "seat" and start bringing it back. Do not allow the dog to get up to you, but drop him immediately and by scolding and rating him make him put the rabbit down and watch it go away. If the dog reaches you, the chances are that he will not put it down, and will be penalized accordingly.

There are times, of course, when you do not know what to do for the best, and you have to take a chance and hope it will turn out all right. I was in such a predicament once, at the Eastern Counties Spaniel Society's Trials at Woburn Abbey, in Bedfordshire. A judge, a keeper who was also one of the guns, and I were in a little copse when I noticed my Spaniel bitch Rozzi working on a line on the far side of a ditch. I saw a hen pheasant creeping just ahead of the Spaniel, and thinking it might be a "runner", and feeling quite safe, I told Rozzi to "push it out". This she did, but whether the pheasant had been pricked, or was just lazy, I do not know, but instead of rising sharply like a normal bird it flew out on to the stubble very low—almost skimming the ground. Rozzi, having retrieved many wounded birds which had acted thus, probably thought that this was a chance for her to shine and went out on to the stubble after the bird. It then promptly rose to a sensible height and carried on. The judge quite rightly put the bitch out of the stake for chasing. I was to blame for not having blown the "stop" whistle the moment the bird broke cover. I suppose I was too keen, and believing it to be a pricked bird I wanted Rozzi to get it. I had taken a chance and lost, so that was that. You might call it bad luck or bad judgment, but it illustrates my point.

When walking in line at a Trial, see that you do not get too far ahead. This is a fault easily committed, especially when handling a Spaniel, and I have often been guilty. It annoys judges, and sometimes makes them think that you are trying to find game for your dog, quite apart from the fact that it may be dangerous to get too far from the line. When your dog is retrieving it is quite permissible for you to move a few steps forward from the line, so that he will recognize you and come straight up to you—no experienced judge will object to this. Do not, however, try to fool the judges and "put one over on them". You may be able to hoodwink an inexperienced man but you will slip up badly if you try tricks too often. There are, we all know, several little dodges which, though quite legitimate, will do you no good in the judge's eye, unless he is so inexperienced that he cannot see through them. Take the case of a bird which your Retriever *should* have marked down. You send the dog out, and he obviously shows that he did not mark it, and starts hunting about in entirely the wrong direction. You should be able to handle him to within reasonable scenting distance of the bird by signals and commands, and if you do this the dog may lose credit for being a poor marker, though you will rise in the judges' estimation for clever handling. The man who cannot handle his dog in this way often resorts to the little trick of waiting until the dog is in such a position that the dead bird lies in direct line between dog and master, and then whistles the dog in so that it will on its return almost walk on the bird, and stands a good chance of winding it, picking it up and making a good retrieve. I have seen plenty of birds found like this—the handler finds the bird, not the dog, and many a poor-nosed, indifferent marker has received undeserved credit from inexperienced judges.

Sometimes a handler tries to fool a judge about a bitten bird. Perhaps the handler knows that his dog is hard-in-the-mouth, and in the habit of killing runners. Such a man, on seeing that the runner the dog has found has no life left in it when the dog comes to hand, snatches the bird and goes through all the actions of killing it before passing it to the judge, pretending that the bird was alive when taken from the dog's mouth. A wise judge will feel such a bird all the more carefully after a performance like this; he will undoubtedly detect crushed ribs or other damage caused by the dog, whereas had the handler not tried to be so clever he *might* have been given the benefit of the doubt—the judge might have decided in conference with his colleagues that the bird had died before the dog got to it and that whatever damage can be felt had been caused by it hitting a tree when falling. A novice judge might be taken in perfectly, but is it worth while? If you have a hard-mouthed dog, or if your dog does happen to bite a bird by chance (as does happen), then why not suffer the penalty in a sportsmanlike manner? What pleasure can it give you to go away from a Trial after having won an award, knowing that really the dog did not deserve it and that had you not been able to fox the judges it would never have been given?

Under Field Trial rules, handlers may not carry any whip, stick, lead or shooting stick in their hand whilst handling a dog in the line, and though not written in the rules it is accepted that one does not punish a dog for doing wrong at Trials. For all this, I have seen a handler seize hold of his dog when it returned from a chase and not only hit it but kick it as well, which earned him a reprimand from the judge and the hostility of everyone present. This sort of thing gets Trials a bad name with the general public and must be ruthlessly stamped out. It is unfortunate that when our dog goes wrong at a Trial we are unable to correct him immediately, as we would in the shooting field (though *not* by kicking him), as this gives the dog the impression that he has "got away with it" and the crime is likely to be repeated. The remedy must be sought and applied at home after the Trials, the sooner the better, or the trouble may become a permanency.

Judges vary a great deal, but, strictly speaking, they should all judge on what they actually see, discounting any prior knowledge or experience of any particular dog or handler, and reckon solely with the stake in progress. There are some who, quite wrongly in my view, seek for weaknesses in a dog which they know from previous experience to exist but which may not become obvious unless certain conditions arise. For instance, a judge may know that a particular dog dislikes retrieving hares, having seen it refuse to do so at a previous Trial. The fair-minded judge will *not* go out of his way to get a hare for this dog to retrieve, or refuse to retrieve, but a less scrupulous man might do so, or might try to poison the minds of his co-judges about the dog. I have also known a judge give wrong directions to a handler about the position of a bird which was down (for reasons of his own, no doubt) and when proved wrong by the handler and his dog put the dog out of the stake. This happened to a friend of mine, who has very naturally sworn never to run under that particular judge again. The number of judges who indulge in practices of this sort is very small, fortunately, and as they become known organizing societies refrain from asking them to judge at their Trials. When these rare cases of flagrant unfairness do arise the best thing is to accept them as part of the game and hope for better luck next time. After all, it would be very difficult to prove to the satisfaction of the committee running the Trials, or to the Kennel Club, that injustice had been done deliberately, and unless you can prove anything it is always best to keep your mouth shut.

The bad loser who goes up and insults the judges after their verdicts have been announced is a despicable character, heartily disliked by everyone concerned. I remember a Spaniel Trial, a two-day meeting, where at the hotel on the evening of the first day a certain handler was loud in his praise of the judges. His dog had done quite well and had got an award.

"The best judges I have ever run under," he exclaimed excitedly, for everyone in the bar to hear. On the following day this same handler received only a Certificate of Merit in the Open Stake, and was he disgusted! Immediately the results were announced he flounced about, noisily proclaiming that the judges did not know their jobs and that the winning dogs were not worthy of Certificates of Merit, let alone prizes! He even went up to the judges and made similar remarks, which was embarrassing for everyone. These two judges are both very knowledgeable men, scrupulously fair and extremely popular, and the handler made himself look ridiculous and increased his already obvious unpopularity.

Some judges will help the handlers more than others, and the understanding, helpful judge is a pleasure to run under. Such a man is usually a trainer himself (often professional) and thus knows just what one is up against when handling. Very often the dog is better than the handler, who is ruining the dog's chances by over-handling (which amounts to hindering). The helpful judge may just murmur "Leave the dog alone" at the right time, with the result that it works better and is given due credit. It may be argued that a judge has no right to interfere in the handling of a dog, and up to a point this is correct. But if a man is obviously a nervous amateur, with quite a good dog, surely the judge is entitled to indicate to the handler that he is ruining the dog's chances? A judge like this will encourage amateurs and give them confidence, whereas the martinet who is either very severe or (worse still) says nothing but keeps on giving black marks frightens the handler and makes matters worse, and quite likely makes the man decide never to run at a Trial again.

Most Field Trial rules read that "judging is entirely at the discretion of the judges, and handlers may work their dogs in their own way, but undue noise, or interference with another handler's dog, will be penalized by the judges", or words to that effect. This surely gives great latitude to both judges and handlers, and I believe that a man who is clearly spoiling the chances of his dog should be warned before being penalized. Some men contend that it is the dogs which should be judged, not the handlers, but I do not see how one can really separate the two. The aim of a Trial is to find the best dogs *and the best handlers*, and though the dog is the main consideration handling cannot be entirely ignored. A good handler can make a mediocre dog appear quite clever; a bad handler can make a good dog look a complete idiot. The discerning judge will be able to discover, before the end of the day, which are the best dogs and the best handlers, by closely watching the two. The winners will usually prove to be good dogs with clever handlers, both working together as a co-ordinated partnership, each understanding the other, and with mutual trust.

In Open Stakes the judges expect to see a higher standard of both handling and dog work than in Puppy and Non-winners' Stakes. This applies to all branches of gundog work, and in Open Stakes the judge is entitled to be particular and ruthlessly eliminate any dog or handler seriously at fault. You just cannot afford to make a mistake when handling in an Open Stake, most of which provide the winning dog with "one leg" towards the title of Field Trial Champion. It would be wrong for judges to be too easy-going in these circumstances; we do not wish to see a lot of "cheap Champions" about—dogs which do not deserve honour. Judges are accordingly apt to be far more severe than when judging the lesser stakes, and the novice handler must be prepared for this. All the same, the understanding judge will help the handler where he can, and the latter can always ask the judge for his advice if in doubt.

Some handlers, having heard so much about noise being penalized, go to the other extreme and seem almost afraid to give a command or blow a whistle. This is very foolish. Provided that the whistle or command is necessary, and that the dog complies with it, a judge will not penalize a handler. Take the case of a Pointer, or a Spaniel, ranging far out when a hare or rabbit gets up. Surely it is "better to be safe than sorry", to stop the dog by blowing the "stop" whistle, than to trust to luck and risk the dog starting a chase, just because the judge might penalize the whistle? When handling at Trials it does not do to trust to luck more than absolutely necessary, and though you should be able to trust your dog to a very large extent, in circumstances when he may be subjected to great temptation a quiet command or whistle may make all the difference between steadiness and a chase, or run-in. Some handlers have a habit of making excuses for their dogs to the judge. This I consider a great mistake, and very irritating to anyone judging. Even if there is some perfectly reasonable explanation for the dog's actions it is extremely unlikely that by telling the judge all about it you will make any difference to his opinions. If he is a discerning judge he will realize without being told that the circumstances are exceptional. If he is not experienced he will probably think you are trying to make excuses, and instead of improving his opinion you make matters worse. One of the most common troubles at Trials crops up when two handlers are using exactly the same type of whistle, and the other man's dog responds to your whistles and *vice versa*. Few judges will need to have this pointed out to them—they have ears and eyes, and will make due allowances for any mistakes which the dogs may make. If there is a very strong reason for pointing anything out to a judge, do so in a tactful manner. Do not give him the impression that you are trying to teach him his job.

On the question of hard mouth, most judges go to great lengths to make sure that the game was not damaged when shot, or in falling, before penalizing a dog for biting. The judges should consult each other in cases of suspected hard mouth, both examine the bird, and in my opinion the dog should be given a second chance unless the damage is so bad and so obviously caused by the dog that there cannot be any other explanation. In matters like this the experienced judge is likely to be much more understanding than a novice judge. At one Spaniel Trial a while ago my dog was running in the Puppy Stake, and brought back a hen pheasant which felt to me, and to the judge, to have been bitten. I was fully expecting to be put out of the stake, but the judge said: "We'll give you another chance. I noticed the way that bird fell and I was suspicious, so I don't feel like penalizing your dog. The bird was shot at close range and the shot or the fall may have damaged those ribs." My puppy went on to win third prize in that stake, so it is obvious that he did not damage any birds, or he would have paid the penalty by being put out.

The man I loathe at Trials is a judge's officious steward. Most men detailed for this job are quite content to be just stewards; others try to interfere with the judging and to influence the judges, and sometimes give orders to the handlers "off their own bat". I have heard a steward tell a judge what he saw a dog doing, and what decision the judge should make. This is all wrong. The steward should take no part in discussions concerning awards. The judge must work on what *he sees*, not upon *hearsay*, and I am glad to say that on the occasion mentioned the judge told the steward in no uncertain terms to mind his own business, and paid no attention to a story which may, or may not, have been true. A steward once gave me an order which I took to be from the judge, and which resulted in my being put out of a stake. This was when my bitch had caught a rabbit and was bringing it back. I told her to stop and was on the point of making her let it go when a voice said, "All right, call her up." I let her come on and took the rabbit from her then, only to find that it was the steward, not the judge, who had spoken. I found out afterwards, when it was too late for the decisions to be altered, that the judge did not know the steward had spoken, and having seen my bitch deliver a live rabbit, put me out. Had I been allowed to make the bitch put it down and see it away, all would have been well, and this I should have done if the officious steward had kept his mouth shut. It was no use being aggrieved and making myself unpleasant to the steward, so I said no more about it, but ever since I have been very careful to take orders only from the judge or to make certain that orders the steward gives *are* official.

To the man who is going to handle at Trials, my advice is to work the dog as on a shooting day as far as possible, pay attention to nothing but the dog and the judge, and to try to remain as cool as a cucumber. Use your brains as well as your whistle when things go wrong, and avoid drawing unfavourable attention to yourself or your dog by giving *unnecessary* commands and signals. Try to adopt the attitude that it is only a sport, after all, and if things go wrong it will not be so terrible really, though you should always go in with the intention of winning. Make the most of every chance, and remember that you can have good, as well as bad, luck.

To a new judge I would suggest that he tries to make his mind a perfect blank concerning anything he may know about a particular handler or dog. I suggest that he tries always to see the handler's and the dog's points of view, which should be easy if he trains dogs himself, and to be fair and to rely upon only what he sees for himself. He should not let himself be bullied by one of the other judges into agreeing to a decision that he has reason to believe unfair. He must not allow a steward do the judging for him, and whenever possible he should help the handler, especially if the handler is an amateur and obviously nervous.

CHAPTER X

HOUSING, FEEDING AND GENERAL MANAGEMENT

Housing. Materials and Benches. Size of Kennel. Runs. Raw Meat. Diet. Supplements. House Training. Kennel Routine. Exercise.

Housing.

THE man who has only one dog or puppy to deal with may decide to keep it indoors, but many owners keep even single puppies in a kennel for some part of the day, or at night, and this practice has a lot to recommend it. I am a great believer in an owner seeing as much of his puppy as he can, and having it with him whenever possible, but at the same time unless the owner, or a responsible member of the household, can actually keep the puppy under his eye a dog is better off in a good kennel. Dogs are happier if they have "a home of their own" in which they can rest when not actually with master, and as far as training is concerned the kennel has much in its favour. A puppy kept in a kennel will not have opportunities to go off self-hunting or foraging and, more important still, the exercise and training spells will be the highlight of the puppy's day, and will therefore be eagerly awaited and much enjoyed. A dog which has been roaming about all day has not the same attitude towards the training period, apart from the harm which may be done to training if it should start self-hunting and getting out of control.

Materials and Benches.

The kennel should be a good one, and if possible have an exercise yard, generally called a "run", attached. It is impossible to lay down hard and fast rules as to what should be built or adapted; conditions today prevent the use of many materials, and the depth of the owner's purse will in all likelihood be the deciding factor. I shall therefore content myself with making general suggestions in the hope that these, or some adaptation of them, will prove of use. The actual kennel, or sleeping house, should be constructed of either brick or wood. Corrugated iron is too cold in winter and too hot in summer, and asbestos is all right except that it is so breakable, especially if more than one dog is kept in a kennel so constructed. The sleeping kennel should contain either a raised bench or a "box type" bench, for the inmate to rest on. For a good, draught-proof kennel the ordinary plain bench is probably best. This should be of a convenient size so that the dog can lie comfortably fully stretched out if he feels so inclined, and should be raised six inches or more from the floor. A puppy's bench should be almost on floor level and be raised as he gets older. Jumping down from a height is liable to cause the front legs to become distorted by the sudden jarring impact with the floor, and I believe over-high benches to be a common cause for dogs being "out at the elbows". If the bench can be movable for cleaning, so much the better. I favour the type which stands upon four legs, or runners, and has a six- or eight-inch board all round to retain the straw or other bedding in winter. Another good type is that which utilizes three sides of the kennel as sides and back, and requires only a front board to retain the straw. These can easily be made removable. The side boards to a bench should be covered with tin or zinc sheeting, to prevent damage by the puppy; many will gnaw at bench fronts and any convenient battens out of sheer boredom or when teething or suffering from lack of bones in the diet. Any projecting battens or quartering in a kennel are best covered in this way to prevent damage. There should be a window or other form of ventilation in the kennel, a good door and a dog exit with a sliding shutter. The bench should be so placed that direct draughts from exit and window do not blow upon it. If small, the kennel run should be paved with concrete, bricks or wood; a large run can be of grass—this is undoubtedly better and more natural, though more difficult to keep clean. If a grass run is used, it should be periodically rested and limed if necessary, so it is a good scheme to have two runs to each kennel, which can be used alternately. A small run which is paved should have a good fall to ensure drainage, and should also be sheltered and have shade. A southern aspect is best for a kennel, provided that shade is obtainable in hot weather.

Size of Kennel.

The dimensions of the kennel will depend upon the material and capital available. For one dog a convenient size is 4 feet square, the height being about 4 or 5 feet, with a sloping roof. For two dogs a kennel 6 feet by 4 feet by 5 feet high is sufficient, if a good exercise run is available. If no run is provided, and the dog or dogs will have to be in the kennel for a large part of the day, the building should be considerably larger. It is best to have two separate compartments, a small one for sleeping and the larger one for use as a daytime run. Both compartments should have a door. The sleeping part should have a ventilator or window and an exit into the daytime compartment, the latter having an open side with iron bars or strong chain-link netting, and a removable shutter. There are many firms who specialize in the manufacture of good, sectional timber kennels, which can be obtained in various sizes suitable for all breeds and purposes, and I suggest that before making a final decision the reader should obtain catalogues and decide upon the most suitable type and size for his requirements. Stables and loose boxes can easily be adapted to make excellent kennels if you are fortunate enough to have such buildings available.

Where a fairly large daytime, open run is available, a single puppy, or two puppies, will do very well in what I always call a "fox box"—because I first got the idea from a silver fox farm where the animals were kept in large enclosures and bred in these specially built kennels. The boxes I bought are raised on concrete blocks a few inches from the ground, are strongly built of tongued and grooved timber, and lined with the same material, there being an air space between the inner and outer walls. These are warm in winter and cool in summer. Quite suitable for two Spaniels or one Retriever, the dimensions of my own boxes are 4 ft 6 in long by 2 ft 2 in wide; height 2 ft 6 in at front, 2 ft at back. The roof is hinged for easy access and cleaning and is of timber covered with asbestos, the whole resting on a separate floor so that the box can be lifted off and the floor cleaned and scraped, or reversed. There is an exit at one side of the front so that the inmates can keep well out of draughts, and there are ventilation holes just beneath the roof. These box kennels I use in the summer quite extensively, and they are excellent for puppies and adults if the open run is a good size. My own grass runs in which these boxes are placed are about 70 or 80 square yards in area.

RUNS.

The dimensions for the outside runs to be used in conjunction with large kennels will depend upon the room available. My concrete runs are 9 feet each way, giving an area of 81 square feet. I find this sufficient for two or three dogs—they are of course given daily running exercise in the fields, and are also let out twice daily into a larger grass compound in front of the main kennel range. There is little point in having excessively large kennel runs. Young puppies will certainly gallop about and play in them, but as they grow up they will sit about and wait to be taken out for exercise. Consequently, all that is necessary is a run of sufficient size for the dog to take a moderate amount of exercise and get plenty of fresh air. If expense is no object, the outside run can be roofed so that the dog can make use of it in all weathers. It can even be provided with a "sliding head" which can be pushed back on fine days. In my opinion, however, gundogs are better if kept in open runs, where they can be during the day in all but the very worst weather. If mollycoddled too much a gundog will not be able to withstand the rigours of a hard day's shooting in winter, when it may have to sit about in the wet for hours on end, and face icy water without any chance of immediate drying.

If the run has a concrete floor the provision of a raised wooden bench is essential; the dog can lie on this away from the cold, damp floor. The bench should be placed in the shade in warm weather, and will be much appreciated by the inmates of the kennel. Such a bench is advisable in any type of run, really, though for young puppies it should not be more than a few inches from the ground—older dogs will prefer a higher bench. The runs should be well enclosed, either by iron bars or with strong chain-link netting, and if in an exposed position the bottom three feet should be boarded or walled up to provide protection from the wind. My concrete runs have a low wall made of concrete blocks, above which are corrugated-iron sheets that can be removed on mild days. The fencing is of 12-gauge wire netting, known as Sommerfield Track, which also has steel bars to reinforce it every nine inches. The netting is of three-inch mesh, though this is really too large—2-inch mesh is better. This netting was extensively used on aerodromes during the war, and I bought mine at a sale. Probably it is unobtainable now. I recommend the use of either iron bars, about two inches apart, or chain-link netting of strong gauge and 2-inch mesh for the run enclosures. The door should be of convenient size and can open inwards or outwards, according to the preference of the owner. My own doors open inwards and are wide enough to permit the passage of a wheelbarrow or a big bench, which is an advantage.

Anyone who has not had much experience of dogs will perhaps not realize what escapologists they can be. Many dogs will quite easily leap a five-foot fence, and many more will climb like a cat even higher fences and so escape. To prevent this I have wired in the tops of several of my runs, which is also useful to prevent the unwelcome attentions of dogs to bitches when in season, and my other runs nearly all have the wire turned-in at the top for about 9 or 12 inches, so that if a dog climbs up he still cannot get over the top. All runs should be covered at the top, and big, open grass runs should have the wire turned-in all the way round, and a board nailed across the top of the gate to prevent a dog climbing out. Runs should be 5 or 6 feet high for gundogs, and the only way to prevent the inmates from burrowing out is to turn-in the bottom 12 inches of wire, or, better still, dig a trench, bury three or four inches of wire, and fill the trench with concrete, thus cementing the wire to the ground and providing a barrier beyond which the dog cannot burrow.

Chain-link fencing, of 12 or 14 gauge, and 2-inch mesh, is ideal for the larger, open grass runs. The corner posts should be well braced, and the whole supported every few feet by strong chestnut stakes or, preferably, steel angle-iron. Do not forget to provide a concrete strip across the gateway to prevent burrowing at this point, and it is not a bad idea to have a concrete path in front of the gate and running all round the wire inside the run. This should be about 2 or 3 feet wide, and will prevent the ground becoming a quagmire in wet weather where the dogs constantly parade up and down along the netting.

I think that puppies should always be reared on grass runs and as far as possible I try to avoid putting youngsters in concrete ones. Up to the age of five or six months the more space they have to play about in the better. After that age they will, as I have already said, sit about and wait to be taken out for exercise. Large grass runs do not get nearly so muddy and bare as small ones; indeed, a small earth run is a menace and should not be used. It may start off as grass but the dog's urine and constant wear and tear will soon kill it, and the bare earth will become a quaking bog in wet weather, the inmate never clean or dry. If, therefore, you are restricted for space, concrete or brick your run, at any rate after the puppy is a few months old. The necessity for this can be avoided if you can arrange for two runs, to be used alternately, so that one can be rested every few weeks and the grass given a chance to recover. Dogs can be shut up in the kennel at night if desired, but I do so only in the worst weather. At other times they are free.

Raw Meat.

On the subject of the correct diet for dogs I hold very strong views indeed, and my articles in the sporting Press have given rise to many controversies. I have even been labelled "crank", but this worries me not at all. I have had ample evidence, both from my own dogs and from those of other owners who hold similar views, that the diet I use and advocate is the best one. It is the only natural one. Why the unfortunate dog should have come to be regarded as a sort of dustbin on legs, to finish up our unwanted table scraps, I do not know. "Anything is good enough for a dog" is not a true statement by any means, yet this seems to be the basis upon which many people feed their dogs, and even try to rear puppies. No wonder that we see so many weakly animals about, and that contagious diseases are even more rampant now than they were twenty or thirty years ago.

At one time I fed my dogs just as so many others do: white flour biscuits and biscuit meal, scraps, cooked meat and thick, greasy gravy, cooked porridge, boiled bones, all mixed up together and given as one glorious, sticky mess. In those days I had my quota of kennel troubles—"eczema" was a common skin complaint, fits and hysteria were nothing out of the ordinary, especially in teething puppies, and the mortality rate when a distemper outbreak occurred was alarming. Then one day a lady for whom I was training some Welsh Springers introduced me to the work of Miss Juliette de Bairacli-Levy, and showed me the results of Natural Rearing methods in her own dogs, which were always in superb condition. I immediately bought and read every book which Miss de Bairacli-Levy had written, adopted her methods of feeding, and now, after three years or more, I would not revert to more orthodox methods for the world. In fact, I have got to the stage where if I could not get raw meat for my dogs I would rather give up keeping them!

It is not my intention to go deeply into the whys and wherefores of the system. Instead, I will recommend readers to purchase and study for themselves Miss de Bairacli-Levy's works, and content myself with a few essential remarks. In the first place, a dog living naturally is a carnivorous animal, feeding upon the flesh of such animals as it can catch and kill, or which it may find dead in the course of its travels. To cook meat, or other food, for a dog is simply wasteful. Cooking destroys a large part of the goodness contained in food, especially meat. Apart from this, it "pre-digests" the meat in a sense, leaving the powerful digestive juices of the dog less to do. These digestive juices were intended by nature to deal with raw flesh, bones, hair and other natural food, and by feeding cooked stuff the juices are left with little to do. The result is that all sorts of troubles arise, the most common of which are skin troubles ("eczema"), hysteria and fits. I have not had one case of hysteria in the kennel since I started raw-meat feeding, neither have any puppies whelped or reared here ever developed the "teething fits" that are looked upon by many breeders as inevitable. "Eczema" is a rarity now, though occasionally dogs which come in from outside do develop it—always ones which have not been Naturally Reared. I have even brought into the kennels a Retriever which was having serious attacks of hysteria at a keeper's kennels, but after being fasted and put on to raw meat this bitch never had another attack. All this has proved to me that I am on the right lines, and it is my wish that other dog owners shall be similarly blessed.

Another result of feeding cooked and unsuitable food to the dog is that the stomach and intestines become mucous-lined and worms thrive and give rise to further troubles, which most owners try to counteract by violent purgings with vermifuges which may expel the worms but which also inflame and irritate the intestines and generally weaken the constitution of the animal concerned.

Of Miss de Bairacli-Levy's disease treatments, which are entirely natural and herbal, I will say nothing other than that I use and recommend many of them. This is not supposed to be a veterinary chapter, nor am I qualified to write one. I am writing simply as a result of my own experiences and those of others with similar views, but I will say that I do now inoculate my dogs against distemper, using one of the modern "egg-adapted" living virus vaccines. Experience of these "new" vaccines has taught me that they give a high degree of immunity to distemper and hard pad or, if a dog does contract the disease, it is likely to be of mild character. I can also with confidence recommend the modern methods of immunization against hepatitis and leptospirosis canicola. Naturally Reared and fed dogs have a very high resistance to the disease and often do not develop it at all, even when brought into close contact with it. This applies to other highly infectious diseases as well.

By going on to a natural diet one cannot expect to turn a sickly dog into a fit one immediately; the ravages of past mismanagement cannot be repaired as easily as that. It may take a generation or two of Natural Rearing and feeding before the results become obvious, for so many generations of dogs have been wrongly reared and fed that weaknesses have been inherited. However, all dogs do benefit by being put on a natural diet, and will give proof within a few weeks by a distinct improvement in coat and condition and, more important still to the gundog man, by increased and improved stamina. A raw-meat fed dog will keep going faster and for a far longer period than the "biscuit and scrap" dog, and this fact alone will appeal to shooting men.

DIET.

To get down to practical facts, the reader will be anxious to know how I recommend that dogs should be fed. In the first place, I never feed meat and cereals together—these are always given as separate meals. The adults mostly have two meals a day—at noon and in the evening. The first meal consists of wholegrain cereal soaked (not cooked) in green-water (usually nettle- or spinach-water). The main meal given in the evening consists of raw meat, including paunches (uncleaned), cut up in large lumps, plus chopped parsley or grated onions, and a dessertspoonful of veterinary cod liver oil (in winter). If I am feeding a high proportion of paunches, the green vegetable is omitted, as this is obtained in the natural state from the paunches. Puppies and young dogs receive more meals a day, and the meat is cut up much smaller. Nothing is cooked and cereal and meat are never fed together—the principle remains the same. On one day each week, generally Sunday, the adult dogs are fasted on water only, a practice carried out with carnivorous animals in most zoos as it has been found necessary to rest and cleanse the internal organs and this method appears to be most effective. Young dogs have a shorter period of fasting once a week. When cereals such as oatmeal, barley meal or wheatmeal cannot be obtained, stale whole-grain brown bread, slightly crisped, is fed instead. I use no biscuits or biscuit meal in any form whatever, though when whole-grain biscuits can be obtained they are excellent.

Raw bones are allowed to all dogs from weaning onwards, but not poultry or rabbit bones. Rabbit and hare flesh can be fed raw to *non-gundog* breeds, but cannot be recommended for gundogs, for the obvious reason that such meals might make them start to eat what they should be retrieving in the field! Many authorities seem against the feeding of bones on the grounds that they wear away a dog's teeth. So they will if given in excess. Nevertheless they are a very natural and necessary food, keeping the teeth free from tartar and supplying the system with calcium and other minerals, and if not given too freely have everything to recommend them.

Meat supplied by knackers for kennel use is usually old horse or cow, or from such animals that have had to be destroyed or have died from disease. The usual argument used in favour of cooking meat before feeding it to dogs is that the cooking will destroy harmful germs, which is quite correct. However, the dog has a digestion well able to deal with most of the germs it may encounter; I have never had a dog made ill through eating raw flesh. Any drugs administered to a sick animal before its death or slaughter may remain in the blood-stream and might seriously affect a dog which eats the flesh, so if you feed your meat raw you should deal with a reliable knacker, explain that the meat will be used raw, and obtain from him an assurance that he will supply only suitable stuff for feeding in that state. If this is done you need have no fears that your dogs will receive anything but benefit from a raw meat diet.

When plenty of meat, including the ever useful paunches, is available adult dogs do excellently on one meal a day, given in the evening or at midday. The diet has the time-saving advantage that all one has to do is to cut up the meat in suitably sized lumps, which I do by hanging it from a hook at a convenient height and cutting it with a *very* sharp knife. The lumps are then dropped into buckets, which are taken round the kennels at feeding time and scooped out with a metal scoop, each dog being given sufficient for his particular requirements. The dose of veterinary cod liver oil is added immediately before feeding, as is the finely chopped vegetable. Dogs vary greatly both in appetite and requirements, and it is almost impossible for me to give the amounts that are fed. Scientists tell us that a dog requires from one half to one ounce of food a day for every pound in body weight, and I believe this to be roughtly correct. My adult Retrievers and Spaniels receive between one and two pounds of meat daily if on meat only, rather less if receiving a morning feed of cereal as well. The slow eaters and "poor-doers" are fed separately from their kennel mates, but where dogs with even appetites are kennelled together they are fed together. Certainly fights do, from time to time, develop but these are generally only minor affairs and are quite natural. If a dog shows that he has a real fighting nature, then he is kennelled separately, or with another of his kind who can be relied upon to stand up for himself.

SUPPLEMENTS.

A very valuable addition to the diet of puppies, in-whelp and nursing bitches, convalescent dogs and those which are in poor condition, is vitamin B. This is best given in the form of the wheat germ extracted from flour and sold under various names, "Bemax" and "Froment" being the two best known. An even better vitamin B group supplement is dried brewers' yeast, easily obtained in either tablet or powder form from chemists' and dog shops. It is extremely valuable where dogs are in poor coat, have deficient appetites or are generally ailing, but I do not consider it essential for dogs in normal health once the adult stage is reached.

HOUSE TRAINING.

The puppy or dog which lives indoors must be trained to be house-clean. To some people this seems to prove very difficult, but nearly always because they omit to let the puppy out of doors often enough, and feed it at wrong times. Dogs are naturally clean animals, and once the early puppyhood stage has been passed are reluctant to "foul their own beds". Usually all that is necessary in order to induce cleanliness indoors is to let the puppy out several times a day, *always* after meals and *especially first thing in the morning and last thing at night*. Only dry food should be given late in the day, and as a result of having water constantly at hand the puppy will not drink large amounts at one time and as a consequence "puddle" all over the place. There are bound to be a few accidents at first, with a young puppy, especially when he is in strange surroundings. A point should be made of putting him outside *immediately* he offends, after having clearly indicated that he has erred by scolding him and showing him the "puddle". Dogs kept in kennels where they have constant access to their runs seldom, if ever, empty themselves in the actual kennel, preferring to go outside to do so. My dogs are never shut in, even at night, except in the very worst of weather. This automatically teaches them to be clean, and if and when they are taken to live indoors they are house-clean.

Kennel Routine.

Dogs living in kennels should be cleaned out first thing in the morning, and again later in the day if necessary. Kennels and runs benefit from an occasional swill down with a good disinfectant, especially in hot weather, and the runs can be hosed down with water as often as desired. I find the war-time stirrup-pump an excellent means of disinfecting a kennel as the fluid can be got into all corners and crevices, which helps to keep the kennels free from both dirt and vermin. After attacks of infectious or contagious ailments in dogs their kennels should be thoroughly disinfected, and for this purpose I adopt the following routine: First of all the kennel is well sprayed with strong disinfectant and allowed to dry out. Then it is completely closed up, all cracks and openings sealed, and a "sulphur candle" of suitable size is burnt, the kennel remaining sealed for twenty-four hours, and afterwards allowed to have a good airing before being again occupied by dogs.

In wooden kennels the inside walls can be painted, white-washed or creosoted, according to choice. Whitewash looks nice at first but is apt to peel and flake—paint is better and can be washed down. Creosote is probably the most hygienic of all, though it does darken the interior of the kennel. It is cheap and very easy to apply. Any kennel which is creosoted inside should be allowed to dry thoroughly before dogs are put in, for dogs are very susceptible to creosote poisoning. The exteriors of all kennels built of wood can be either painted or creosoted, and creosote has much to recommend it. Floors, if of wood, should also be treated with the same preservative and will then last for years.

Exercise should be given first thing in the morning whenever possible, either before or after the cleaning-out routine, and bedding, when used, renewed as often as desirable. I have found that my dogs prefer to do without bedding during the warm weather, so this is dispensed with from about April to October. Many dogs will indicate dislike for bedding by scratching it out on to the floor and lying on the bare boards of their bench. Bedding in hot weather encourages skin vermin and is very overheating. My kennel benches and sleeping compartments are always kept dusted with a good insecticide, and in the winter when I use straw or hay for bedding this is dusted once a week as well. In this way the dogs keep remarkably free from lice and fleas, but if these do appear the dogs are dusted with the same powder, with immediate and excellent results.

Where no outside run is provided and the dogs have to be kept shut in for long spells, or during bad weather, or when the dogs are sick, the floor of the kennel should be sprinkled with clean, dry sawdust. Pine sawdust, on the coarse side, is best for this purpose; it promptly soaks up any moisture and prevents the kennel from becoming smelly. The soiled sawdust should be removed and renewed at least once a day. Very fine sawdust is unsuitable. It blows about everywhere, gets into the dogs' coats, eyes and noses, and spoils food and drinking water. This latter, by the way, should be always available, and should be changed often.

The only time when it is really necessary to bath a dog is for treatment of skin disease or skin vermin which have got the upper hand. I do not believe in bathing for its own sake, though of course all my dogs do very frequently swim in rivers and ponds in the course of their training. Brushing and combing are necessary at times, especially when the dogs are casting their coats and can be helped considerably by grooming. Periodical and regular grooming of the long-haired breeds (Spaniels and Golden or Flat-coated Retrievers, and Setters) may be necessary, and I am guided by the condition of the coat and skin. I think grooming can easily be overdone, and may become a fetish, as is the bathing of dogs with some people. Provided the skin and coat are clean and healthy, my advice is to leave well alone, though all breeds should be inspected after work in cover, and burrs, "sweethearts" and other odds and ends embedded in the coat and skin removed. At such times it is well also to examine the eyelids for thorns, and to look into the lower lids for dust and weed seeds which may have collected there. These should be promptly removed or they will set up irritation and cause inflamed and sore eyes, which the dog will aggravate by rubbing and pawing. The long-haired breeds will probably be troubled from time to time by mud-balls forming between the pads, collecting on the long hair. The hair here should be kept short, especially during snow, when it can be a positive nuisance as miniature snowballs form and are uncomfortable for the dog, which keeps stopping and biting at them.

Kennel ventilation should be carefully attended to. Dogs require plenty of fresh air but draughts should be avoided. In the winter they need to be snug and warm, yet the air in the kennel should be fresh and clean. In summer all ventilators and shutters should be kept open, day and night. I find that many dogs prefer to sleep on the outside run benches in the hot weather, which is all the better. Dogs can withstand a good deal of cold, if it is a *dry* cold, but damp cold is very bad for them and can lead to all sorts of troubles, from rheumatism to pneumonia.

Exercise.

Exercise—free running exercise—is most important to the health of a dog. A gundog, *during the shooting season*, probably gets far more exercise than the average household pet, but it is quite hopeless to shut a dog away in kennel for eight months of the twelve and expect him to remain fit and hardy. In the types of run I have mentioned a dog will get a certain amount of exercise which will suffice in bad weather or when it is otherwise impossible to take him out. At all other times he should have free exercise in fields and open spaces, where he can gallop at will. I suggest that whenever possible the gundog should be exercised early in the morning and again in the evening, with a midday spell as well, except in very hot weather. Training, when it starts, will provide wonderful exercise, and during this period separate exercise may not be necessary. But before training is begun, and when it is over, give as much exercise as you can. A trained dog is very easy to exercise—he can be sent back over long distances for the dropped dummy, or sent to range out and "worked" in different directions whilst the owner stands still, or be left sitting on the drop and called up after the owner has walked on for a couple of hundred yards or so. This sort of thing cannot be said to be very hard on even the most tired owner, and if there are several dogs to be taken out they can all go together. In the summer this work should be carried out early in the morning and late in the evening, when it is cool and there is a dew on the ground. Dogs will be found to be much keener then, and have twice as much life and energy than if exercise is attempted during the heat of the day.

Some authorities recommend an owner to use a bicycle to exercise dogs. He is advised to ride very slowly at first, and to have short spells of really fast work. This can be done only on roads and tracks where there is little traffic, and for this reason the very early morning is about the only time that it is safe to indulge in road exercise with dogs. Certainly road work is very excellent for hardening pads and especially valuable prior to the opening of the shooting season, but dogs kept in kennels with hard runs, and exercised over hard, arable land, will not require road work to the extent needed by dogs kept on softer ground.

A Retriever or Spaniel can be given a good deal of exercise of the kind I have recommended. I always carry a ball in my pocket, so when I have a dog out I am able to give him some retrieves at odd moments, which is wonderful exercise. A ball can be thrown farther than the dummy, and as it rolls and bounces for some distance after it has fallen quite long retrieves can be arranged. Another advantage is that a ball is more difficult to find than a dummy, and requires greater use of nose. Therefore you are doing really useful work when exercising dogs this way. However, these thrown retrieves should not be overdone or they will sicken the dog, as explained in the Training Chapters. You will have to be guided by the keenness of the individual dog, but the suggestion is offered as from experience I know that the rubber ball can be helpful and is easy to carry, which cannot be said of the regular training dummy. A Spaniel is probably least trouble of all to exercise; he is constantly on the move, even in the open, and tireless in cover.

CHAPTER XI

LIFE IN A TRAINING KENNEL

The Business Side. Selling a Trained Dog. "Approval". Conclusion.

The Business Side.

WHENEVER anybody asks what I do for a living, and I reply that I am a gundog trainer, the usual comment is: "What a wonderful life that must be!" Certainly it has its advantages, and I cannot think offhand of anything I would rather do, but the average man or woman simply has no idea of what the job entails. The popular conception of life in a gundog training kennel is that the proprietor spends all his time out shooting with the sweet little dogs. Nobody ever thinks about the feeding, cleaning-out, grooming, nursing, carpentry and butchery that these same sweet little dogs necessitate. And the layman thinks that vast profits are made in the dog training business.

A visitor to my kennel sometimes asks what my training fee is, and when I tell him he looks round the kennels, does some quick mental arithmetic on "fifteen dogs at £5.00 a week" lines and comes to the conclusion that I am making a *profit* of about £75.00 a week! No thought is given to the feeding bill, cost of labour, car, telephone, stationery, rates, rents of shooting! Neither is it ever imagined that dogs can be sick or need attention other than feeding, and the mental picture of me spending hours each week cutting up meat, skinning casualty calves and sheep, writing long "report" letters to owners and answering training queries is never painted!

Wear and tear on kennels is a serious item. Dogs chew and bite their benches and projections in the kennels; timber rots; wire rusts. All of these have to be replaced from time to time. I think that I spend almost as much of my time doing carpentry and odd jobs round the kennel as I do training. Cutting up the meat, and skinning and boning the casualties farmers let me have, occupies a good many hours each week. I am usually chained to the typewriter for at least an hour a day, frequently longer, and the telephone never seems to stop ringing. There are visits from owners to arrange time for; dogs have to be taken to and fetched from the station. The rabbit pen entails a good deal of work—the wire has to be kept in good order to retain the inmates, the sexes have to be sorted out and, in winter, mangolds and hay have to be fed to them. New runs and kennels have to be put up from time to time, all buildings creosoted, hinges renewed and fasteners replaced as they wear out. When all these, and many other things, have been attended to I can get on with the training and attend Field Trials.

I never try to work to a time-table. It is quite hopeless and is sure to be upset if arranged. I train when I feel like it and when the weather is right, my favourite times in spring and summer being before ten in the morning and after tea in the evening. In winter I do as much training as possible in the morning. On days when I feel irritable or impatient I do no training at all. It is worse than useless to train when you are not in the mood, as I have found to my cost in the past, and you can always make up for it on days when you are feeling fit. In the hot weather I do not have dogs out in the middle of the day, but devote this time to conserving my energies for the evening training period, or to writing and odd jobs about the kennels. The only training carried out during the heat of the day is water-work; at that time I often pack four or five dogs into the back of my Utility and take them down to the river and marshes.

One of the greatest headaches in a training kennel is fitting in the pupils at the dates required by owners. Far too many people leave arrangements much too late, with the result that I am often telephoned and asked to take a puppy for training the very next week, or even the next day. If there is no room available at the particular time it may be possible to get the owner to wait a few weeks until I have a vacancy, but very often he feels that his puppy is getting on in age and needs immediate attention. I wish shooting men would realize that it is much wiser, and certainly very helpful to the trainer, to book up in advance, giving at least four to six weeks' notice of their intention to send a puppy for training. In a training kennel it is quite futile to take on too many pupils at once. The result is that they are cramped for room, and that they cannot possibly all get the attention they require. This is unsatisfactory to all concerned. Every proprietor of a kennel knows just how many dogs he can comfortably house, feed and train, and he tries as far as possible to keep numbers within the maximum. In the spring and summer, when days are longer, more dogs can be comfortably dealt with, though much depends on the weather. This is the time of year when most people want their dogs trained, so that they will be ready for the shooting season, and each year in July and August quite a lot of dogs are sent back to training kennels for "refresher courses", a very wise and sensible thing, as even the best trained dogs are liable to get into bad habits during the summer if not kept well in hand. A brief course at the training kennels is usually sufficient to guarantee that when shooting starts again they will be fit, steady and reliable once more.

The most common question asked by an owner, and a very natural one, is: "How long will you take to train my dog?" This is rather like asking the length of a piece of string and the answer depends upon many factors. All one can say is that given good weather, good luck and a pupil with natural ability, the dog should be at a fair standard of training at the end of sixteen to twenty-four weeks. We just cannot afford to tie ourselves down about this time business. It is impossible to set a time limit in training. Even if everything goes well at the outset you never know when some snag is going to pop up, such as the dog developing a fault or peculiarity which may need a lot of time for eradication. One of the worst risks we have to run is that a dog may be sent to us which has been allowed to self-hunt, or which has been taken out shooting and allowed to run wild before initial obedience training has been given. Naturally a dog like this gives much more trouble and takes far longer to train than one which comes into kennel with an open mind, so to speak—in other words, untampered with. Whenever possible I avoid taking on dogs which have been allowed to self-hunt or which have been taken shooting too early, though some owners foist such animals on one without admitting that there is a past history of this nature, which is as unfair as it is foolish. Trying to reclaim a spoilt dog is a thankless task. Even if you are successful it more often than not reverts to its wicked ways when it gets back to its owner and former surroundings. It often occurs to me that if some owners, instead of begrudging the fee that is asked, would be prepared to pay really handsomely for training, the result would be that trainers could manage to live by taking fewer dogs, which in most cases would result in dogs being trained better and quicker. However, most owners are reasonable men who quite appreciate the overhead costs of running a kennel, and also realize that to send their dog to the cheapest kennel is false economy. Whilst on the subject of owners,

I cannot refrain from remarking that, on the whole, they are very genuine, sporting and understanding, and aware of all the difficulties with which we have to cope. They are also, as a class, "good payers", which is most important to anyone running a small business.

In the handling capabilities of owners much variety is displayed. I have often heard trainers declare: "If only we could have the owners in kennel to train as well as the dogs, life would be a lot easier!" There is a lot of truth in this. Yet most of them have the sense to realize that they should come down and collect the dog at the end of the training course, and learn as much as possible of the handling methods, commands, signals and whistles used. In this way they learn much, and the likelihood of the dog being a success and doing the trainer credit is greatly increased. Some men never will be good handlers, no matter how much tuition they receive or how well their dog is trained in the first place. Others, the men with "dog sense", are a pleasure to work for, and when handing over a pupil the trainer has the feeling that not only will it remain a good worker but will go on improving as experience is gained under its considerate owner.

Nothing is more exasperating than to train a dog to quite a high standard, only to learn later that it has been allowed to degenerate and is as wild as a hawk and completely out of control when out shooting. Such dogs cannot be other than bad advertisements for a trainer. Anyone seeing the dog out shooting may enquire who trained it, and on being told make a mental note to avoid that trainer when requiring a dog. There is nothing to tell him that it is the owner, not the trainer, who is at fault, though doubtless anyone who knows dogs and has "dog sense" will quickly discern that the owner is a poor handler and make due allowances. The wise trainer therefore makes a point of refusing to train dogs for people he knows to be bad handlers and who are likely to become bad advertisements.

Personally, I have no objection to the owner having carried out a certain amount of preliminary training before sending a dog to me, provided that this has been on the right lines and the dog has not been allowed to see game and rabbits or been taken shooting. If a man who intends having a dog trained makes a point of teaching it to be a good retriever of the dummy, to be unafraid of the gun, to drop to command, and to respond to whistle or call, then a good deal of time can be

[Horace Hall

A range of outdoor kennels suitable for gundogs

[Horace Hall

Raw material for the trainer

[Horace Hall

Outside benches are appreciated by the kennel inmates

[Horace Hall

Gnawing of woodwork makes a lot of extra work for the kennelman

[Horace Hall

The end to which the trainer has been working. A typical shooting-day scene

[P. R. A. Moxon

A spaniel holding the Turner-Richards feathered wing dummy

[P. R. A. Moxon

The finished product. Clean delivery right up to hand

saved when the dog comes into kennel. Beyond this he should not go, and even this should not be attempted unless he knows how to set about it. I like a dog to come to me confident and unafraid of people and things, and for this reason one which has been taken about in a car, and allowed to live indoors, is often an easier pupil than one which has spent his early life in kennel without company or affection. Some trainers, I know, like a puppy to come to them completely unhandled. I am merely stating my personal views about this.

One thing about which I am most insistent with owners of dogs I am training is that they shall not visit them until sufficient time has elapsed for the animal to have forgotten his previous home and master. To visit a dog before it has completely settled down and "taken to" the trainer is asking for trouble, and likely to delay training. It is just the same as sending a boy to boarding school and then visiting him before he has had a chance to become acclimatized. The unsettling effect will "put the clock back" possibly weeks, and is unfair to both trainer and dog. Once at the trainer's kennels, the dog must forget about his previous home and master, settle down and accept the trainer as master and the kennels as his home. Some dogs may take weeks to do this, others settle in almost immediately and quite hurt their owners by the apparent callousness of the ready transfer of affection from themselves to the trainer! Really, this is desirable and necessary, and will be understood and appreciated by any owner who gives the matter thought.

I never attempt to handle a dog in the training sense until he gives proof that he is completely at home with me and trusts and loves me. To try to train a dog which is pining and unhappy is both foolish and impracticable, and will lead only to the development of an "inferiority complex" in the dog. Owners who are in such a hurry that they are not prepared to allow for this inevitable lapse of time should not send a dog away for training. Dogs vary greatly in this respect. Most settle down and eat well within a day or two of coming into kennel, others may take considerably longer—I have known six weeks to pass before a shy puppy gave evidence that he was completely "at home". When a new pupil first comes in for training I try to see as much as possible of him in order to win his affection and trust, and make a point of exercising him personally (on the lead at first, for obvious reasons), so that he can get to know me and accept me as master. A dog always seems to have the greatest affection for the man who gives him exercise, especially free running exercise, and for this reason if my kennel assistant does do any exercising the dogs have to be on a lead with him. I must be the one to whom they look for the really enjoyable spells of freedom. I have found this policy to pay handsomely, and I am thankful to say that dogs take to me quickly yet also seem to realize that I intend to be boss from the start. I like to have all the dogs out from time to time in the large exercising compound in front of the kennels, and to stay there with them for a while, making a fuss of each and generally showing that I have affection for them. I do not allow undue liberties from the dogs, of course, but at first I do not mind them jumping up and pawing me, licking my hands and in other ways demonstrating their friendliness, for they need to be bold and confident, and unafraid to come right up to me fearlessly. Otherwise, how am I going to get a dog to retrieve to hand with confidence?

As the risk of infection being brought in from outside by newcomers to the kennel cannot be disregarded I insist that any new dog goes into an isolation kennel, away from the main range, for the first ten or fourteen days of its stay with me. In this way I am able to deal with any trouble immediately it becomes evident. Distemper may easily be in the incubation stage in a dog which comes in to kennel, and to put a dog straightway in the main range, in contact with all the others, might start an outbreak which could not be controlled at that stage. Therefore I regard all new pupils as contagious and rigorously enforce the isolation rule, which so far has proved successful. The newcomer is not deprived of exercise, of course, but he is taken well away from the usual grounds for his walks, and is watched closely. Any suspicious symptom which develops is promptly noted, the dog's temperature taken and the owner contacted if this remains high, or if further suspicious signs become apparent. The source of most of the outbreaks of distemper that have occurred in my kennels has been traced to infection having been brought in by new pupils, or to the too early mixing of freshly inoculated dogs with healthy ones. I insist that, before coming to me, a dog is inoculated against hard pad and distemper and that at least three weeks should elapse between the last injection and the date of admission into my kennel. The live virus system of inoculation means that to all intents and purposes the dog is suffering from a mild form of distemper for a period subsequent to the injections, and such dogs should be strictly isolated and watched. I consider this rigid isolation of newcomers the only fair way of protecting both myself and other owners from the possibility of an outbreak occurring which, in a kennel of any size, is expensive and worrying. Even if an inmate of my kennel is taken away for just one day by the owner, to attend a Show, as sometimes happens, the isolation period is enforced again upon his return, as I regard Dog Shows as hotbeds of infection and one of the chief causes of the widespread outbreaks of distemper and allied diseases about which we hear so much. If any dogs in kennel here do develop suspicious symptoms, such as loss of appetite, lassitude, diarrhoea and sickness, temperatures are immediately taken and anti-distemper precautions at once enforced. My treatment, which I have found to be very effective, of distemper is "naturopathic" as recommended by Miss de Bairacli-Levy, and consists, in the main, of fasting the dogs whilst fever is present, and dosing with specially prepared herbs. I always inform any owner whose dog is affected and ask him to decide whether the animal is to receive orthodox veterinary treatment or be treated as I see fit.

When accepting a dog for training it is quite impossible to give any guarantee as to the success of the course. Owners understand this, presupposing that every attempt will be made by a trainer to make a good job of a dog entrusted to him. None of us likes failures, but not every dog turns out well by any means—so much depends upon the breeding and other circumstances. My policy is to advise an owner about once a month how his dog is shaping in training, and always to err on the pessimistic side. To give glowing reports of pupils, which may not be substantiated by their performance when the owner comes, is foolish and misleading. Any dog which does not promise well at the end of about six weeks is usually removed from the kennels at my request, unless there are exceptional reasons for the lack of promise. I do not like to cause a man to spend money without there being a reasonably good prospect of my being able to hand over a worth-while gundog at the end of the training period. That many dogs do come on well subsequent to being "sent down" as unpromising I do not doubt, but in no case can an owner accuse me of wasting his money, as he would be entitled to do if I had retained a dog without it improving as far as work was concerned.

SELLING A TRAINED DOG.

When the training course is finished, I like owners personally to collect the dog and thus be afforded the opportunity of seeing him working for me, and learning my handling methods and words of command, signals and whistles. The owner can also state whether the standard of training reached is satisfactory; if it is not, the dog can remain with me for a further period. To send a dog home by rail with merely written instructions about handling, etc., is a most unsatisfactory conclusion to a rather expensive business, and an owner who insists that this is done rather than go to the trouble of visiting his trainer can blame only himself if the dog proves unsatisfactory. In just the same way, when offering a trained or partly trained dog for sale I consider it essential for the prospective buyer to see it working with the vendor. In this way there can be no possibility of fraud and deception, and an opportunity will be given for ensuring that the dog is "as stated". Trained dogs cannot be bought today for much less than £100, or even more if experienced; partly trained dogs from £35–£50, and it appears rather futile to spend as much money as this on an "unknown quantity". Quite apart from this, the buyer can learn the handling methods and words of command when watching the vendor handling the dog, rather than rely upon written instructions. I make a point of supplying with any which I have trained a whistle of the type to which he is accustomed. This I consider absolutely essential.

"APPROVAL".

The sending of a trained dog "on approval" is a practice in which I refuse to take part. It is a perfectly ridiculous procedure and likely to cause all sorts of trouble—that is, unless you are personally acquainted with the buyer, and know that he knows your methods thoroughly and can handle a dog. It is one thing to show what a dog can do *for you*—it is quite another to guarantee that it will do as well, or indeed do *anything*, for a stranger. The more so if the stranger has never seen you handling a dog and does not know your system. To send a valuable trained dog on approval may well result in its training being completely ruined by mishandling, and the value of the dog seriously reduced. That risk is not worth running. If a man will not or cannot come to see a dog working for me he must take my word for it that all is "as stated", and if not satisfied with the dog that is just too bad. I will not take it back except in most exceptional cases. All too many men get a trained dog one day by rail, take it out shooting the next, and are horrified if it either runs wild or refuses to work for them at all! A dog needs several days, maybe several weeks, to get used to a new owner and new surroundings, and to attempt to work the dog until after it has settled down is plain foolishness. Yet every year scores of buyers are disappointed through lack of attention to the very elementary principle that *a dog should be seen working for its trainer before purchase or acceptance.*

Few, very few, men would dream of buying a car, a gun or a typewriter, for instance, without seeing and trying it out, yet many will run the risk of losing anything from £35–£200 on a dog by not going to see it working. This does not make sense to me; I have no sympathy for the man who gets "bitten" in this way, or for the trainer who indulges in the pernicious "on approval" system of selling trained dogs. The best dog in the world can become a bad advertisement in the wrong hands, and it is a short-sighted policy for anyone with a reputation to agree to "approval". Except, as I have written, when the buyer is known to be a good handler, and is acquainted with the trainer's methods and commands.

From what I have written the reader will be able to get some idea of the varied, interesting and at times worrying life of a gundog trainer. That the life is not all milk and honey will, I hope, be obvious. Anyone who goes in for training dogs for a living requires, in large measure, a sense of humour and a thick skin. In this sphere one becomes something of a student of human as well as canine psychology, and soon learns the types of owner and how to deal with them. Luckily, nearly all are good fellows, and know that we are doing our best, often in very difficult circumstances. Costs in this business have trebled since the war, yet fees are generally not quite double what they were pre-war; which proves that we trainers are doing our best to keep the cost of training gundogs within reach of the average shooting man. This is, of course, a semi-luxury trade, and if fees were to go too high the ordinary man would not be able to afford to have a gundog trained. We are saved probably only by the fact that gundogs are an essential part of the sport of shooting, and because, human nature being what it is, many men are prepared to make sacrifices in order to have their four-footed companions trained for their jobs. I know the struggle some people have in order to be able to afford their sport and gundogs and I admire them all the more for it, for field sports are one of the heritages of the British way of life. Without them this would be a poor country indeed.

CONCLUSION TO THE FIRST EDITION.

Before taking leave of the reader, and packing my Remington away in its case after its valiant survival of my daily assaults for many weeks, I would like to express the sincere hope that this book will prove of some use to the sportsman and dog lover. That it has many imperfections I am quite aware, and that many things I have written will prove unacceptable to a lot of readers I do not doubt for one moment. If some of my recommendations and methods appear at variance with those advocated in previous books and articles of mine, I would point out that this is because I am constantly learning, and that I do not hesitate to change if I find something better in training, feeding, treating or managing dogs. Where, therefore, a disparity between this and any of my previous writings is noted, it should be accepted that the ideas now put forward have proved better than the old ones. I apologize to readers for any omissions; in a work of this nature it is well-nigh impossible to deal with every query that may arise during the training of a gundog, or at a Field Trial, but as far as practicable I have included enough of the main essentials to put the amateur trainer on the right track, and to give the uninitiated some idea of how Trials are conducted. There are many other, and possibly better, training methods than those I have advocated, but the simplicity and success of the suggested system encourages me to believe that the average man will find it easy to operate and, above all, that the average dog will find it easy to assimilate. If this book is responsible for the introduction of but one newcomer to the sport of Training and Field Trials, and if it helps to improve the standard of training of a single gundog, then my effort will not have been fruitless.

CHAPTER XII

THE SCENE TODAY

Trials and Tests. Modern Training Aids. Feeding. Vaccination

TRIALS AND TESTS.

SINCE this book was first conceived, some eighteen years ago, the sport of gundog training—for both practical work in the shooting field and competition at field trials—has continued to grow in popularity. Increasing general prosperity, more leisure time and a very natural desire to "get away from it all" has contributed to this, and the emergence of gundog working tests almost as a sport in their own right has also played a very large part. Naturally I am very happy about this state of affairs, all the more so because I know, through correspondence with readers, that my own enthusiasm and writings on gundogs have been partly responsible for helping and encouraging beginners to appreciate good dog work in the shooting, test and trial fields.

Of course, things have changed a bit over the years. There is now a wider appreciation of psychology in dog training and handling, and also of the "finer points" of education which go to produce a more efficient and attractive working gundog. Unfortunately, the modern trend in gundogs (especially at field trials) seems to place undue emphasis upon the handler and the handling ability of the dogs, and many of us older hands believe that specialization is tending to go too far, with the inevitable result that trial dogs and ordinary shooting dogs are becoming two distinct types. Much of this—especially in retrievers—is due to the influence of the American market, which, certainly among professional and quite a lot of semi-professional trainers, provides an incentive which is not in the best interests of the British sporting fraternity, who demand initiative and *natural* gamefinding ability from their dogs.

There is also widespread criticism of gundog working tests—sometimes unjustified—from a section of the dedicated working gundog fraternity because these events are encouraging some owners to train their dogs for test work and subsequently to enter them for field trials proper *without first giving them the essential practical experience of working on shoots, or being shot over.* It should be realized that working tests were originated as jumping-off grounds for field trial dogs and handlers—a sort of halfway house—and that the good test dog is not necessarily a potential trial winner, and *vice versa*. If you are content to train and keep your dog for tests (which are all artificial), fair enough. If, however, you aspire to competition in trials proper, for heaven's sake give it practical experience in the shooting field before applying for a trial nomination. Otherwise, you will be sadly disappointed, and may also be depriving a much more worthy dog of the opportunity of competing at the meeting.

There have been no major developments in training technique since this book was first written, and I have found no reason to change my methods in a general sense. Such minor alterations of procedure as have become necessary are entirely due to the continuing scarcity of rabbits, thanks to the ghastly, artificially introduced disease of the coney population, myxomatosis, and to the availability of various artificial aids to training which have been invented in the last few years.

Ever since gundogs were first trained for practical use, the ubiquitous bunny has provided ideal "real thing" practice at all seasons of the year. Spaniels could be encouraged to hunt at an early age, and to face cover; retrievers and "bird dogs" could be put under temptation and steadied and, for natural retrieves, rabbits were always readily available. Today, unfortunately, rabbits are something of a rarity on most shoots, with the result that it proves more difficult, and takes longer, to get dogs on to the real thing.

Those of us who are fortunate enough to have a rabbit pen are in a rather better position than the ordinary shooting man, for pen rabbits can be caught up periodically and vaccinated against myxomatosis. But, at best, the rabbit pen is only a means to an end and not the end in itself, and all shooting dogs have *got* to have experience and practice on game in its natural surroundings. As we have to rely upon pheasants and other game birds, it is obvious that our training season is seriously curtailed and opportunities for getting scent into the noses of young dogs are strictly limited. Whereas, in pre-myxomatosis days, you could train-up and have a spaniel ready for shooting and/or open field trials by the time it was ten months to a year old, it is now extremely difficult to reach the same stage of training before the dog is eighteen months to two years of age.

One result of this sorry state of affairs is that it costs more to produce a trained gundog; another being that the enthusiastic owner-trainer may be (and often is!) tempted to shoot over his young dog in company before it has been thoroughly grounded in good manners and given sufficient experience of "battle conditions" in less exacting circumstances. The trainer of today has to be more patient and more ingenious, and a greater improviser, than he was fifteen or twenty years ago.

MODERN TRAINING AIDS.

In some respects, however, the present-day gundog trainer has never had it so good. There have been some notable advances in various training aids, which considerably lighten his burden and increase the efficiency of his pupils and, in some instances, save him both time and money.

In my opinion, the greatest boon has been the introduction of the American-invented dummy launcher. This device is very similar in appearance and performance to the well-known "beer-can launcher" which many keen shooting men use for target practice. Known as the "Windrush Retriever-Trainer" (available from Windrush Guns Ltd., Witney, Oxon. at £12.50 complete with dummy) it fits conveniently into a gamebag, and fires a blank .22 cartridge, giving a realistic "bang", and ejects for a considerable distance (up to 100 yards, according to wind force and direction) an almost indestructible dummy of suitable size and composition for the average retrieving dog.

The advantages of this dummy launcher are immediately apparent to the enthusiastic gundog trainer, and its possibilities are almost limitless. Not only does it accustom the canine pupil to gunfire and arouse its interest in the lofted dummy in the most natural way possible, but enables the handler to give his dog wide and varied practice—from "towered birds" and straightforward marking to bolted rabbits (if fired so that the dummy bounces along the ground). It can be fired behind the dog, in front of the dog, over a hedge or across water. In the earlier stages of training it saves the handler having to lug a shotgun around with him, and, at around 2p per bang, it is considerably cheaper than having to use ordinary shotgun cartridges for gunfire and dropping to shot lessons. Such is my enthusiasm for the dummy launcher that I often wonder how on earth we ever managed without it in the past!

Another time and money saving innovation is the "Acvoke" shotgun adapter, which enables a cheap .25 blank cartridge to be fired from the ordinary shotgun. These blanks give a good "bang" and not the rifle-shot "crack" of which many puppies show fear, and are available in varying strengths. The manufacturers, Messrs Accles & Shelvoke Ltd., Talford Street Works, Aston, Birmingham 6, can also supply a very handy 8-shot pistol which accepts the same blank cartridges, and can be used for firing "doubles" or a succession of quick shots. I make wide use of both the adapter and the pistol for both early and advanced training, and unhesitatingly recommend them to the trainer who wishes to train his dog, efficiently and cheaply, to the various aspects of gunfire to which it must, ultimately, be subjected.

We do not seem to be able to get away from plastics and nylon today, and these, too, have their application to gundog training. Plastic material—either a strong polythene sheet or even a piece of old plastic mackintosh—makes an ideal covering for the core of the homemade retrieving dummy, and helps to waterproof it, with obvious advantages. Nylon stockings, when your wife has finished with them, are excellent for encasing a dead pigeon or game specimen for the early retrieving lessons, making a very effective sort of "halfway house" between artificial dummy and "the real thing". The dog which is chary of picking up feather in its natural state will often oblige if the bird is stuffed into an old nylon stocking and thrown out, or placed, like its usual retrieving dummy. When success has been achieved once or twice, and confidence built up, the bird can be thrown naturally and, nine times out of ten, you will find that the dog will pick up and retrieve happily and cleanly.

Nylon cord is available in differing sizes and strengths, and the very narrow-gauged, stringlike stuff makes ideal whistle lanyards, washable and long-lasting. Heavier gauges provide very superior check cords, being virtually rot-proof, lighter and much stronger than ordinary cords, and far less liable to kinking in use.

For ordinary slip or choke leads, nylon cord has completely replaced leather in my affections. I now have these made up of this material by the local saddler and use them in preference to leather leads. They are much lighter and stronger, and roll up small to fit conveniently in the pocket. Admittedly, they are no more chew-proof than leather, but they are certainly less prone to be chewed by dogs and, if they are, they are cheaper to replace than the leather article.

Plastic tubing, foam insulating material and the like can

help to make very useful retrieving dummies. I have referred above to the absence of rabbits and the necessity for getting dogs on to "feathered" game earlier than has hitherto been necessary. Old car radiator hose or heavy plastic tubing, cut into lengths of 12 to 16 inches, can be utilized to accustom dogs to carrying feather in the following manner. First of all, make a couple of small holes at one end and thread through these a nylon cord to make a "throwing tail", by which the dummy can be flung. Around the body of the dummy, by means of wide rubber bands cut from old cycle inner tubes, fasten a number of pheasant, duck, partridge or grouse wings, cut off your dead game and thoroughly dried out so that they are blood-free. Once young gundogs have been accustomed to retrieving this type of dummy, far less difficulty is experienced when the time comes for them to lift and carry the real thing. Rabbit-skin dummies still have their uses, and I would not be without them but, under modern conditions, feather dummies probably have a far more practical application to work in the field.

FEEDING.

Although my views upon feeding have not radically altered over the years—I still maintain that, for a carnivorous animal like the dog, raw meat in one form or another is essential—experience and necessity have *modified* them to a certain extent. One must try to be realistic, and all sorts of factors decide what can and should go to make up a suitable canine diet which is both convenient and economic for the individual owner. Recent legislation, which orders that all "knacker's" meat must be sterilized before sale, has meant that it is now virtually impossible to obtain fresh raw meat for dogs except that which is fit for human consumption. As a result, there is not enough cheap meat and offal to go round, prices have soared and many owners are completely unable either to afford or obtain adequate supplies.

The "prepared" pet food industry is, these days, very big business indeed, and the proliferation of brands (especially of canned foods) now on the market is quite bewildering to the novice dog owner! As these are now subject to a crippling 22 per cent purchase tax, the cost of feeding a dog, by any means, has risen savagely since 1969. I doubt if, nowadays, it is possible for most people adequately to feed a gundog for less than between 75p and £1.25 per week (according to breed, size and age), and for that sort of money the animal has got to earn its keep! Which should provide an incentive for shooting men to obtain first-class stock in the first place and to train it very thoroughly.

Although by no means a lover of canned foods for dogs, I must admit to their convenience for the average owner and, if I am honest, allow that most dogs that I have seen which are regularly fed upon them do not appear to be taking any harm!

Dry feeding, in meal or pellet form, long beloved by dog fanciers in America and Canada, is now available in this country and gradually catching on. I have, myself, carried out quite serious controlled experiments with several different products, especially as regards *ad lib.* hopper feeding for young puppies. These foods usually contain natural whole-grain cooked cereals, meat meal, fish meal, dried milk, oil and added vitamins and minerals. Results obtained have been most encouraging, so much so that I am rapidly being converted and, whilst still maintaining that raw meat (especially ox tripes and sheep's paunches) constitute the ideal canine diet *if you can obtain and afford it*, have, for several months past, been feeding almost the entire kennels on the "all-in" system of dry, pelleted food. The two most palatable and satisfactory products being "Evenlode Dog Food", manufactured by Evenlode Products Ltd., "Stonewalls", Evenlode, Moreton-in-Marsh, Gloucestershire, and "Wuffitmix" from Messrs. B. Dugdale & Son Ltd., Clitheroe, Lancashire. These foods are available in both puppy and adult formula and are not only easy and convenient to feed but also economical and labour-saving. In my experience, this type of food is best given in two meals, instead of the traditional one per day; scattered rather than bowl or trough fed and—supremely important—dogs fed by this method *must have drinking water always available*. Raw and tinned meat contains around 60 to 70% water, whereas these dried foods have a moisture content of only eight to ten per cent. So the precaution should be obvious.

Vaccination.

Advances in the veterinary field over the last fifteen or twenty years have been most impressive. Improved drugs (particularly antibiotics) and vaccines, as well as surgery techniques, have made life much easier for dog owners in general and kennel proprietors in particular. Thanks to "all-in" vaccination against distemper, hepatitis and two forms of jaundice, these diseases no longer pose the threat that once they did and, indeed, give every evidence of being on their way out. At one time, and with very good reason, I was strongly anti-vaccination, and made this abundantly clear in early editions of this book. However, things have changed so much that nowadays I regard the veterinary surgeon as the dog owner's best friend, and am so pro-vaccination that I will not accept into my kennels any dog which has not been immunized in the modern manner. Any owner who does not take advantage of distemper, jaundice and hepatitis immunization for his dog is a fool to himself and a traitor to his dog and other owners.

From all that I have written above, readers will, I hope, realize that I am not afraid of changing my opinions in the light of experience and circumstances, and of admitting that I *can* be wrong! As I have stressed throughout this book, with dogs you *never* stop learning, and the man who thinks he knows it all is a fool to himself, and sooner or later is going to be in for a very big shock. This applies both to training and general care and management of the dog, and I hope and believe that I shall go on learning from my dogs—and "the dog business" generally—for many years to come. Perhaps one of the best pieces of advice that I can offer readers is always to keep an open mind and (forgive the pun) not to become too dogmatic!

APPENDIX A

GUNDOG SOCIETIES

and the names and addresses of Secretaries at March 1978

BORDER COUNTIES GUNDOG CLUB.
Mrs. P. Beardsworth, Knott Edge, Preston Patrick, Milnthorpe, Cumbria, LA7 7NR.

BRISTOL AND WEST WORKING GUNDOG SOCIETY.
Mr. R. A. Davis, Fairlawn, Back of Kingsdown Parade, Cotham, Bristol 6.

CORNWALL GUNDOG CLUB.
Mrs. L. Mabey, Treranke Cottage, Roche, St. Austell, Cornwall.

DUKERIES (NOTTS) GUNDOG CLUB.
Mrs. R. Davies, The Paddocks, Clumber Park, Worksop, Notts., S80 3BQ.

EAST RIDING GUNDOG SOCIETY.
Mr. G. E. Abbot, 9 Westwood Close, Tweenydkes Road, Sutton-on-Hull, HU7 4XH.

FORTH AND CLYDE WORKING GUNDOG ASSOCIATION.
Mrs. M. Paton, Loanside Cottage, Clackmannan, Central.

GOYT VALLEY GUNDOG SOCIETY.
Mr. R. A. Hibbs, 8 Overdale Road, New Mills, Nr. Stockport, Cheshire, SK12 3LJ.

GUNDOG SOCIETY OF WALES.
Mrs. S. Ashbourne, 43 Penrhiw, Rhiw-Fwr, Swansea, W. Glamorgan.

HAMPSHIRE GUNDOG SOCIETY.
Mrs. K. E. French, Church Cottage, Week, Winchester, Hants,

HIGHLAND GUNDOG CLUB.
Mr. B. Easton, 110 Springfield Road, New Elgin, Scotland.

LEICESTERSHIRE GUNDOG SOCIETY.
Mrs. A. Webster, 90 Ashby Road, Kegworth, Leics.

LOTHIAN AND BORDERS GUNDOG ASSOCIATION.
Mr. W. D. Knox, 37 Wester Broom Drive, Edinburgh 12.

MERSEYSIDE GUNDOG CLUB.
Mr. J. H. Corrin, Mann Villa, Prescot Road, Melling Mount, Melling, Liverpool.

MIDLAND GUNDOG SOCIETY.
Mrs. J. Haywood, 171 Baginton Road, Styvechale, Morton, Malvern, Worcs.

MID-WESTERN GUNDOG SOCIETY.
Mr. R. Hall Jones, The Captains, Castlemorton, Malvern, Worcs.

NATIONAL GUNDOG ASSOCIATION.
Mrs. Anne Webster, 90 Ashby Road, Kegworth, Derby, DE7 2DJ

NORTHERN COUNTIES GUNDOG CLUB.
Mr. D. I'Anson, 24 Harrowgate Village, Darlington, Co. Durham.

NORTH OF SCOTLAND GUNDOG ASSOCIATION.
Mr. D. M. Douglas, Frogfield, Laurencekirk, Grampian.

NORTH RIDING GUNDOG SOCIETY.
Mr. A. Wood, 11 Kilton Close, Ings Farm, Redcar, Cleveland, TS10 2NH.

SCOTTISH GUNDOG ASSOCIATION.
Mr. M. M. Jamieson, Greenbank, Auchterarder, Tayside.

SHROPSHIRE GUNDOG SOCIETY.
Mr. C. M. Brown, Poplars Cottages, Brockton, Much Wenlock, Salop.

SOUTH EASTERN GUNDOG SOCIETY.
Mrs. A. Carden, Eastwood Farmhouse, Ulcombe, Kent.

SOUTH OF ENGLAND GUNDOG CLUB.
Mr. D. J. Williams, 26a Dennis Park Crescent, West Wimbledon, London, SW20 8QH.

SOUTH WESTERN GUNDOG CLUB.
Mrs. K. G. Holmes, Monkton House, Pinhoe, Exeter.

SOUTH WEST SCOTLAND GUNDOG ASSOCIATION.
Mrs. G. S. Campbell, Montgreenan Kennels, Kilwinning, Strathclyde.

STRATHMORE WORKING GUNDOG CLUB.
Mr. R. Methven, Lauriston, Inchture, Tayside.

ULSTER GUNDOG LEAGUE.
Mr. A. C. M. Rountree, Lisanelly House, Gortin Road, Omagh Co. Tyrone.

UNITED GUNDOG BREEDERS ASSOCIATION.
Mr. R. W. Moseley, Laburnum, Cottage Woodseaves, Stafford, ST20 0NP.

UTILITY GUNDOG SOCIETY.
Mrs. E. Henbest, Bank Green Cottage, Bellingdon, Chesham, Bucks.

WAVERLEY GUNDOG ASSOCIATION.
Miss P. H. Anderson, 66 Findhorn Place, Edinburgh, EH9 2NW.

WEST DARTMOOR WORKING GUNDOG CLUB.
Mr. E. V. Thomas, Padiva, 69 Longmead Road, Paignton, TQ3 1AX.

WESTWARD GUNDOG SOCIETY.
Mrs. M. J. Curgenven, Keepers Lodge, Burlescombe, Tiverton, Devon, EX16 7JU.

WINDSOR GUNDOG SOCIETY.
Mrs. V. E. Banks, Oaklands, Basingstoke Road, Spencers Wood, Reading, Berks.

Yorkshire Gundog Club.
Mrs. M. Backhouse, 121 Silcoates Lane, Wrenthorpe, Wakefield, W. Yorks.

SETTERS

Belfast and District Irish Setter Club.
Mr. W. Connery, 46 Dunbeg Park, Hillsborough, Co. Down.

British Gordon Setter Club.
Mrs. L. Jackson-Richmond, Garden Cottage, Sutton Park, Guildford, Surrey.

English Setter Association.
Mr. J. Bowen, 10 St. Cleres Way, Danbury, Nr. Chelmsford, Essex

English Setter Club.
Dr. J. B. Maurice, Batts Farm, Wilton, Marlborough, Wilts.

Gordon Setter Association.
Mrs. J. W. Allan, Finella, Drumtochty, Auchenblae, Grampian.

Irish Setter Association (England).
Mr. W. J. Basbridge, 105 Manor Green Road, Epsom, Surrey.

Irish Setter Breeders Club.
Mrs. A. I. Ashton, Greystones House, Horbury Road, Ossett, W. Yorks.

Irish Setter Club of Scotland.
Mrs. I. Munro, Station House, Innerleithen, Borders, EH44 6PD.

Northern Counties Pointer and Setter Society.
Mrs. E. J. Buist, Katewell, Evanton, Highlands.

Northern English Setter Society.
Mrs. P. A. Justice, 206 Sheffield Road, Killamarsh, Nr. Sheffield, S31 8ED.

Pointer and Setter Society (International Gundog League).
Dr. M. S. Good, Alwyn Lawn, Stone, near Aylesbury, Bucks.

Setter and Pointer Club.
Mr. B. Coupe, Timadon Kennels, Woodside, Ashton, Chester.

Ulster Irish Red Setter Club.
Mr. J. V. Courtney, Slieve Muire, Culmore, Omagh, Co. Tyrone.

POINTERS

Northern Counties Pointer and Setter Society.
Mrs. E. J. Buist, Katewell, Evanton, Highland.

Northern Ireland Pointer Club.
Mr. W. R. Gardiner, 12 Swanston Crescent, Glengormley, Newtonabbey, Co. Antrim.

Pointer and Setter Society (International Gundog League).
Dr. M. S. Good, Alwyn Lane, Stone, near Aylesbury, Bucks.

The Pointer Club.
Mrs. S. M. Rhodes, Hazelborrow, Walseker Lane, Woodall-in-Harthill, Nr. Sheffield, S. Yorks.
Setter and Pointer Club.
Mr. B. Coupe, Timadon Kennels, Woodside, Ashton, Chester.
Southern Pointer Club.
Mrs. G. Woollard, Stonehouse Pointers, East Grinstead, Salisbury, Wilts.

GERMAN SHORTHAIRED POINTERS

German Shorthaired Pointer Association.
Mr. H. Fisher, Firhouse, 32 Cherry Lane, Lawton Heath End, Alsager, Stoke-on-Trent.
German Shorthaired Pointer Club.
Mr. W. K. Simpson, Northwold House, Northwold, Thetford, Norfolk.

RETRIEVERS

Curly Retriever Club.
Mr. J. F. Spooner, 104 Lovely Lane, Warrington, Lancs.
East Anglian Labrador Retriever Club.
Mrs. L. G. Kinsella, The Mount, Fingringhoe, Nr. Colchester, Essex.
Eastern Counties Retriever Society.
Mrs. A. Wentworth-Smith, The Old Rectory, Swardeston, Norwich, NOR 95W.
Flat-Coated Retriever Society.
The Hon. Mrs. D. Jessel, The Grove House, Droxford, Hampshire, SO3 1PT.
Golden Retriever Club.
Mrs. B. Webb, 116 Cambridge Road, Great Shelford, Cambridge.
Golden Retriever Club of Scotland.
Mrs. M. Smart, 5 Strathearn Terrace, Perth, PH2 OLS.
Golden Retriever Club of Wales
Mrs. M. Hunton-Girling, Sarelle, Ponthir, Newport, Gwent.
Herts., Beds., Bucks. and Hants. Retriever Society.
Miss A. Hill-Wood, Knipton Lodge, Knipton, Grantham, Lincs.
Labrador Club of Scotland.
Mr. William Hogg, Rhuallan, Buchlyvie, Central.
Labrador Retriever Club.
Mr. T. J. Glover, Valley Cottage, Milton Abbey Gardens, Milton Abbas, Blandford, Dorset, DT11 ODA.
Labrador Retriever Club of Northern Ireland.
Mr. A. J. Kilpatrick, 16 Corby Drive, Lisburn, Co. Antrim, N. Ireland.

MIDLAND COUNTIES LABRADOR RETRIEVER CLUB.
Mr. F. Whitbread, Rose Cottage, Cat and Fiddle Lane, West Hallam, Derbys.

NORTH WEST LABRADOR RETRIEVER CLUB.
Mr. R. Gregory, The Poplars, Kitty Lane, Marton, Blackpool, Lancs.

NORTHERN GOLDEN RETRIEVER ASSOCIATION.
Mrs. M. Dawson, The Poplars, Donnington Northorpe, Spalding, Lincs.

NORTHUMBERLAND AND DURHAM LABRADOR RETRIEVER CLUB.
Miss E. Smith, 29 High Street, Gosforth, Newcastle-on-Tyne 3.

RETRIEVER SOCIETY (INTERNATIONAL GUNDOG LEAGUE).
Mr. J. W. Taylor, 61 Peterborough Road, Castor, Nr. Peterborough.

SOUTH WESTERN GOLDEN RETRIEVER CLUB.
Mr. R. Coward, Greenacres, Ibsley Drive, Nr. Ringwood, Hants.

THREE RIDINGS LABRADOR CLUB.
Mr. B. Daly, 135 Blacker Lane, Netherton, Wakefield, W. Yorks.

ULSTER GOLDEN RETRIEVER CLUB.
Mr. W. Hosford, 76 Ballybunden Road, Killinchy, Co. Down, BT23 6RX. N. Ireland.

ULSTER RETRIEVER CLUB.
Mr. H. A. Wilson, Nesfield House, 71 Queensway, Co. Antrim, N. Ireland.

UNITED RETRIEVER CLUB.
Mr. J. J. Tiranti, Garthfield, Mumbery Hill, Wargrave, Reading, Berks, RG10 8EE.

WEST OF ENGLAND LABRADOR RETRIEVER CLUB.
Mr. L. J. Harding, Coombe Cross, Dittisham, Nr. Dartmouth, Devon.

YELLOW LABRADOR CLUB.
Mr. H. W. Clayton, Ardmargha Cottage, Brighthampton, Standlake, Witney, Oxon.

YORKSHIRE RETRIEVER FIELD TRIAL SOCIETY.
Mr. R. F. Bilton, Rolston Hall, Hornsea, N. Humberside.

SPANIELS

AMERICAN COCKER SPANIEL CLUB OF GREAT BRITAIN.
Mrs. A. M. Jones, The Captains, Castlemorton, Malvern, Worcester.

ANTRIM AND DOWN ENGLISH SPANIEL CLUB.
Mr. R. B. McClean, 10 Parkland Avenue, Lisburn, Co. Antrim, N. Ireland.

BLACK COCKER SPANIEL SOCIETY.
Mr. M. Chivers, Whitegates, Alton Road, Odiham, Basingstoke, Hants.

CHESHIRE COCKER SPANIEL CLUB.
Mrs. N. Curtis, Cornerways, London Road, Prestbury, Nr. Macclesfield, Cheshire.

CLUMBER SPANIEL CLUB.
Mr. R. W. Henson, Fatpastures, Donington-on-Bain, Lincoln, LNH 9RG.

COCKER SPANIEL CLUB.
Mrs. E. S. Robertson, "Nostrebor", Pikes Pool Lane, Finstall, Bromsgrove, Worcs.

COCKER SPANIEL CLUB OF LANCASHIRE.
Mrs. D. M. Schofield, Cobbles, Norcott Brook, by Warrington, Lancs.

COCKER SPANIEL CLUB OF SCOTLAND.
Mrs. J. Braid, Craigallian, Dunure Road, Ayr, Strathclyde.

COVENTRY COCKER SPANIEL CLUB.
Mr. C. Gardner, Chrisolin, 112 Hinckley Road, Coventry, CV2 2EV.

EAST ANGLIAN COCKER SPANIEL SOCIETY.
Mrs. O. B. Norfolk, "Tarlings", West Hanningfield, Essex.

EAST OF SCOTLAND COCKER SPANIEL CLUB.
Mrs. E. Johnston, Knock Tower, Newbridge, Lothian.

EASTERN COUNTIES SPANIEL SOCIETY.
Mrs. A. Wentworth-Smith, The Old Rectory, Swardeston, Norwich, NOR 95W.

ENGLISH SPRINGER SPANIEL CLUB.
Mrs. I. B. Hampton, Larkstoke Cottage, Bourton-on-the-Hill, Moreton-in-Marsh, Glos.

ENGLISH SPRINGER SPANIEL CLUB OF NORTHERN IRELAND.
Mr. R. E. Clemiston, Fairacres, 1 Holywood Road, Newtownards, Co. Down, N. Ireland.

ENGLISH SPRINGER SPANIEL CLUB OF SCOTLAND.
Mrs. E. K. Thomson, Rivington Lodge, Castle Douglas, Dumfries and Galloway.

ENGLISH SPRINGER SPANIEL CLUB OF WALES.
Mrs. E. Green, 45 Heoltawe, Abercrave, Swansea, SA9 1XP.

FIELD SPANIEL SOCIETY.
Mr. R. Hall Jones, The Captains, Castle Morton, Malvern, Worcs.

HOME COUNTIES COCKER CLUB.
Mrs. E. Samuels, 24 Kennedy Avenue, Hoddesdon, Herts.

IRISH WATER SPANIEL ASSOCIATION
Mrs. J. W. Johnson, 77 Russell Road, Horsell, Woking, Surrey, GU21 4UY.

LONDON AND HOME COUNTIES ENGLISH SPRINGER SPANIEL SOCIETY.
Mr. D. Miller, 283 Desborough Avenue, High Wycombe, Bucks

LONDON COCKER SPANIEL SOCIETY.
Mr. R. W. Crisp, 84 Wembley Hill Road, Wembley, London.

MIDLAND COCKER SPANIEL CLUB.
Mr. R. M. Pain, 30 Alvechurch Highway, Lydiate Ash, Bromsgrove, Worcs.

MIDLAND ENGLISH SPRINGER SPANIEL SOCIETY.
Mrs. M. Backhouse, 121 Silcoates Lane, Wrenthorpe, Wakefield, W. Yorks.

NORTH MIDLAND AND EASTERN COUNTIES COCKER SPANIEL CLUB.
Mrs. W. M. Prince, Bowbridge Fields Farm, Ashbourne Road, Mackworth, Derby.

NORTH OF ENGLAND COCKER SPANIEL ASSOCIATION.
Mrs. R. Tyson, 71 Egerton Road South, Chorlton, Manchester, M21 1XJ.

NORTH OF ENGLAND SPANIEL CLUB.
Mrs. F. Curran, Glen View, Stannerford Road, Crawcrooke, Co. Durham.

NORTH OF IRELAND COCKER SPANIEL CLUB.
Mrs. D. M. Yeames, 74 Bawnmore Road, Belfast, BT9 6CD.

NORTH WALES COCKER SPANIEL CLUB.
Mr. D. A. Milburn, 8 Llwyn Derw, Mynydd Isa, Mold, Clwyd.

NORTH WEST ULSTER SPANIEL CLUB.
Mr. J. Stewart, 92 Rainey Street, Magherafelt, Co. Londonderry.

NORTHERN COUNTIES AMERICAN COCKER SPANIEL CLUB.
Mrs. M. F. Slapp, 2 The Crescent, Broadwater, Fleetwood, Lancs.

NORTHERN ENGLISH SPRINGER SPANIEL SOCIETY.
Mrs. E. Dobson, Teesview Gundogs, Neasham, Co. Durham. (new society).

PARTI-COLOURED COCKER SPANIEL CLUB.
Mr. W. R. Blythe, Lincoln Flats Kennels, Foggathorpe, Nr. Selby, N. Humberside.

RED AND GOLDEN SPANIEL CLUB.
Mr. R. M. Pain, 30 Alvechurch Highway, Lydiate Ash, Bromsgrove, Worcs.

ROTHERHAM AND DISTRICT COCKER SPANIEL CLUB.
Mrs. M. E. Stevens, Leabank Kennels, Fulshaw Cross, Nr. Thurlstone, Sheffield.

SCOTTISH SPANIEL CLUB.
Mr. D. M. Douglas, Frogfield, Laurencekirk, Grampian.

SOUTH WALES AND MON. COCKER CLUB.
Mrs. T. M. Bebb, Bona Vista, 148 Cefn Road, Rogerstone, Gwent, NP1 9EX.

SOUTHERN ENGLISH SPRINGER SPANIEL SOCIETY.
Mr. D. Miller, 283 Desborough Avenue, High Wycombe, Bucks. (new society).

Spaniel Club.
Mr. C. Sutcliffe, Newlands Cottages, Blithbury, Rugeley, Staffs.

Sussex Spaniel Association.
Mrs. Lancaster, Moss Cottage (Nursery Road), off Close Lane, Alsager, Stoke-on-Trent.

Ulster Cocker Spaniel Club.
Mr. T. J. Cardy, Mount Keepe, Glen Road, Lower Castlereagh, Belfast 5.

Welsh and English Counties Spaniel Club.
Mrs. M. M. Leopard, Lower Kimbolton Farm, Leominster, Hereford, HR6 0JA.

Welsh Springer Spaniel Club.
Mrs. A. Walton, Hill Park, Farm Wrotham, Sevenoaks, Kent.

West of England Cocker Spaniel Club.
Mr. T. E. W. Heavisides, Kirkdon, 26 Moorland, Road Yate, Nr. Bristol.

Western Counties and South Wales Spaniel Club.
Mr. A. M. Peace, 23 Durleigh Road, Bridgwater, Somerset.

Yorkshire Cocker Spaniel Club.
Mr. E. Walker, 158 Warminster Road, Sheffield, S8 8PQ, S. Yorks.

WEIMARANERS

Weimaraner Club of Great Britain.
Mrs. M. Holmes, 78 The Byeway, West Wittering, Sussex.

HUNGARIAN VIZSLAS

Hungarian Viszla Club.
Mrs. D. Hunt, Hunter's Lodge, Glen Close, Hindhead, Surrey.

Hungarian Vizsla Society.
Mr. A. J. Gray, Park Gate, Donhead St. Mary, Shaftesbury. Dorset.

LARGE MUNSTERLANDERS

Large Munsterlander Club.
Mrs. P. A. Perkins, Barge Farm House, Taplow, Maidenhead, Berks.

APPENDIX B

FIELD TRIAL SOCIETIES

and the names and addresses of Field Trial Secretaries at March 1978.

ANTRIM AND DOWN ENGLISH SPRINGER SPANIEL CLUB.
Mr. R. B. McClean, 10 Parkland Avenue, Lisburn, Co. Antrim, N. Ireland.

BRISTOL AND WEST WORKING GUNDOG SOCIETY.
Mr. R. A. Davis, Fairlawn , Back of Kingsdown Parade, Cotham, Bristol 6.

BRITISH STEEL CORPORATION PORT TALBOT (FIELD TRIAL SECTION).
Mr. J. Carter, Home Farm Cottage, Coldbrook Park, Abergavenny, Gwent.

CAMBRIDGESHIRE FIELD TRIAL SOCIETY.
Mrs. M. J. Curtis, The Moors, Whittlesford, Cambridgeshire.

CHESHIRE, N. WALES AND SHROPSHIRE RETRIEVER AND SPANIEL SOCIETY.
Mr. Hobley Heaves, Keren, St. Hilary's Drive, Deganwy, Llandudno Junction, LL31 9SS.

CHILTERN GUNDOG TRAINING CLUB.
Mr. R. K. Bradbury, 2 The Hale, Wendover, Bucks.

CLWYD RETRIEVER CLUB.
Mrs. J. G. Bailey, Gunstock Kennels, Whitford, Holywell, Clwyd, CH8 9AL.

COCKER SPANIEL CLUB.
Mr. G. W. Tickner, Upper House, Helions Bumpstead, Haverhill, Suffolk.

DUKERIES (NOTTS.) GUNDOG CLUB.
Major A. Scott, Croft House, Tideswell Lane, Eyam, Sheffield, S30 1RD.

EAST ANGLIAN LABRADOR RETRIEVER CLUB.
Mrs. I. G. Kinsella, The Mount, Fingringhoe, Nr. Colchester, Essex.

EASTERN COUNTIES RETRIEVER SOCIETY.
Mrs. C. A. Wentworth-Smith, The Old Rectory, Swardeston, Norwich, NOR 95W.

EASTERN COUNTIES SPANIEL SOCIETY.
Mrs. C. A. Wentworth-Smith, The Old Rectory, Swardeston, Norwich, NOR 95W.

ENGLISH SETTER CLUB.
Dr. J. B. Maurice, Batts Farm, Wilton, Marlborough, Wilts.

ENGLISH SPRINGER SPANIEL CLUB.
Mr. F. J. Robinson, The Cottage, Canwell, Sutton Coldfield, W. Midlands.

ENGLISH SPRINGER SPANIEL CLUB OF NORTHERN IRELAND.
Mr. R. E. Clemiston, Fairacres, 1 Holywood Road, Newtownards, Co. Down.

ENGLISH SPRINGER SPANIEL CLUB OF SCOTLAND.
Mrs. E. K. Thomson, Rivington Lodge, Castle Douglas, Dumfries and Galloway.

ENGLISH SPRINGER SPANIEL CLUB OF WALES.
Mr. K. Bell, 23 Welland Circle, Bettius, Newport, Dyfed.

ESSEX FIELD TRIAL SOCIETY.
Mr. L. G. Kinsella, The Mount, Fingringhoe, Nr Colchester, Essex.

FLATCOATED RETRIEVER SOCIETY.
Mrs. J. M. Marsden, Brock Cottage, Claughton-in-Brock, Preston, PR3 OPP.

FORTH AND CLYDE GUNDOG ASSOCIATION.
Mrs. M. Paton, Loanside Cottage, Clackmannan, Central, Scotland.

GAMEKEEPERS' NATIONAL ASSOCIATION.
Mr. M. Pattinson, c/o The Kennels, Loch Inch, Stranraer, Dumfries and Galloway.

GERMAN SHORTHAIRED POINTER ASSOCIATION.
Mr. H. Fisher, Firhouse, 32 Cherry Lane, Lawton Heath End, Alsger, Stoke-on-Trent.

GERMAN SHORTHAIRED POINTER CLUB.
Mrs. S. Kuban, The Hawk's Nest, Prey Heath, Mayford, Woking, Surrey.

GOLDEN RETRIEVER CLUB.
Mr. C. Lowe, Meadowcroft, Furnace Lane, Brenchley, Kent.

GOLDEN RETRIEVER CLUB OF SCOTLAND.
Mr. R. McDonald, Gaidrew Bungalow, Drymen, by Glasgow, G63 ODN.

GWYNEDD SPANIEL TRAINING CLUB.
Mrs. V. M. Davies, Coedfryn, Lower Halkyn, Holywell. Clwyd.

HERTS., BEDS., BUCKS., BERKS. AND HANTS. RETRIEVER SOCIETY,
Miss A. Hill-Wood, Knipton Lodge, Knipton, Grantham, Lincs.

HIGHLAND GUNDOG CLUB.
Mr. M. Smith, Norleigh Kennels, Drybridge, Buchie, Grampian

HUNGARIAN VIZSLA CLUB.
Mrs. D. Hunt, Hunters Lodge, Glen Close, Hindhead, Surrey, GU26 6QF.

HUNGARIAN VIZSLA SOCIETY.
Mrs. L. Petrie-Hay, Lower Bouts Farm, Inkeberrow, Worcs.

INTERNATIONAL GUNDOG LEAGUE POINTER AND SETTER SOCIETY.
Mr. and Mrs. A. Town, Rosebank, Borrowby, Thirsk, N. Yorkshire.

INTERNATIONAL GUNDOG LEAGUE RETRIEVER SOCIETY.
Mr. J. W. Taylor, 61 Peterborough Road, Castor, Nr. Peterborough.

IRISH SETTER ASSOCIATION.
Mrs. A. E. Mason, Acornbank. Bayford, Nr. Hertford, SG13 8PP.

KENNEL CLUB.
Lt.-Cdr. J. S. Williams, 1 Clarges Street, London, W1Y 8AB.

LABRADOR CLUB OF SCOTLAND.
Mr. R. J. Montgomery, Cedar Lodge, Kilsyth, Glasgow, G65 0GA.

LABRADOR RETRIEVER CLUB.
Lt.-Cdr. P. A. Whitehead, Brookmead, East Grimstead, Salisbury, Wilts.

LABRADOR RETRIEVER CLUB OF NORTHERN IRELAND.
Mr. A. Thompson, 16 Dromara Park, Old Warren, Lisburn, Co. Antrim.

LOTHIANS AND BORDERS GUNDOG ASSOCIATION.
Mr. I. Glass, Oaklands, West Road, Haddington, Lothian.

MIDLAND COUNTIES FIELD TRIAL SOCIETY.
Mrs. M. Bertrand, Cadge & Colman Ltd., East Station Road, Peterborough.

MIDLAND COUNTIES LABRADOR CLUB.
Mrs. R. H. B. Hayes, Humby Mill, Nr. Grantham, Lincs.

MIDLAND ENGLISH SPRINGER SPANIEL SOCIETY.
Mrs. J. A. Oakey, Takoradi, Eydon, Daventry, Northants.

MIDLAND GUNDOG SOCIETY.
Mr. G. A. O. Jenkin, Llangunnock, Three Ashes, S. Hereford, HR2 8LU.

MID-SUSSEX WORKING SPANIEL AND TRAINING CLUB.
Mrs. G. Newbury, 27 Balaclava Road, Surbiton, Surrey.

NORTH OF SCOTLAND GUNDOG ASSOCIATION.
Mr. D. M. Douglas, Frogfield, Laurencekirk, Grampian.

NORTH WEST LABRADOR RETRIEVER CLUB.
Mrs. N. Thornton, 6 Skippool Avenue, Poulton-le-Fylde, Lancs.

NORTH WESTERN COUNTIES FIELD TRIAL ASSOCIATION.
Mr. M. K. Walsh, 8 Patterdale Avenue, Rossall, Fleetwood, Lancs.

NORTHERN COUNTIES POINTER AND SETTER SOCIETY.
Mrs. E. J. Buist, Katewell, Evanton, Highland.

NORTHERN GOLDEN RETRIEVER ASSOCIATION.
Mrs. M. Dawson, The Poplars, Donington, Northorpe, Spalding, Lincs.

NORTHERN IRELAND POINTER CLUB.
Mr. W. R. Gardiner, 12 Swanston Crescent, Glengormly, Newtonabbey, Co. Antrim.

North West Ulster Spaniel Club.
Mr. J. Stewart, 92 Rainey Street, Magherfalet, Co. Londonderry.

Northumberland and Durham Labrador Retriever Club.
Miss E. Smith, Brooklands, 29 High Street, Gosforth, Newcastle-on-Tyne 3.

Pointer Club.
Major A. Scott, Croft House, Tideswell Lane, Eyam, Sheffield, S30 1RD.

Scottish Field Trials Association.
Mr. J. Blair, 1 Abbotsford Road, Bearsden, Nr. Glasgow.

Scottish Gundog Association.
Mr. M. M. Jamieson, Greenbank, Auchterarder, Tayside.

Scottish Spaniel Club.
Mr. D. M. Douglas, Frogfield, Laurencekirk, Grampian.

Setter and Pointer Club.
Mrs. M. Jarosz, Daneshill, Great North Road, Baldock, Herts.

South Eastern Gundog Society.
Mrs. P. Hales, White Cottage, North Chailey, Lewes, Sussex.

South West Scotland Gundog Association.
Mrs. G. S. Campbell, Montgreenan Kennels, Kilwinning, Strathclyde.

Southern and Western Counties Field Trial Society.
Mrs. M. L. Barrenger, Lane End House, Woodlands, St. Mary, Newbury, Berks.

Southern Pointer Club.
Mrs. M. Blackburne, St. Aldwyns, Milton Tundergarth, Lockerbie, Dumfries and Galloway.

Spaniel Club.
Mr. C. Sutcliffe, Newlands Cottages, Blithbury, Rugeley, Staffs.

Strathmore Working Gundog Club.
Mr. R. Methven, Lauriston, Inchture, Tayside.

Three Ridings Labrador Club.
Mr. C. W. Chase, Holly Bank, Barton on Humber, S. Humberside, DN19 7DF.

Ulster Golden Retriever Club.
Mrs. S. V. Robinson, "Erinville", 179 Monkstow Road, Newtonabbey, Co. Antrim.

Ulster Gundog League.
Mr. A. C. M. Rountree, Lisanelly House, Gortin Road, Omagh, Co. Tyrone.

Ulster Irish Red Setter Club.
Mr. J. V. Courtney, Slieve Muire, 1 Glenard Road, Culmore, Omagh, Co. Tyrone.

Ulster Retriever Club.
Mr. H. A. Wilson, Nesfield House, 71 Queensway, Lisburn, Co. Antrim, N. Ireland.

United Gundogs Breeders Association.
Mr. R. W. Moseley, Laburnum Cottage, Woodseaves, Stafford, ST20 ONP.

United Retriever Club.
Mrs. D. Compton, Fox Close, Stonely, Huntingdon, PE18 OEH.

Utility Gundog Society.
Mrs. P. Steele, Gosdens Heath, Lodsworth, Petworth, Sussex.

Weimaraner Club of Great Britain.
Mr. C. L. Church, St. Mary's, Plummers Road, Fordham, Colchester, Essex.

Welsh and English Counties Spaniel Club.
Mrs. M. M. Leopard, Lower Kimbolton Farm, Leominster, Hereford, HR6 OJA.

Welsh Kennel Club.
Mrs. M. M. Leopard, Lower Kimbolton Farm, Leominster, Hereford, HR6 OJA.

West Dartmoor Working Gundog Club.
Mr. I. T. Gussey, Brooking Lodge, Meavy Lane, Yelverton, Devon.

West Midland Field Trial Society.
Mr. C. Sutcliffe, Newlands Cottages, Blithbury, Rugeley, Staffs.

Western Counties and South Wales Spaniel Club.
Mr. A. M. Peace, 23 Durleigh Road, Bridgwater, Somerset.

Yellow Labrador Club.
Mr. H. W. Calyton, Ardmargha Cottage, Brighthampton, Witney, Oxon, OX5 7QQ.

Yorkshire Gundog Club.
Mr. B. G. Spencer, Moor Lane, Scawby, Brigg, N. Humberside, DN20 9NG.

Yorkshire Retriever Field Society.
Mr. R. F. Bilton, Rolston Hall, Hornsea, N. Humberside, HU18 1XJ.

APPENDIX C

KENNEL CLUB FIELD TRIAL RULES

Reproduced by kind permission of the Kennel Club,
1 Clarges Street, London, W.1.

10 March 1977
Amended 13 September 1977
Amended 14 December 1977

1. Definitions.—In these Rules and in any Regulations for the time being in force, unless the contrary intention appears:—

(*a*) Words importing the male sex shall include the female.

(*b*) Words in the singular shall include the plural, and words in the plural shall include the singular.

(*c*) The word 'month' shall mean a calendar month.

(*d*) The General Committee means a duly constituted meeting of the General Committee of the Kennel Club, and in so far as any powers of the General Committee have been delegated includes the delegated authority.

(*e*) Delegated Authority means a duly constituted meeting of a Sub-Committee of the General Committee of the Kennel Club, or other body to whom powers have been delegated by the Committee.

(*f*) A Society means any Club, Society or Association promoting a Field Trial and its duly appointed Committee responsible for the executive work of the Society.

(*g*) A Field Trial is a meeting for the purpose of holding competitions for the work of dogs in the field.

(*h*) A Stake is a competition held at a Field Trial.

(*i*) A Nomination is the right to enter at some subsequent date a dog to compete in a stake.

(*j*) The Draw is the selection by ballot of the order in which dogs in a stake should compete.

(*k*) A Prize is a money prize or prize of any description won in a stake, other than a Special Prize.

(*l*) An Award of Honour is not a prize but may be awarded at the discretion of the Judges to the dog officially placed reserve in any stake.

(*m*) A Diploma of Merit is not a prize, but may be awarded at the discretion of the Judges at a Championship Meeting.

(*n*) A Certificate of Merit is not a prize, but may be awarded at the discretion of the Judges in any stake.

(*o*) The Breeder of a dog is the Owner of the dam at the time of whelping, unless a variation of this definition has been effected under the Regulations for Loan or Use of Bitch for Breeding purposes.

(*p*) An Open Stake is a stake open to all dogs of a named breed, without restriction as to age or residential qualificaton of the owner, but it may be limited to a prescribed number decided by ballot.

(*q*) An All-Aged Stake is an Open Stake, but restricted by the regulations of the Society promoting the Field Trials.

2. Registrations.—The following registrations must be made at the Kennel Club prior to the date of closing of applications for nominations or of the closing of entries if no application for nomination is required and must be made on forms supplied for the purpose and in accordance with the conditions thereon. (All persons making any registration shall be considered as thereby agreeing to be bound by these rules and regulations, including particularly Rules 13 and 14):—

(*a*) The name of a dog and the particulars required on the form. When at the date of closing of applications for nominations or of entries a competitor has applied for but has not received the Kennel Club Certificate of Registration, the dog shall be entered in the name shown as first choice on the registration form and the name should be followed by the letters 'N.A.F.'

(*b*) The last transfer of ownership of a registered dog.

(*c*) Any change of the registered name of a dog.

(*d*) Re-registration in connection with any error in a previous registration.

(*e*) A name assumed for competition or breeding purposes.

(*f*) The affix of an individual or a partnership.

(*g*) The loan of a bitch for breeding purposes.

The General Committee may decline an application for any registration or cancel any registration already made.

3. Regulations.—The General Committee shall have power to make, amend, or cancel Regulations for the following purposes:—

(*a*) For classification of the breeds.

(*b*) For the registration of dogs' names, affixes, pedigrees and other registrations under Rule 2.

(*c*) With regard to entries in the Kennel Club Stud Book.

(*d*) For conducting Field Trials.

4. Stud Book Entries.—Any dog which has won a prize or Reserve or been awarded an Award of Honour, Diploma of Merit, or Certificate of Merit at Field Trials held under Kennel Club Field Trial Rules and Regulations, who complies with the Regulations for entry into the Kennel Club Stud Book, is entitled to free entry in the Stud Book.

5. Refusal of Entries.—A Society may reserve the right to refuse any entries they may think fit to exclude, without assigning any reason for so doing.

6. Nominations.—A person applying for a nomination renders himself liable for such fee or fees as are mentioned in the Schedule in accordance with the conditions stated therein.

7. Prize Money.—All prize money must be paid within one month of the date of a Field Trial, and paid subject to return in the event of a subsequent disqualification.

8. Objections and Disqualifications.—An objection to a dog must be made to the Secretary of the Society in writing at any time within twenty-one days of the last day of the meeting upon the objector lodging with the Secretary the sum of £2·00, which shall be forfeited if the objection prove frivolous. Should any objection be made which cannot at the time be substantiated or disproved, the dog may be allowed to compete under protest, the Secretary retaining any winnings until the objection has been withdrawn or decided upon.

Any appeal to the General Committee of the Kennel Club must be lodged within fourteen days of the decision being given against which it is desired to appeal.

No spectator, not being the owner of a dog competing, or his accredited representative has the right to lodge any objection to a dog or to any action taken at the meeting unless he be a member of the Committee of the Society, or the General Committee of the Kennel Club or a Steward.

A dog may be disqualified by the General Committee of the Kennel Club from winning any award, whether an objection has been lodged or not, if proved amongst other things to have been:

(*a*) Entered at a Field Trial not recognized by the General Committee of the Kennel Club.

(*b*) Entered by a person disqualified or suspended under Kennel Club Rules.

(*c*) Not entered for the Field Trial in accordance with the Regulations of the Kennel Club and the Trial and with the details recorded at the Kennel Club.

If a dog is entered in a stake for which it is ineligible and is not withdrawn before the commencement of the stake, the dog will be disqualified.

The owner of a dog disqualified for any of the above reasons is liable to forfeit all nominations and entry fees made for and all prize money won by such a dog.

The General Committee of the Kennel Club shall have power to inflict fines upon owners and handlers who have made breaches of Kennel Club Field Trial Rules or Regulations or the Regulations of the Trial, and in the event of such fines or prize money not being paid within the time stipulated by the General Committee, the owner or handler may, at the discretion of the General Committee, be dealt with as if a complaint under Field Trial Rule 13 had been lodged against him, or them and proved to the satisfaction of the General Committee.

9. The Title of Field Trial Champion.—The following dogs shall be entitled to be described as Field Trial Champions:—

Pointers and Setters.

(i) The winner of the Pointer and Setter Championship Stake

or

(ii) A dog which wins two first prizes at two different Field Trials in Open or All-Aged Stakes for Pointers and Setters in which there are no fewer than 8 runners.

One of these wins must be in a stake open to Pointers and all breeds of Setters.

Retrievers.

(i) The winner of the Retriever Championship Stake

or

(ii) A dog which wins two first prizes at two different Field Trials in Open or All-Aged Stakes for Retrievers.

One of these wins must be in a stake open to all breeds of Retrievers. In order to qualify both stakes must be for not more than 12 nominations with one day allotted for judging and not more than 24 nominations with two days allotted for judging. In 12 dog stakes there must be no fewer than 8 runners and in 24 dog stakes no fewer than 16 runners in order for the stakes to qualify.

Before a Retriever is entitled to be described as Field Trial Champion it must also have sat quietly at a drive and have passed a water test. These conditions must have been fulfilled at the Championship, in a Field Trial Stake before two Panel A Judges or at a subsequent special test before two Panel A Judges.

Cocker Spaniels.

(i) The winner of the Cocker Spaniel Championship Stake

or

(ii) A dog which wins two first prizes at two different Field Trials in Open or All-Aged Stakes for Cocker Spaniels or open to any breed of Spaniel. With the exception of the Spaniel Championship all stakes must be limited to 16 dogs and not more than 16 dogs may run on any one day, irrespective of the number of stakes. In order for the stakes to qualify there must be no fewer than 8 runners in Stakes for Cocker Spaniels and no fewer than 12 runners in Stakes open to any breed of Spaniel.

Spaniels (Other than Cocker).

(i) The winner of the Championship Stake for Spaniels (other than Cocker)

or

(ii) A dog which wins two first prizes at two different Field Trials in Open, or All-Aged Stakes for Spaniels.

With the exception of the Spaniel Championship all stakes must be limited to 16 dogs and not more than 16 dogs may run on any one day, irrespective of the number of stakes. In order for the Stakes to qualify there must be no fewer than 12 runners in each stake.

Before a Spaniel is entitled to be described as a Field Trial Champion, it must also have satisfied the requirement of Regulation 16 of the General Regulations for the Conduct of Field Trials. These requirements must have been fulfilled at the Championship, in a Field Trial Stake before two Panel A Judges or at a subsequent special test before two Panel A Judges.

Breeds which hunt, point and retrieve.

A dog which wins two first prizes at two different Field Trials in Open or All-Aged Stakes in which there are no fewer than 8 runners.

One of the above wins must be in a stake open to all breeds which hunt, point and retrieve.

For pointers and Setters, Retrievers and Spaniels, all the above wins are confined to stakes which carry a qualification for the Championship Stakes.

10. Championship Stakes.—The conditions governing Championship Stakes shall be decided by the General Committee and these conditions shall be published as early as possible each year.

11. Order of Merit following Disqualification.—If a prize winner be disqualified the dogs next in consecutive order of merit, if so placed by the Judge, and awarded not less than Reserve, shall be moved into the higher places in the Prize List and such placings shall thereupon become the awards.

12. The Kennel Club Disciplinary Sub-Committee.—The General Committee shall appoint a Sub-Committee (to be known as the Disciplinary Sub-Committee). It shall be the duty of such Disciplinary Sub-Committee to make preliminary investigations into the matter of any complaints or allegations which any person or body may seek to prefer under Rules 13 or 14. In the event of the Secretary of the Kennel Club becoming aware of any matter or matters in respect of which he is of the opinion that consideration should be given with a view to action being taken under Rules 13 or 14, he shall report the same to the Disciplinary Sub-Committee, who shall instruct him whether or not he shall prefer any complaint against any person or persons. No member of the Disciplinary Sub-Committee shall take part in any proceedings which may be brought before the General Committee under Kennel Club Field Trial Rules 13 or 14, and no person who has assisted the Sub-Committee in accordance with the provisions of Rule 9, Part III of the Constitution of the Kennel Club shall take any further part in any proceedings that may be taken in any case in which he has assisted.

13. Disciplinary Powers of the General Committee.

(i) The General Committee shall have power to inquire into and deal with any complaint which may be made against any person who has submitted to the jurisdiction of the Kennel Club. A complaint may be in respect of either:—

(*a*) Any act or conduct in regard to a dog or any matter connected with, arising out of or relating to a Field Trial, or to these Rules or any Regulations made by the General Committee which in the opinion of the General Committee is discreditable or prejuducial (or calculated to be prejudicial) to the interests of the canine world: or,

(*b*) Any default or omission in regard to any matter connected with a Field Trial or to these Rules or any Regulations made thereunder.

(ii) *Penalties.*

(a) The General Committee, if any complaint under paragraph (i) (*a*) of this Rule is proved to their satisfaction, shall have power to inflict any or all of the following penalties:—

(1) To suspend the person concerned from taking part in or having any connection with or attending any Show, Field Trial, or Working Trial or from acting as an officer for any Canine Society.

(2) To disqualify from registration or competition at the discretion of the General Committee, all dogs owned by him or registered in his name, or owned or registered by him jointly with another or others, or owned or registered in the name of a nominee, or the progeny of any dogs owned by him or owned or registered by him jointly with another or others, or owned or registered in the name of a nominee.

(3) To disqualify him from judging at, or taking part in the management of a Show, Field Trial or Working Trial.

(4) To censure and/or warn any such person.

The suspensions and disqualifications under this Rule may be for life or such shorter period as the General Committee shall fix, and the General Committee shall have the power from time to time to remove or modify any suspension or disqualification.

Any person suspended shall, during the period of such suspension, be not eligible to become or remain a member of any Club or Society registered at or affiliated with the Kennel Club. If any persons suspended under this Rule shall attend any Show, Field Trial or Working

Trial, the General Committee shall have power to increase the period of suspension and disqualification. Any person who shall employ any persons suspended or disqualified under this Rule in any capacity in connection with dogs will, if it is proved to the satisfaction of the General Committee that he knew of such suspension or disqualification, be liable to be dealt with as an offender within the meaning of the Rule.

(5) To impose a fine payable at such time and, in the event of non-payment, subject to such penalties as the General Committee may determine.

(b) The General Committee may, if any complaint under paragraph (i) (*b*) of this Rule is proved to their satisfaction, censure and/or warn any person guilty of any such default or omission, or inflict on him a fine, payable at such time as they may determine and if the person makes default in payment he shall, so long as such default shall continue, be liable to be dealt with as if he had been suspended under Rule 13 (i) (*a*).

(c) The General Committee shall have power in any case under this Rule to publish an account of the same, together with the proceedings in respect thereto in the official organ of the Kennel Club, viz. THE KENNEL GAZETTE, together with the name, description and address, and further, to publish the names of such disqualified or suspended persons under this Rule, in two separate "black lists", which they shall have power to forward to any person or persons concerned, as they may think fit.

(iii) If, on the hearing of any complaint under paragraph (i) (*a*) of this Rule, the General Committee are not satisfied that the complaint is proved but are satisfied that a default or omission under paragraph (i) (*b*) of this Rule has been proved they may find accordingly and impose the penalties (or any of them) set out in paragraph (ii) (*b*) of this Rule.

(iv) Any complaint under this Rule may be made by the Secretary of the Kennel Club on the direction of the Disciplinary Sub-Committee, or by the representative of any registered Canine Society on behalf of a Committee of the Society or by an individual who is not suspended or disqualified. Any complaint if made by an individual must be accompanied by a deposit of £5·00 which may be wholly or partly awarded, if the complaint is dismissed, to the person against whom the complaint is preferred or otherwise dealt with as the General Committee shall think fit. In any case, except under paragraph (vi) or (vii) of this Rule, the complaint shall first be referred to the Disciplinary Sub-Committee who shall give such directions as they think proper to enable the same to be brought before and heard by the General Committee.

(v) (*a*) When hearing complaints referred to it, the General Committee may appoint a solicitor or barrister to attend the meeting, who need not be a member of the Kennel Club and who may, but need not be, elected as Chairman to preside over the hearing.

(*b*) Both the complainant (whether or not the complainant is the Kennel Club) and the person complained against may be represented in the proceedings before the General Committee.

(*c*) Proceedings before the General Committee may be attended by representatives of the Canine Press and the Press Association unless both the complainant and the person complained against object in writing to the Kennel Club seven days before the hearing.

(vi) If the General Committee is satisfied that any person has been suspended or disqualified by an overseas Kennel Society with which a reciprocal agreement is in force and which has jurisdiction over him they shall suspend or disqualify that person.

(vii) If the General Committee is satisfied that any person has been convicted by a court of cruelty to a dog or of an offence involving dishonesty with regard to a dog, any competition under Kennel Club Rules or a Canine Society, or of an offence which in the opinion of the General Committee is prejudicial to the interests of the canine world, they shall inform the person concerned in a registered letter to his usual or last known place of address of his right to deliver to the General Committee within a period of twenty-one days a written statement regarding any circumstances of his case which he may wish the General Committee to consider. After considering such written statement or after twenty-one days have elapsed without such statement being received, the General Committee shall decide on the action if any to be taken and shall have power to impose any or all the penalties listed in paragraph (ii) (*a*) of this Rule.

14. Where any person who has not agreed to submit to the jurisdiction of the Kennel Club is alleged to have done any act, or been guilty of any conduct or omission in respect of which a complaint could have been made under Rule 13 if such person had submitted to the jurisdiction of the Kennel Club, such allegation may be referred to the Disciplinary Sub-Committee who, if satisfied that it would be proper to bring the matter of such allegation before the General Committee, may direct the Secretary of the Kennel Club to invite such person to attend before the General Committee. Any allegation under this Rule may be made in like manner as a com-

plaint under Rule 13 and the Disciplinary Sub-Committee shall give such directions as they think proper to the person or body making such allegation to enable the same to be brought before and heard by the General Committee. The General Committee shall have power to inquire into the matter of any such allegation, and if the same is proved to their satisfaction may impose on the person or body concerned such penalty or penalties as set out in Rule 13 as would be applicable were the act, default or omission the subject-matter of a complaint under Rule 13 save that the General Committee shall have no power to impose any fine on any such person.

15. Delegated Powers.—The powers conferred on the General Committee under these Rules, except Rule 3 (*a*, *b* and *c*), are delegated to the Field Trials Committee, but subject to a right of appeal to the General Committee from a decision under Rules 13 and 14.

16. General Committee the Sole Authority.—The General Committee of the Kennel Club shall be the final court of appeal or umpire in all questions or disputes of any kind whatsoever arising from the competing of any dog at any Field Trials held under the Kennel Club Field Trial Rules, and whether such dispute be between two or more subscribers, or between subscriber or subscribers and the General Committee or Secretary, Veterinary Inspector, or Judge or Judges, of such Field Trials, or between any or more of such parties and another or others of them, and any person or persons acting in any of the capacities above mentioned at any Field Trials held under the Kennel Club Field Trial Rules shall be deemed thereby to agree to refer any disputes which may arise between them or any of them to the General Committee of the Kennel Club whose decisions shall be final and binding.

GENERAL REGULATIONS FOR THE CONDUCT OF FIELD TRIALS

Definitions.

(i) A Puppy is a dog whelped not earlier than the 1st January in the year preceding the date of the Field Trials, but in any stake run in January a dog which was a puppy in the previous month shall be deemed to be a puppy.

(ii) Novice or Non-Winners Stakes for Spaniels, unless otherwise stated, are confined to dogs which have not won a First Prize other than in Puppy, Brace or Team Stakes prior to the closing of entries.

(iii) A Brace Stake is a stake for two dogs of the same breed entered as a Brace by the same owner.

(iv) A Team Stake is a stake for three or more dogs of the same breed entered as a Team by the same owner.

1 (a) THE SCHEDULE.

A Society holding a Field Trial must issue a Schedule which is to be treated as a contract between the Society and the public. No modification may be made except by permisssion of the Kennel Club, followed by advertisement in suitable papers if time permits before the closing of entries. The Secretary of the Society shall send a copy of the Schedule to the Kennel Club within 3 days of printing. The Schedule must contain:—

(i) The date and place of the Field Trial, and number of nominations accepted.
(ii) The latest date for applying for a nomination if such is required.
(iii) The latest date for receiving entries.
(iv) The amounts of nomination and/or entry fees and of prize money.
(v) The conditions for the Draw and for intimating acceptance or refusal of a nomination.
(vi) A statement that the Field Trial is held under these Rules and Regulations.
(vii) A definition of any Stake not defined in these Rules, or Regulations.
(viii) The names of the Judges, where possible.
(ix) The order in which the Stakes will be run.
(x) A statement of the proportion of entry fee to be returned to entrants should any stake have to be abandoned owing to the weather being unfit.
(xi) For Retrievers and Spaniels, if the Trial includes an Open or All-Aged Stake, an indication of whether that Stake carries a qualification for the Championship.

THE CARD.

A Society holding a Field Trial must publish a Card which must contain:

On the front outside cover
(i) The name of the Society.
(ii) The breed(s) for which stakes are run at the Trial.
(iii) Date(s) of the Trial.
(iv) For Retrievers and Spaniels, if the Trial includes an Open or All-Aged Stake, an indication of whether that Stake carries qualification for the Championship.
(v) Names of the Judges.
(vi) Venue of the Trial.

Contents
(i) A definition of each stake to be run in the Trial.
(ii) The prizes offered.
(iii) Entries listed in numerical order as follows:
Registered name of dog.
Name of Owner.
Breed of dog.

Sex of dog.
Date of birth.
Registered names of sire and dam.
Name of breeder.
Name of handler.

(iv) A list of the names and addresses of owners of all dogs in the Trial in alphabetical order.
The Secretary of the Society shall send to the Kennel Club within one week of the meeting a copy of the entry card with all awards marked thereon.

(v) A statement that the Trial is held under Kennel Club Field Trials Rules and Regulations.

(vi) A statement that the Society accepts no responsibility for injury, loss or damage to person or property however occasioned.

2. Copy of Rules.—The Secretary of the Society shall send a copy of these Rules to any applicant and shall have a copy with him or his representative on the ground during a meeting.

3. Awards.—Equal awards for any of the prizes offered at a Field Trial are prohibited.

4. Record of Entries.—The Secretary shall preserve all entry forms for six months after the meeting, and produce any of them to any official body inquiring into an objection or dispute.

5. Appointment of Judges.—The Judges shall be appointed by the Society. The Committee shall issue to Field Trial Societies Panels of Judges for Field Trials for Retrievers, Spaniels, Pointers and Setters, and breeds which hunt, point and retrieve. Before a Judge can be considered for addition to any panel he must be recommended by a Field Trial Society for which he has judged. The qualifications required before a Judge can be added to a Panel are:—

Panel A. Retrievers and Spaniels.

Before a Judge can be added to this Panel he must have judged at least two Open Stakes and two other Stakes run under Kennel Club Field Trial Rules and Regulations and held by two different Societies registered with the Kennel Club.

Panel A. Pointers and Setters.

Before a Judge can be added to this Panel he must have judged at least two Stakes.

Panel A. Breeds which hunt, point and retrieve.

Before a Judge can be added to this panel he must have judged at least two Stakes, one of which must be an Open Stake.

Panel B. Retrievers and Spaniels.

Before a Judge can be added to this panel he must have judged at least two Stakes.

Panel B. Pointers and Setters.

Before a Judge can be added to this Panel he must have judged at least one Stake.

Panel B. Breeds which hunt, point and retrieve.

Before a Judge can be added to this panel he must have judged at least two Stakes.

The compulsory number of Panel A Judges for the various Stakes is as follows:

	Retrievers	Spaniels	Pointers and Setters	Breeds which hunt, point and retrieve.
Championship	All A	All A	All A	——
Open and All-Aged Stakes	2 A	1 A	1 A	1 A
Non-Winner and other Stakes	1 A	1 A	1 A	1 A

The General Committee shall have power to add names to the Panels from time to time and also to remove names at their discretion.

The General Committee may at its discretion take into account the experience of Judges at Field Trials held under the Irish Kennel Club Field Trial Rules and Regulations when considering the addition of names to the Panels.

When there are four Judges for a Stake they must judge in pairs, each pair watching the work jointly of one dog at the same time. Each pair of Judges must decide between themselves which of them is to give the commands.

If only two of the four Judges are on Panel A they must not judge together but must each take one of the Judges not on Panel A as their co-Judge.

No judge shall shoot at a Field Trial at which he is judging.

The Secretary of a Field Trial must include a copy of the Guide to Field Trial Judges R(3), issued by the Kennel Club Field Trials Committee, in the Judges' book.

6. Nominations.—A nomination is the right to enter at some future date a dog owned and registered at the Kennel Club in the name of the applicant for the nomination. If a partnership of two or more persons make application for a nomination for the partnership, then only one of the partners shall be permitted to apply for a separate nomination for a dog registered at the Kennel Club in his sole ownership. If applications exceed the number of nominations available, the right to a nomination shall be decided by ballot. If a nomination be not returned to the Secretary of the Society by a date specified in the Schedule the applicant will be held to have accepted it and be liable for the full entry fee, unless the Secretary can transfer the nomination to some other applicant.

7. Reducing Prize Money.—If the full number of nominations be not applied for or nominations not accepted cannot be transferred to other applicants, the prizes may be reduced at the option of the Society.

The amount of Prize Money offered by a Society may be made to depend on the number of entries received.

8. ORDER OF RUNNING,—The Draw shall take place at such time and in such conditions as are stated in the Schedule, and at it each dog must be given the number that accords with its place in the Draw, and every dog must be tried in order of draw.

9. MANAGEMENT AT FIELD TRIALS.—The management of a Field Trial shall be entrusted to the Society, who shall decide any disputed question by a majority of those present.

Secretaries of Field Trials must ensure that a handler and dog are always available to pick up wounded game when required.

10. WEATHER CONDITIONS.—If the Society considers the weather unfit for holding the Trial, the stake or stakes may be cancelled and a proportion of the entry fees, decided by the Society and published in the Schedule, shall be returned to entrants; or a fresh draw may be made and a fresh date fixed for the abandoned stake or stakes.

11. HANDLING OF DOGS.—If a deputy handles a dog, the owner may be in the line but must take no part in the working of the dog. All handlers must obey the orders of the judges. Handlers will not be allowed to carry in their hand gun, stick, whip, shooting stick, or lead, whilst handling their dogs, but in cases of physical disability a shooting stick may be carried with the permission of the Judges. A Spaniel Society may, however, hold a Special Stake in which it is compulsory for all handlers to shoot over their dogs.

No handler may handle more than 3 dogs in any single dog Stake for Retrievers or Spaniels, or more than 5 dogs in any single dog Stake for Pointers and Setters.

When there are four Judges at a Retriever Trial there is no objection to relatives of Judges running dogs.

When called up by the Judges, a handler may wear only the armband relevant to the dog being judged.

12. DOGS UNDER TRIAL.—The control of all matters connected with dogs under trial shall rest with the Judges of the meeting, but they may call the Secretary to their assistance if they think fit.

The Judges are empowered to turn out of the Stake any dog whose handler does not obey them, or wilfully interferes with another conpetitor or his dog.

13. PHYSICAL CONDITIONS.—Should the members of the Committee present, after consultation with the judges, consider a dog is unfit to compete by reason of sexual causes or of any contagious disease or from an attack of hysteria occurring on the ground or any other cause which interferes with the safety or chance of winning of his opponents, such dog must be removed immediately from the ground and from the Trials. Any such case is liable to be reported to the Kennel Club and dealt with under Rules 13 or 14.

If a dog competes which has been exposed to the risk of any

contagious or infectious disease during the period of six weeks prior to the Field Trial and/or if any dog shall be proved to be suffering at a Field Trial from any contagious or infectious disease, including contagious results of inoculations against distemper, the owner thereof shall be liable to be dealt with under Rule 13.

14. UNPUNCTUALITY.—A dog which is not present when required by a Judge may be disqualified.

15. DISCARDING DOGS.—No dog shall be discarded until it has been tried by two Judges except that it shall be discarded if it has run in or chased or refused to enter water or if two Judges concur that the dog is out of control of his handler or is held to have a hard mouth; but all the Judges must have examined the injured game before the dog is discarded for hard mouth.

The handler should be given the opportunity of examining the damaged game in the presence of the Judges, but the decision of the Judges is final.

A dog which whines or barks in the opinion of a Judge shall be discarded from the Stake.

In the Retriever Championship Stake the discarding of dogs shall be entirely at the discretion of the Judges.

16. WATER TEST.—A Water Test requires a dog to enter water readily and swim. In Retriever and Spaniel Stakes and Stakes for Breeds which hunt, point and retrieve, a dog which fails a Water Test shall not receive an award in that Stake. If a Water Test is held, all dogs placed in the awards must have passed this test. A handler is not entitled to ask for a shot to be fired. A Special Water Test conducted in accordance with the provisions of Field Trial Rule 9—Title of Field Trial Champion must be held between 1 October and 1 February.

17. AWARDS OF HONOUR, DIPLOMAS OF MERIT AND CERTIFICATES OF MERIT.—Judges shall be empowered to award Diplomas of Merit in Championship Stakes and Certificates of Merit in all other Stakes to those dogs, apart from the prize winners, which have, in their opinion, acquitted themselves sufficiently well to warrant them.

A dog officially placed Reserve shall receive an Award of Honour or a Certificate of Merit at the discretion of the Judges. At a Championship meeting a dog officially placed Reserve shall receive an Award of Honour or a Diploma of Merit at the discretion of the Judges.

18. WITHHOLDING PRIZES.—The Judges are empowered and instructed to withhold and prize or award if, in their opinion, the dogs competing do not show sufficient merit.

19. WITHDRAWAL OF DOGS.—No dog entered for competition and once under a Judge at the Trial may be withdrawn from competition without the consent of the Society.

No competitor may leave the field without the permission of the Judges or Society and any dog so removed is liable to disqualification.

20. Impugning Decisions.—Anyone taking part in a Trial openly impugning the decision of the Judge or Judges shall render himself liable to be reported to the Field Trials Committee of the Kennel Club under the provisions of Kennel Club Field Trial Rule No. 13.

21. Qualifying Certificates.—A Gundog which has won one or more Challenge Certificates at Shows may be entered for a Qualifying Certificate at a Field Trial Meeting for its breed provided that:—

1. For Retrievers, the Society holding the Meeting is recognized for the Retriever Championship Stake and that two of the Judges awarding the Qualifying Certificate appear on the Official Judges Panel "A" for Retrievers.
2. For Spaniels, the Society holding the Meeting is recognized for the Spaniel Championship Stake and that one of the Judges awarding the Qualifying Certificate appears on the Official Judges Panel "A" for Spaniels.
3. For Pointers and Setters, that the Society holding the Meeting is recognized for the Pointer and Setter Championship Stake and that one of the Judges awarding the Qualifying Certificate is on the Official Judges Panel "A" for Pointers and Setters.
4. For breeds which hunt, point and retrieve, that one of the Judges awarding the Qualifying Certificate is on the Official Judges Panel "A" for these breeds.
5. (*a*) The permission of the Society holding the Trial must be obtained and the dog must be entered on the entry form of the meeting. The fee charged by the Society must not exceed £5.00.

(*b*) A dog may not run for a Qualifying Certificate more than three times in all and not more than twice in any one Field Trial season.

(*c*) All dogs entered for Qualifying Certificates must be tested during the morning.

(*d*) The granting of Qualifying Certificates shall be at the discretion of the Judges at the meeting and all Judges must sign the Certificate.

(*e*) Before signing a certificate the Judges must be satisfied that the dog fulfils the following requirements:—

(1) that the dog has been tested in the line; (2) that the dog has shown that it is not gun-shy and was off the lead during gun-fire; (3) for a Pointer or setter that it hunts and points; (4) for breeds which hunt, point and retrieve that it hunts, points and retrieves tenderly and enters water and swims; (5) for a Retriever, that it hunts

and retrieves tenderly; (6) for a Spaniel, that it hunts, faces covert and retrieves tenderly; (7) Steadiness is not absolutely essential for a Qualifying Certificate.

6. A Gundog which has won one or more first prizes in a Class for its breed at a Show where Challenge Certificates are offered for the breed, may be entered for a Qualifying Certificate at a Specialist Club Qualifying Trial provided that Judge of Judges of the Trial are on Panel A for the breed and subject to Regulations 5 (*d*) and (*e*) above.

22. Contingencies.—Any event not provided for in these Rules and Regulations shall be decided by the members present of the Committee of the Society assisted by the Judges, and their decision shall be final.

FIELD TRIAL REGULATIONS FOR VARIOUS BREEDS

POINTERS AND SETTERS

Arrangements for Conduct of Field Trials.—Immediately before the dogs are drawn at any meeting, and before nine o'clock on every subsequent evening during the continuance of such meeting, the time and place of meeting on the following morning shall be declared. A card or counter bearing a corresponding number shall be assigned to each entry. These numbered cards or counters shall then be placed together and drawn indiscriminately. At the conclusion of each round the judges shall select such dogs as they consider have shown enough merit to entitle them to remain in the stake, and a fresh draw shall be made among these dogs for the next round. When not more than six dogs are left in the stake no further draw shall take place, but the judges shall run such dogs in such pairs as they think fit, and place them in order of merit.

2. Order in which Stakes shall be Run.—The stakes shall be run in the order they are given on the programme, unless the competitors, or their representatives, in the various stakes may agree otherwise—in which case the order may be changed, with the consent of the stewards of the meeting.

Plural Nominations.—When more than one nomination in a stake is taken in one name, the dogs, if *bona fide* the property of the same owner, shall be guarded in every round, where possible, when a draw takes place.

4. Byes.—When in any round in a stake the number of dogs is unequal, the dog whose number is drawn last shall be given a bye. No dog shall have a second such bye in the stake unless it is unavoidable.

5. Order in which Dogs are to be Brought Up.—Every dog shall be brought up in its proper turn, without delay. If absent for more than a quarter of an hour, when called, that dog shall be liable

to be disqualified by the judge or judges, and its opponent shall run a bye if required by them to do so. If both dogs be absent at the expiration of a quarter of an hour after being called, the judge or judges shall have the power of disqualifying them both.

6. REGULATIONS REGARDING HANDLING.—A person handling a dog may speak, whistle, and work him by hand as he thinks proper; but he can be called to order by the judge or judges for making any unnecessary noise, and if he persists in doing so they can order the dog to be taken up, and put him out of the stake.

Dogs must be worked together, and their handlers must walk within a reasonable distance of one another, as though shooting together. After a caution, the judge or judges may have the power of fining the handler the sum of £1, or of disqualifying the dog whose handler persists in neglecting this Rule.

7. DOGS MAY BE REQUIRED TO WEAR COLLARS.— The judges may require any brace of dogs to wear distinguishing collars of red and white. The red collar shall be placed on the dog which has the smaller number on the card.

8. COMPETING DOGS MUST BE SHOT OVER.—Every competing dog must have been shot over before it can gain a prize or certificate of merit, and satisfy the judges that it is not gun-shy.

RETRIEVERS

1. COMPETING.—The dog with the lowest number under each Judge shall be placed on his right. After all the competing dogs have been tried under two Judges, the judges may call up at their own discretion any dogs they require further and try them again.

2. RETRIEVING FUR AND FEATHER.—All dogs running in stakes other than Puppy, will be expected to retrieve fur as well as feather. In a Puppy Stake they will not be compelled to retrieve fur.

3. "DRIVING" and "WALKING-UP".—Where possible, all dogs should be tested, driving, walking-up and in water.

4. Dogs must not wear any form of collar when under the orders of the judges.

SPANIELS

1. ENTRIES, NOMINATIONS, ETC.—The Committee of the Field Trial meeting may make its own arrangements as regards dates of closing of entries, filling of nominations and conditions of stakes. Subject to the following a Society may give preference to its own members.

Preference in the draw for Open and All-Aged Stakes which qualify for the Spaniel Championships shall be given in the following order:—

(*a*) Members' dogs which have been placed First, Second or Third in an Open or All-Aged Stake or First in a Novice Stake.

(*b*) Non-members' dogs which have been placed First, Second or Third in an Open or All-Aged Stake or First in a Novice Stake.

(*c*) Members' dogs which have gained other awards.

(*d*) Non-members' dogs which have gained other awards.

The foregoing awards must have been gained during the season then current or in the two seasons preceding it in a Stake qualifying for entry in the Kennel Club Stud Book.

The Stake may then be filled by other dogs. The entry form for a Qualifying Open or All-Aged Stake at a Field Trial shall provide a space where the owner must state the highest award obtained by his dog and its date. The application to enter a dog in such Stake applies to that named dog and is not an application for a nomination. Should the dog be drawn to run in the Stake and then be withdrawn for any reason, the owner may not run a substituted dog in its place even though it may have gained the same qualification unless all the reserve dogs have had the opportunity to run in the Stake.

2. Running of Dogs in Single Stakes.—Dogs must be run either singly or in pairs but not more than two dogs may be tried at the same time, even should there be more than two Judges. With the exception of the Spaniel Championship all stakes must be limited to 16 dogs and not more than 16 dogs may run on any one day, irrespective of the number of stakes.

3. Judges may call up any Dog.—After the first round of a stake being completed the Judges may call up any dogs they please and in any order.

4. Dogs must not wear any form of collar when under the orders of the Judges.

5. At all Spaniel Field Trials, a referee shall be appointed in addition to the judges and his identity disclosed to the competitors.

BREEDS WHICH HUNT, POINT AND RETRIEVE

1. Dogs shall be run singly under two judges.

2. Dogs shall be required to quarter ground in search of game, to point game, to be steady to flush, shot and fall, and to retrieve on command.

3. Water Retrieve.—Dogs shall be required (i) in Puppy, Novice and Non-Winner stakes to retrieve from or across water a seen bird which has been thrown and shot at whilst in the air, (ii) in all other stakes to make a blind retrieve of a bird from across water, re-entering the water, where practicable, with the bird and with no shot fired.

4. Dogs must not wear any form of collar when under the orders of the judges. All dogs must be kept on a lead when not competing.

5. Any dog which in the opinion of the judges fails to hunt, point, retrieve tenderly, complete the water test, is gun-shy, or is out of control shall not receive any prize. Any dog in any stake must have been tried at least twice in the line, excluding the water retrieve, before receiving a prize.

6. Eliminations.—Whining or barking, out of control, chasing: failure to hunt, point, retrieve, enter water and swim, face cover: hard mouth: deliberately catching unwounded game.

APPENDIX D

GUIDE TO FIELD TRIAL JUDGES
25th July, 1972

Issued by the Kennel Club Field Trials Committee

These notes are designed to assist Judges in selecting the best shooting dogs. They are not intended to be rules, as these have already been laid down by the Kennel Club. The Field Trial Rules and Regulations and also the Field Trial Council recommendations, approved by the Kennel Club Field Trials Committee, can be obtained from the Kennel Club free of charge.

No Judge should accept an invitation to judge Trials unless he is fully conversant with these Rules and Regulations and has studied the Guide to Field Trial Judges.

The Secretary of a Field Trial should ensure that each of the Judges at a Field Trial has a copy of this Guide.

RETRIEVERS

1. At the start of a Field Trial, Judges should make sure that they have the correct dogs in the line, lowest number on the right.

2. Judges should take gamefinding to be of the first importance in Field Trials.

3. Judges at Open Retriever Stakes are advised to ask their Guns not to shoot directly over a dog when it is out working. In Puppy, Novice and Non-Winner Stakes, Judges are advised to ask their Guns not to shoot when a dog is out working.

4. All wounded game must be gathered as expeditiously as possible and must be killed at the earliest opportunity. Wounded game must be recovered before dead game. If a Judge cannot gather wounded game, he must be careful to depute this task to the official handler and dog appointed for this purpose.

5. If a bird is shot very close to a dog which would make the retrieve of no value, the Judge should pick the bird by hand or offer it to another Judge. During the first round of the Stake, dogs should have the opportunity on game shot by their own guns.

6. After all the dogs have been tried once, Judges may call up for trial any dog at their discretion.

7. Judges should be most careful to see that each dog gets its chance in the correct order, starting with the lowest number on the right. Should dog No. 1 fail, and dog No. 2 be successful, No. 2 still has the first chance in the next retrieve. It is quite unfair to give a dog two first chances in succession and the other dog two second chances. If the two dogs fail on a bird, the Judge should not call

fresh dogs into the line to try for the bird until dogs already in the line have been tried. In the concluding stages of a Trial, Judges may use their own discretion as the situation arises.

8. In the first round of a Stake, if the amount of game permits, a dog should have a minimum of two opportunities to retrieve before the next dog is called up, but the actual number of retrieves is at the discretion of the Judges according to the merit of the work done.

9. When a number of dogs have been tried and have failed on a bird, the Judge should not look for it unless all the Judges agree that no more dogs should be tried. Once Judges have looked for and found a bird, no more dogs should be tried on it.

10. Handlers should be instructed where to try from and given reasonable directions as to where the game fell.

11. Good marking is essential in a Retriever as he should not disturb game unnecessarily. Judges should give full credit to a dog which goes straight to the fall and gets on with the job.

12. At a drive, the placing of the dogs shall be at the discretion of the Judge with the lowest number on the right. The Kennel Club Field Trial Rules state that a dog which whines or barks in the opinion of a Judge shall be discarded from the Stake.

13. A dog must walk steadily to heel.

14. The perfect pick-up should be quick with a fast return. The handler should not snatch or drag the game from the dog's mouth. Judges should not penalize a dog too heavily for putting a bird down to get a firmer grip, but this must not, however, be confused with sloppy retrieving. A good gamefinding dog should not rely on the handler to find the bird. He should, however, be obedient and respond to his handler's signals when necessary. Dogs showing gamefinding ability and initiative should be placed above those which have to be handled on to their game. Usually, the best dog seems to require the least handling. He appears to have an instinctive knowledge of direction and makes difficult finds look simple and easy. Steadiness to fur is most important and, where possible, dogs should be given fur to retrieve.

15. If a dog is performing indifferently on a runner, it should be called up promptly. If three or more dogs are tried on a runner, the work of all these dogs must be assessed in relation to the order in which they are tried.

16. If a bird is known to have run, the handlers of the second and subsequent dogs down should be allowed to take their dogs towards the fall, and the first dog also if he has not had a chance to mark the bird.

17. A dog which has its eye wiped on a dead bird should be penalized but all eye-wipes should be treated on their merits.

If a dog shows ability by acknowledging the fall and making a workman-like job of the line, it should not automatically be barred from the prize list by failing to produce the bird providing that the bird is not collected by another dog tried by the Judges on the same bird.

18. All game should be examined for signs of "hard mouth". A hard-mouthed dog seldom gives visible evidence of hardness. He will simply crush in one or both sides of the ribs. Blowing up the feathers will not disclose the damage. Place the bird on the palm of the hand, breast upwards, head forward, and feel the ribs with finger and thumb. They should be round and firm. If they are caved in or flat, this is definite evidence of hard mouth. Be sure the bird reaches your co-Judges for examination. There should be no hesitation or sentiment with "hard mouth"—the dog should be discarded. A certain indication of a good mouth is a dog bringing in a live bird whose head is up and eye bright. Superficial damage, if any, in this case can be ignored. At times, the rump of a strong runner may be gashed and look ugly. Care should be taken here, as it may be the result of a difficult capture or lack of experience in mastering a strong runner by a young dog. Judges should always satisfy themselves that any damage done has been caused by the dog, not by the shot or fall, and in cases of doubt, the benefit should be given to the dog. Handlers should be given the opportunity of inspecting the damaged game in the presence of the Judges, but the decision of the Judges is final.

19. If more than one bird is down and the dog changes birds on his way back, he should be severely penalized.

20. The standard of work in Stakes carrying Field Trial Championship status should be higher than in Novice, Non-Winner and Puppy Stakes, where more leniency is allowed.

21. Judges should keep their opinions strictly to themselves and act on what happens on the day or days of the Trials at which they are judging, forgetting past performances at previous Trials.

22. Judges are advised to place each dog in a category such as A, B and C, according to the work done at the end of each round.

23. In the concluding stages of a Trial, the dogs should all be in the centre under all the Judges.

24. It is advisable to take short notes of each dog's work and not to trust to memory.

25. It is in the interests of all Field Trial supporters that Judges should be as courteous and co-operative as possible with the Host and Steward of the Beat and fall in with their arrangements. This goes a long way towards making a success of the Trial and the possibility of receiving an invitation for another year.

26. Summary of Points.

Eliminating faults: Hard mouth—Whining or barking—Running in and chasing—Out of control—Failing to enter water.

Major faults: Failing to find game—Unsteadiness at heel—Eye wipe—Disturbing ground—Slack and unbusinesslike work—Noisy handling—Poor control—Changing birds.

Credit points: Natural gamefinding ability—Nose—Marking ability—Drive—Style—Quickness in gathering game—Control—Quietness in handling—Retrieving and delivery.

SPANIELS

NOTE: The attention of Judges is particularly drawn to paragraph 11 of this section which deals with duties of a Referee.

1. Before starting a Trial, Judges should ask the Steward of the Beat what the game position is likely to be and regulate the number of retrieves to each dog accordingly. They should also satisfy themselves that arrangements have been made for the collection of dead or wounded game which they do not require.

2. A Field Trial should be run as nearly as possible to an ordinary day's shooting, and artificial retrieves should be restricted to a minimum.

3. A Spaniel should at all times work in range with good treatment of ground; under no circumstances should it pass over game on the beat it is working. A Spaniel's first job is to find game and flush within range of the gun. The direction of the wind has a considerable influence on the way a dog will work ground. With a head-on wind, the dog should quarter the ground systematically left to right and *vice versa*, making good all likely game-holding cover, but keeping within gunshot distance of the handler. With a following wind it will be very different. The dog will often want to pull well out, then work back towards the handler. Judges should regulate the pace of the line to allow the dog to do this and make good his ground. Often a dog has been penalized for missing game when, in fact, the line has been moving forward too fast to permit the dog to make good the ground. Lines and foot scents should be ignored. Persistent "pulling on" on foot scents is annoying and unprofitable, resulting in game being missed. During this period, the Judge can assess the gamefinding ability and nose of the dog, also pace, drive, treatment of ground and possibly courage.

4. A dog which catches un-shot game should be discarded unless in the opinion of the Judges there are extenuating circumstances. Should a dog indicate or strike at game without effect, the handler may "stop" his dog and appeal to the Judges for permission to flush the game.

5. If a dog points or hesitates slightly before flushing, this is an added refinement, but the dog must flush on command.

6. A dog should "stop" to game and shot automatically, but if a dog moves a little in order to mark the fall, if this is obscured, this shows intelligence and should be credited. For instance, in thick cover, a dog should push game into the open and check after doing so.

7. Good marking should always be looked for and given full credit, and bad marking penalized.

If a dog shows ability by acknowledging the fall and making a workman-like job of the line, it should not automatically be barred from the prize list by failing to produce the bird providing that the bird is not collected by another dog tried by the Judges on the same bird.

8. A Spaniel should pick up cleanly, return quickly and deliver well up to hand. Such a retrieve is desirable, but too much should not be made of a momentary check, particularly through cover, as the dog may have had a long, gruelling hunt up to the time of flushing and thus making the retrieve possible, and this should be allowed for.

On no occasion should a dog be sent on a long, blind retrieve, but should be taken to within a reasonable distance of the fall, bearing conditions in mind, Normally, it is unwise to try more than two dogs on one retrieve.

9. All game should be examined for signs of "hard mouth". A hard-mouthed dog seldom gives visible evidence of hardness. He will simply crush in one or both sides of the bird. Blowing up the feathers will not disclose the damage. Place the bird on the palm of the hand, breast upwards, head forward, and feel the ribs with finger and thumb. They should be round and firm. If they are caved in or flat, this is definite evidence of hard mouth. Be sure the bird reaches your co-Judges for examination. There should be no hesitation or sentiment with "hard mouth"—the dog should be discarded. A certain indication of a good mouth is a dog bringing in a live bird whose head is up and eye bright. Superficial damage, if any, in this case can be ignored. At times, the rump of a strong runner may be gashed and look ugly. Care should be taken here, as it may be the result of a difficult capture or lack of experience in mastering a strong runner by a young dog. Judges should always satisfy themselves that any damage done has been caused by the dog, not by the shot or fall, and, in cases of doubt, the benefit should be given to the dog. Handlers should be given the opportunity of inspecting the damaged game in the presence of the Judges but the decision of the Judges is final.

10. A dog should have drive and thrust and face cover well, and, at the same time, should be amenable and gay—in short a pleasure to watch. It should show good treatment of ground with the minimum of help from its handler. All things being equal, the stylish dog should be given the credit. Judges should, however, be satisfied that the fast stylish dog is also the best gamefinder.

11. A Referee should not take any part whatever in the judging of a Stake unless the Judges appeal to him to settle a point or an award on which they cannot agree, but he should make notes on the work of the dogs. When a dog has been under two Judges and they both agree, and feel certain that this is their best dog, they are quite

in order in putting it on one side and running off for the remaining places.

12. Judges are advised to place each dog in a category such as A, B and C according to the work done at the end of each run, and usually they will find little difficulty in getting down to the placings. With dogs of equal merit, they can be divided by running them side by side. The main consideration should now be style, pace, ground treatment, and the dog's response to the handler. Judges should walk side by side, and the dogs work wide by side, but not encroach on each other's beats.

13. A Judge should refrain from talking to anyone while the dog is actively competing under him. From the moment the dog starts questing, he should make every effort to keep that dog in view and so place himself, when the dog is sent out for a retrieve, to enable him to observe every move of the dog until the game is delivered to hand.

14. It is advisable to take short notes of each dog's work and not trust to memory.

15. SUMMARY OF POINTS.

Eliminating faults: Hard mouth—Whining or Barking—Running in and chasing—Out of Control—Failing to enter water—Deliberately catching unwounded game (elimination for this fault is at the Judges' discretion.)

Major faults: Failing to find game—Not quartering and not making ground good—Not stopping to shot and game—Disturbing ground—Noisy handling—Poor control.

Credit points: Natural gamefinding ability—Nose—Drive—Marking ability—Style—Control—Quickness in gathering game—Quietness in handling—Retrieving and delivery.

POINTERS AND SETTERS

1. The task of Judges is to find the dog which, on the day, pleases them most by the quality of its work from the shooting point of view.

2. It is the duty of Judges to give the dogs every opportunity to work well by seeing that conditions are in their favour as far as possible, and also, where feasible, to demonstrate to competitors and spectators how their decisions are reached. It is the better dogs who should be fully tried and not the hopeless ones.

3. The first round, having been drawn in accordance with the rules, should be proceeded with as rapidly as possible. Each brace, except in cases of undoubted lack of merit, should be tried for at least 15 minutes. "Undoubted lack of merit" is behaviour which convinces the Judges that no Certificate of Merit can be awarded to the dog concerned. When this has been confirmed by consultation

between the Judges, the brace should be picked up, or a bye dog, if available, tried with the survivor.

4. Stickiness on point should be severely penalized.

5. If a dog deliberately gallops into game up wind, he should be discarded, but if, on the other hand, he is coming down wind and drops immediately the birds rise, this does not constitute a flush. Chasing live game, be it fur or feather, must put a dog out of the Stake.

6. Dogs should be penalized if they do not drop to shot.

7. Judges should appreciate that different breeds have different styles of working, and should make themselves conversant with these styles.

8. Persistent false point should be severely penalized.

9. Full credit should be given to a dog which backs naturally.

10. Noisy handling should be penalized.

11. Finding the winner should consist of taking into consideration the whole quality of the dog's work, not just the number of points he has made. Gamefinding, of course, is essential, but the dog's whole method of working should be a pleasure to watch, such as quartering his ground methodically, and making it all good, natural backing, steadiness and style on point, and pace. Though the Trial should not be run as a "knock-out" competition, it is desirable, if possible, that the winner should have run against the second and the third against the fourth. Otherwise, variation in the conditions of scent and presence of game make too great a difference in the results and tend to over-emphasize the luck of the draw.

12. Judges should exercise considerable control over the proceedings and endeavour to get the dogs running in favourable wind. They should also conserve the ground by being as decisive as possible.

13. Judges should keep up with the handlers and try to see everything that takes place at a Trial. Frequently, a Judge is two or three hundred yards behind and is unable to see all the work. This does not mean that he should try and keep up with a dog that is obviously running out of his ground.

14. It is advisable to take short notes of each dog's work and not trust to memory.

15. Judges are advised to place each dog in a category such as A, B and C, according to the work done at the end of each round.

16. SUMMARY OF POINTS.

Eliminating faults: Flushing up wind—Out of control—Chasing fur or feather.

Major faults: Not quartering and not making ground good—Not dropping to shot—Stickiness on point—Not dropping to flush down wind—Missing birds.

Credit points: Game finding—Natural backing—Style on point—Pace—Quartering.

BREEDS WHICH HUNT, POINT AND RETRIEVE

1. Trials should be run as nearly as possible to an ordinary day's shooting. Judges are responsible for the proper conduct of the Trial in accordance with Kennel Club Regulations and with the Schedule for the Stake. They should co-operate with the Host and the Steward of the Beat to achieve the best result in an atmosphere of friendliness and confidence. If conditions force them to depart from usual practice they should explain the reasons to handlers and spectators. Guns and handlers should be briefed at the start.

2. Judges at Open and All-Aged Stakes should ask the guns to shoot everything, except *directly* over a dog out working. In other stakes judges should ask the guns to shoot only over the "point" and when the handler is beside his dog, unless otherwise directed.

3. The first round should be taken as drawn. For subsequent rounds judges may call forward dogs at their discretion, so that those showing merit will be thoroughly tested and given every opportunity in roughly comparable conditions of wind, scent and ground. Dogs which are not forward within 15 minutes of being called may be disqualified.

4. Judges should so position themselves that they can see every move of the dogs while in the line. They should regulate the pace of the line to the handler and dog to avoid game being flushed on a part of the beat not yet covered by the dog. Game so flushed should not be counted as missed by the dog.

5. Judges should accede to a request from the handler of a puppy in a Novice or Puppy Stake who asks to be excused from retrieving fur.

6. If a dog catches game and the judges are satisfied that the game was unwounded and undamaged, the dog should be eliminated. When it appears that game will not flush for the dog, the handler may ask permission to take up his dog, and should only be marked down for handling if subsequently shown to have been wrong.

7. Judges must confirm the arrangements for the collection of unretrieved and unwanted game.

8. Judges may discuss situations that arise and must agree the categories to be marked, but must not discuss the actual marks they award as these represent their opinions and should be kept strictly to themselves. The marks should represent the work seen on the day, and should not be influenced by past performances.

9. The standard of work in Open and All-Aged Stakes carrying Field Trial Championship status should be higher than for other stakes. A prize should not be awarded unless the dog has had a productive point, a retrieve in the field and has completed the water

retrieve, whatever the conditions of the day. Other stakes may be judged more leniently, but a prize should not be given unless the dog has proved himself a pointer, and a retriever on land or at the water, and has swum. Certificates of merit are not prizes and may be awarded at the judge's discretion to dogs showing all round qualities and that they swim.

10. Judges should mark the following categories:—

(i) *Ground Treatment.*—The dog has to hunt the beat allotted thoroughly, making good all ground, missing no game and using the wind correctly. A dog that deliberately runs into game up wind should be discarded, but if he drops to birds rising down wind of him, this is a credit.

(ii) *Pointing.*—The dog should point game staunchly, and work out only on word of command. He must be steady to flush, shot and fall. Persistent false pointing should be severely penalized, but an unproductive point, where the dog indicated by nose down and wagging tail where departed game lay should not be marked, but may be credited as a "point" for the award of Certificate of Merit. It is accepted that hares and rabbits in their forms may not give off scent for the dog to point. Judges should not penalize dogs for failing to point in such conditions.

(iii) *Retrieve.*—The retrieve must be on command. If game is shot over the point, and is marked, the dog should go straight to the fall, and any diversion marked down. With blind retrieves, judges should indicate to the handler where the game fell. The dog should go directly as indicated by the handler and any diversion from that line, with consequent waste of time and risk of disturbance of game, should be marked down. On a long blind retrieve, the dog should be taken towards the fall. A handler should be allowed to position himself where he can see to direct the dog according to conditions, but he should be beside the judges for the delivery.

In the case of a strong runner, the judge should give the immediate order for a dog to be sent. Wounded game should be retrieved before dead game. The seen dead game lying in the open does not really test a good dog, should not be highly marked, and should be avoided except in stakes other than Open and All-Aged. Not more than two dogs should be tried on the same bird. When a judge goes forward to locate the game, no further dog should be tried on it. If more than one bird is down, and the dog changes birds on the way back, he should be severely marked down. The pick up should be clean with a quick return and delivery to hand. A dog that puts game down to take a firmer grip should not be severely marked down as he may have had a gruelling stint quartering, but sloppy retrieving and finishing should be penalized.

All game should be examined for "hard mouth". A hard mouthed dog seldom gives evidence of hardness. He will simply crush in one or both sides of the bird. Blowing up the feathers will not disclose the damage. Place the bird on the palm of the hand, head forward, and feel the ribs with finger and thumb. They should be round and firm. If they are caved in or flat, this is definite evidence of hard mouth. Be sure the bird reaches your co-judge and the handler for examination. There should be no hesitation or sentiment with "hard mouth"—the dog should be eliminated. A certain indication of a good mouth is a dog bringing in a live bird whose head is up and eye bright. Superficial damage, if any, in this case can be ignored. At times the rump of a strong runner may be gashed and look ugly. Care should be taken here, as it may be the result of a difficult capture, or lack of experience in mastering a strong runner by a young dog. Judges should always satisfy themselves that any damage done has been caused by the dog, not by the shot or fall, and in cases of doubt the benefit should be given to the dog. Handlers should be given the opportunity of inspecting the damaged game in the presence of the judges, but the decision of the judges is final.

(iv) *Game Finding Ability*.—This is of the highest importance. The judges will be looking for it throughout the dog's work by the manner in which he works his beat, finds his game and responds to scent generally, and by the degree of sense of purpose and drive that he displays.

(v) *Steadiness*.—The dog must in all cases be steady to flush, shot and fall. He may move to mark the fall, and this may be a credit. A dog that runs in to retrieve and is stopped, and then retrieves on command, should be marked down according to the extent of the break, but the dog that does not stop should be eliminated. Dogs should be steady to fur and feather going away.

(vi) *Facing cover*.—There are occasions, e.g. on a grouse moor when this category cannot be marked. Unless all dogs can be marked, none should be. In general the dog should go boldly into reasonable cover when ordered, either to push out game or to retrieve it. The judges should agree what is reasonable.

(vii) *Style*.—This embraces grace of movement, stylishness on point and of the retrieve, and the general appearance of keenness, competence and happiness in what he is doing.

(viii) *Handling*.—Noisy, ineffective and over handling should be severely marked down. Usually the best dogs seem to require the least handling, but the dog should be responsive to his handler's signals.

(ix) *Water Retrieve.*—This should be fully assessed, with special attention to direct, courageous but not suicidal entry, strong swimming, direct emergence and speedy delivery to hand. In Open and All-Aged Stakes the water retrieve is blind across water, and should be judges accordingly, including the re-entry into water carrying game.

Eliminations.—Whining or barking, out of control, chasing; failure to hunt, point, retrieve, enter water and swim, face cover: hard mouth: deliberately catching unwounded game (myxomatosis rabbits excluded).

Major Faults.—Not making ground good, missing birds, unsteadiness, stickiness on point, not acknowledging game going away, failing to find game, disturbing ground, sloppy work, noisy handling, changing birds.

Credits.—Game finding ability, style on point, drive, good marking speed and efficiency in gathering game, good waterwork, quiet handling.

INDEX